Praise for
Hermann Maier: The Race of My Life

"This is the book I was waiting for: A gutsy, honest, straightforward read about one of the best skiers of all time. Hermann is ample proof that there is always hope and his book is destined to be a skiing classic. It's an exciting and captivating read."
—PETER GRAVES, Olympic and World Cup race announcer

"Great insight into a comeback we only thought we understood."
—STEVE PORINO, OLN and NBC Olympic race announcer

"When you read his book, you realize this guy is all about hard work."
—TODD BROOKER, NBC Alpine Skiing Analyst
   and former pro World Cup downhiller

"A tale of mental toughness and recovery."
—*Vail Daily*

"Rarely has there been an athletic comeback story as compelling as that of Hermann Maier. . . . [This book belongs] on the shelf with the best skier biographies, a rarity in a sport that, in America, lives in the margins."
—*Boston Globe*

"What is truly illuminating about the Herminator's story is that it's a warts-and-all tale. It's not like Maier always knew he'd make it back. It's not like he never got frustrated and behaved selfishly or rudely. Like any human who has his livelihood suddenly snatched away from him, Maier at times lashed out, threw things in anger, and wanted to give up. And then he went back to work with the determination of a champion."
—*Dallas Morning News*

"An open diary of Maier's ski career. . . . This book is a lesson in life."
—SportsFeatures.com

HERMANN MAIER

The Race of My Life | AN AUTOBIOGRAPHY

with

Knut Okresek

Translated by Barbara Swartzwelter
Translation edited by David Kramer

BOULDER, COLORADO

VeloPress®
1830 North 55th Street
Boulder, Colorado 80301–2700 USA
303/440-0601 • Fax 303/444-6788 • E-mail velopress@insideinc.com

Distributed in the United States and Canada by Publishers Group West.

Cover design by Stephanie Goralnick
Interior design by Trish Wilkinson

First edition

Printed on acid-free paper

Library of Congress Cataloging-in-Publication Data

Maier, Hermann, 1972–
[Hermann Maier. English]
    Hermann Maier : the race of my life : an autobiography / Herman Maier with Knut Okresek ; translation edited by David Kramer.
        p.   cm.
    ISBN 1-931382-83-4 (pbk. : alk. paper)
    1. Maier, Hermann, 1972– 2. Skiers—Austria—Biography. I. Okresek, Knut. II. Title.
    GV854.2.MA3 2006
    796.93092—dc22

                                                                    2005031043

To purchase additional copies of this book or other VeloPress® books, call 800/234-8356 or visit us on the Web at velopress.com.

Printed in the United States

    06 07 / 10 9 8 7 6 5 4 3 2

My parents, who have had to fear for their children's safety all their lives; Alex, who can always rely on his older brother, and the other way around; Heini, my coaching father, who knows me as well as hardly anybody else does; Petra, my first true love; Gudrun, who held out at my bedside and who had to put up with me during the hard time afterward; Andy, to whom I mean more in my skiing outfit than in my soccer duds back in the old days; Ed, who has to spend more time with my skis than he can with his family; Schipi and Ernst, my friends back in the days before the "Herminator," who travel from race to race, run my merchandising store, and make me proud of my homepage every single day; Artur, who is there for me not only during operations; Harald, who listens to every one of my medical worries; Werner Aufmesser, who did the very right thing at the scene of the accident; Johannes, the doctor whom not only women trust; Vinzent and his healing hands; Nurse Bettina, the good fairy at the Olympic Training Center during my rehab; Peter Schröcksnadel, the bullheaded Tyrolean whose fatherly advice I could always rely on; Prim. Dr. Karlbauer and his team in the hospital of Salzburg, who set the basis for my miracle comeback; Professor Christoph Papp, whose ingenious contribution to my seven-hour operation has not been sufficiently appreciated; Volker Müller, my healing place of refuge when things get rough; Leodegar Pruschak and all of my sponsors, who were there for me even during the times when nobody seemed to believe in my skiing skills anymore; the people from Atomic, who supplied me with great equipment for fifty World Cup victories, the Olympics, and three World Championships; Gerhard Grasser, who taught me how to prepare my skis the right way; Alex Reiner, who, late but nevertheless realized what he had in me; Werner Tautermann, who provided me with *qigong* energy during my times at the Europe Cup; my true fans, who were there for me during my worst times; all of those whom I didn't think of before this got printed; Puschel, my chinchilla, who has been there for me since 1988 every time I visit my parents' house between races.

CONTENTS

FOREWORD

The first time I saw Hermann Maier, he was sailing across the screen. The Spanish TV commentator was saying something about the "Cherminatorrr," and I found myself asking, "Who is this crazy Austrian? And can he do anything besides fly through the air like a madman?" A few days later I had my answer. Hermann won two gold medals and turned out to be the star of the 1998 Olympic Winter Games in Nagano.

At that time in my life I had just won my own personal battle over cancer and was able once again to ride my bicycle on a professional level. I started my comeback with the Ruta del Sol. I still had a rocky path ahead of me before my first Tour de France victory. Again and again I asked myself for the purpose of my striving; I had setbacks and emotional breakdowns that I had to overcome. How did I manage? Through focused and disciplined training.

When I first met Hermann, I was shocked when he showed me the big bulge on his right lower leg. "Unbelievable that you can win races with this thing," I marveled. That was at the 2003 Tour de France prologue in Paris, when the "Herminator" attacked the four-mile course as a forerunner and duly impressed us bicycle pros with his time.

During the preceding months I had read and heard in the U.S. media about Hermann's tragic motorcycle accident. When I realized how closely he avoided a complete amputation of his right leg, I felt for him. I was impressed and glad when I realized how well his comeback was going, and I asked myself, "How did he pull it off?" After looking at excerpts from this book, I knew the answer. Just as with my own comeback, it was hard, un-compromising work and an unshakeable belief in himself. Recovering from a blow like that really shapes you for the rest of your life.

With my books I was able to motivate many people with cancer and keep them from giving up. My readers confirmed this with thousands of letters and e-mails. I reckon that Hermann will also help many people with his book. Especially those who, after a serious injury, run the danger of losing all hope.

There was another parallel that I couldn't help but notice. Just as in Hermann's case, there were many people in my life who said, "He won't ever make it to the top again. He only puts on a show for his sponsors." As we all found out in the meantime, these naysayers were just as wrong about Hermann as they were about me. And I, for one, am excited to see how the race of Hermann's life will continue.

Lance Armstrong
Seven-time Tour de France champion

PREFACE

Actually, I just wanted to be left alone. Aside from my routine of vigorous training, I wanted to savor the summer after my comeback season. Nevertheless, I was somehow compelled to work through the race of my life once more. And believe me, it was not an easy feat.

As we began to work on this book, the difficult hours, days, and weeks after my motorcycle accident came alive for me once again. I was reminded almost daily of the toughest and most prolonged fight of my life. I remembered the shock of possibly losing my leg, the fear of never being able to walk again, the pain, the fainting spells, and the complete frustration at having lost control over my body. I was startled to look again at pictures of myself in the intensive care unit.

I have grown accustomed to the scars—the palm-sized bulge that graces my right calf and the twelve-inch scar on my left upper arm where the skin flap was removed for the transplant. However, the details of my medical history still affect me in such a real way that I need to brace myself before I confront the gruesome details once again.

So, if you are expecting heroic literature with the typical sports phrases, you will be disappointed. The story I am about to tell you is as real as my scar tissue. Which is exactly what I intended. I had to tolerate entirely too much garbage in the media surrounding my comeback. Suddenly, my victories were downplayed and some of my colleagues went so far as to understate the gravity of my injury. "Just broke his leg, that's all," could be heard muttered behind closed doors.

Against such unfair statements I prefer to let the facts speak for themselves: Following my motorcycle accident, my lower leg was hanging on by nothing more than a few pieces of skin, but that was not even the gravest problem from a medical point of view. My body was going into shock, I was facing kidney failure, my liver was shutting down, and nerve trauma made it impossible for me to move my "good" left leg. My hemoglobin count was so low that even simple tasks like talking and eating were almost more than I could handle. I prayed that my body would not reject the skin transplant. I spent 137 hours in intensive care, and I had to learn how to walk again. Even so, I consider myself lucky that I was able to give up my crutches after a mere six weeks, a recovery that is virtually unheard of among those with comparable injuries.

It is my ability to set goals for myself and to pursue those goals with a relentless consistency that has carried me to the point of recovery that I enjoy today. Although some people are amazed to hear me say it, I am grateful for the fate that took hold of me. I am grateful that I was afforded this important life lesson, this experience like no other. Through it I have learned to appreciate the small, seemingly inconsequential things in life. I am grateful for every day that I am allowed to ski down a slope on two legs.

After my accident, as well as after my comeback, I received thousands of personal letters and e-mails. And even now people write to me from the hospital, telling me that my comeback fills them with hope for their own future. If with this book I can make a further contribution toward that end, then it has served its purpose.

HERMANN MAIER

The Race of My Life

PART I

(previous page) Elementary school championships, 1981. Even then, they sent me to race with too high a starting number.

1

BACK TO
THE BEGINNING

My crash at the Olympic downhill in Nagano was completely different. Then, it seemed like I was flying through the air for an eternity. But this time, everything happened like lightning. At once I realized, one wrong move and you're dead! During a ski race, split seconds make the difference between victory and defeat, but now there was much, much more at stake.

I can still see every detail in my mind's eye: I'm riding my brand-new 114-horsepower motorcycle along the state highway in the Austrian town of Radstadt, not far from Salzburg. I see a column of cars slowing to a crawl ahead of me. Traffic slowdown? No problem! I simply accelerate, speed past a few cars, and smoothly scoot back into my lane. Again the coast is clear, so I get ready to move out again. There's nothing to it. I'm on a two-lane highway, the speed limit is 55 mph, and I just passed a traffic sign with a black arrow crossed out in red: no left turn. Then, all of a sudden there's a red Mercedes with a German license plate swerving to the left. This can't be! You're not allowed to make a left turn here! Everything else happens in slow motion: To my left, the traffic island, to my right, the Mercedes, and there seems to be less and less street left. I am in serious trouble. But I feel a flicker of hope: Hey, maybe I can still squeeze by. No, there's not enough room. There's only one chance left: yield to the left!

As a ski racer, my reaction time and reflexes have been finely honed. Time and again I am speeding down a crowded slope, and it's not a rare event that tourists will challenge you to a close call. That's when I react instinctively to avoid a bad collision. It's this daily level of awareness that has prepared me to the nth degree for just such a situation. And I know what has to be done to contain the damage in a worst-case scenario. During my 1998 crash in Nagano, for instance, I worked out a strategy for impact while I was still in the air. To a ski racer that's second nature. In fact, skiing and riding a motorbike are quite similar in this regard: speed, a feel for the curves, the ability to react quickly . . .

What now? Hit the brakes? No, the distance is simply too short. I'll suffer a frontal collision smack into the side of the car. I don't want to end up on his hood, in the driver's door, or on the roof. How about with my backside into the sign on the traffic island, and go home in a wheelchair? No thanks! The car is by now at a right angle to the road, but the driver still hasn't seen me. He simply doesn't know I'm here! Damn! To my right, there's a light pole, next to it the blue metal "23.4 kilometers" sign, and a bit farther off, a rock wall. If I crash into that, it's all over. In my thoughts I'm already beyond, just as in skiing: You're at a gate, but you're already thinking about the next turn. I'm already shifting my weight to the right; now I accelerate and I'm about to pull up with my legs. That guy has *got* to see me by now! But no, the driver seems to have been looking at the oncoming lane, and never behind him. Now I am registering, but only subconsciously, the impact of 750 pounds of flesh and metal hurled against the frame of the car. My right calf takes the brunt, tibia and fibula are being torn apart. Yet I can't feel anything and I'm thinking, half crazed, "Now I'm a goner!" It still hasn't registered that the crash has already happened. It came as a total surprise!

I feel the motorcycle lifting away from me, and I am fighting it with every fiber of my body. Somehow, I want to get control over the 550-pound machine. I squeeze my thighs together with all my strength, so tightly that I dent the gas tank. And now I feel the seat being ripped out of its mounting brackets. I have to sustain an unbelievable amount of pressure in order not to fall over to the left and be thrust underneath the car. The seat gives way, and I take off, and just as in a ski crash, my body is mobilizing enormous defensive forces. Every muscle is tense. I am cata-pulted sixty feet through the air and crash-land in a ditch on the opposite embankment, the motorcycle seat still clenched between my legs. The motorcycle is mowing down the weeds in the ditch and comes to rest in front of the bridge, just as though it had been parked there. The lights are still blinking. For an instant, I don't see anything, hear anything, feel any-thing. But only for an instant. Then I can sense the metallic taste of blood in my mouth. I'm still alive! What happened? Instinctively, I take my right leg into my hands, and I realize that my foot is dangling by little more than a few shreds of skin. It is Friday, August 24, 2001, 7:24 P.M. The race of my life has begun.

THEY ALL HATED ME

In the summer of 2001 I was unbeatable. No matter what I did, no one could hold a candle to me. And moreover (and this unnerved even me), I was getting better with each passing day! It was like a puzzle that was sud-denly piecing itself together: the routine of four and a half years of World Cup experience, as well as the foundation that I had laid through the con-sistent, monotonous, but effective training with Heini Bergmüller at the Olympic Training Center. The incessant training had just about done me in, and I was so tired of it all that for the first time in my career, I was seri-ously questioning why I was putting myself through this torture. Just as the beautiful summer weather was arriving in Austria, I had to head off to Chile, into the South American winter. I was fed up with the whole business.

But when the going gets tiresome, somehow I am able to "flip the switch" and get back on track. And I was truly in my element in the snow. Suddenly, everything seemed easy. Routine, strength, technique: Every-thing fell into place. Everything, that is, until the last two days, when the "skiing school" at the castle in the Andes (which would have made a nice backdrop for a James Bond movie) had me so totally bored that I no longer maintained the necessary level of concentration. Until then, I had been ahead by one second or more during each training run, even the times I was experimenting with equipment or technique. I probably could have whisked down the slope on the wooden planks from the ski museum. I was in better shape than I had ever been in my life. My ski trainer, Andreas Evers, claimed that the racing season could have started for me in August. Probably it would have been best that way. As it was, I had to find other diversions to keep myself in good spirits until winter came.

And so, in the summer of 2001, after my third overall World Cup victory, I granted myself the first true luxury of my life: a "custom bike," which I had ordered from Peter Penz, a motorcycle fabrication specialist in Upper Austria, to my exact specifications. It wasn't cheap, but I felt that my Penz SP 14 Performance with its gleaming red metallic paint was worth the 36,000 euros I had to fork out. A 114-horsepower engine, the seat almost four feet away from the handlebars. The enormous wheel base, the massive fork, and the low clearance gave me that unique roadster sensation when riding it. During the three months it was being built, time and again I would drive up to Altheim in order to personally check up on its progress. I was counting the days until I could launch my new toy. A few days after my metallic dream finally stood in my parents' garage in Reitdorf, I had to take off for Chile to attend the three-week snow camp. Throughout that time I was like a child, looking forward to being reunited with my new red girlfriend.

When I returned to Austria, I was greeted by beautiful late summer weather. I decided to take the first ride on my new bike up into the mountains to my conditioning workout. I know the 21-mile ride from Flachau to Obertauern, which sits 5,700 feet above sea level, by heart. I could almost drive the steep switchbacks blindfolded. Almost every day that I don't ski I drive up there and spend eight to ten hours at the Olympic Training Center before Heini, my trainer, lets me go again.

My workout on that fateful August 24 was almost like a walk in the park. Because I had just recently returned from South America, six time zones away, my slave driver Heini let me sleep in for once. When I arrived at the center, I had to offer up my finger for a blood sample. Every day, my blood levels were tested before I started my routine of mounting my stationary workout bike and pedaling at a constant heart rate of 105 to 110 beats per minute. Half an hour of monotonous pumping the pedals. I can do this as reliably as a metronome. I feel like a good little boy who always eats his spinach, which is probably why my coach likes me so much. If my lactate count, which is an indication of the level of exertion, is correct on top of this, then Heini is the happiest dad—I mean trainer—in the world. The nurse pricked my ear, and put the blood sample into the small apparatus on the table next to me for analysis. Lactate 1.5. Heini was euphoric. "Unbelievable, the shape you're in!" Another thirty minutes of biking. "This sure gets old," I was thinking to myself as I leafed through the newspaper that always sits on the fiberglass stand attached to the bicycle. That's when I discovered that there would be a soccer match in Flachau at eight that night. "Well, that works out nicely," I thought to myself, and called Andy Evers, my ski trainer, and my brother Alex while I was still biking. "Let's go to the game, and afterward we can go out for a beer." After all, I had earned it with my obedient training behavior. I was looking forward to the evening.

When I stepped outside, the sun was already setting behind the mountain, so beautiful it was almost kitsch, like a postcard. How quickly everything was to change. In front of the training center complex my buddies from Obertauern were waiting for me. They wanted me to join them for a barbecue. "Sorry, I've made other plans." If only I had gone to the grill fest! Why on earth did I want to take in yet another sporting event that evening?

I started my Penz, and everyone's jaw dropped. That melodic roar of the engine; none of them had seen such a bike before. I proudly made a loop in the parking lot and rode off into the warm summer night. Nice and easy. I was planning on a leisurely ride down the mountain, since I didn't want to overwork the fully chromed S&S engine during its first 500 miles. I was dressed for biking, including, thank God, a sturdy Harley-Davidson leather jacket. My workout equipment was stored in my special hard-sided backpack, which can be used as a sledding saucer in the wintertime. That backpack would save my life in a few minutes.

While I was meandering down the switchbacks of the mountain pass, I thought about the ski training in Chile and about my top form. I marveled at how easily it all came to me. Nothing could stop me now!

DOC, PLEASE SAVE MY LEG!

A few moments later, my world had turned upside down. I was lying in a ditch, holding my thigh. The people arriving at the accident site saw a grim picture: The bones were protruding from my shredded blue jeans, blood was everywhere, and a foot was dangling from where it didn't seem to belong. One of my sneakers must have been torn off; I could see only the mangled sock. This did not look good! My lower leg was attached by no more than a few shreds of skin and tissue. I was slipping into shock. What did I feel at that moment? It's impossible to describe. The pain wasn't really that bad, but I knew that I had been clobbered.

I needed to take control over this disastrous situation. The first thing I checked was if I could still wiggle my toes. I thought, if that still works, then at least a few nerve and muscle fibers have remained intact. Great, it works. I suddenly felt relieved, because I knew that my spinal cord had probably not been compromised. From the adjacent property, a little old man arrived who wanted to help me. It was Engelbert Erlbacher, an 87-year-old herbalist who is known throughout the Pongau region.

The next thing I registered was the presence of two motorcyclists who had stopped right away. I yelled as hard as I could, "Call a doctor! Call a doctor! An ambulance! A helicopter! My leg is off, but I still need it for work!" Only later did I realize that it was at that moment that I first thought about skiing. I started cursing: "It's illegal to make a left turn here. Why did that jerk try to turn there?" One of my two biker colleagues concurred: "I was in line right behind you and saw the whole thing; it really wasn't your fault!" At that point, I started worrying about my face. I had registered a lamp pole in the background, and now I had a dreadful suspicion. "I must have struck that pole and ripped off my nose and part of my face in the process!" What made things worse was that so much blood was running into my eyes that I couldn't see anything on my right side. I could sense with my tongue that my upper incisors were missing. At that moment my worldview narrowed: How do I look? How are people reacting to my appearance?

An older lady showed up. I was lying in the ditch, and she was bending over me. I looked her right in the eyes and waited in suspense to see if my shattered visage would frighten her. She didn't seem perturbed, though, and so I felt relieved for the second time: "My face must still be there." The lady was trying to help me by putting me in a more comfortable position. But when she noticed my leg, she realized that she was completely out of her league and only said, "Can you move your toes?" Yes, it was a miracle, my toes were still working, even though the foot looked horrible. The protruding bones, the exposed flesh, the blood everywhere. Then another woman came running. She was beside herself: "I'm a doctor, I'm a doctor! Stay where you are! Don't move." Obviously, she was afraid that my back had been injured. By now, my situation was becoming precarious. Since the hillside on which I was lying, in the middle of a bunch of nettles, was quite steep, I had to brace myself with my arms in order not to slide downhill. Time and time again I ran the events of the crash through my mind and tried to reconstruct what exactly had happened. Down the road and to the right I saw the red Mercedes C 180 with the German license plate. He must have kept going before stopping beyond the traffic island. I must have caused the damage to my face myself. Probably with my hand during the time in the air. That's when my watch with the silver casing that I was so proud of must have been ripped off. But that was of precious little concern to me right then.

Another person, brown dress, light-colored tights, hair dyed blond, a little over 60, was struggling to explain: "We are so very sorry, we are so sorry," I could hear her say with a Bavarian accent. The lady must have been with the driver of the Mercedes. I could do nothing but yell at her. With my busted leg and my contorted mouth I had difficulty speaking, but somehow I had no trouble cursing: "You're crazy! You're not allowed to turn there! That was an illegal turn! I can't believe you didn't see me!" She stammered again, "Please forgive us, we are so very sorry!" I yelled and cursed. The fact that I was able to go on like that shows me that I must have been in pretty good mental shape, given the circumstances. If it had been up to me, I would have gotten up right away. In fact, for a short time I considered hopping down the embankment on my left leg. But the terrain was too rocky.

Finally, someone came who was really able to help me. It was Werner Aufmesser, the brother of my physician at the Olympic Training Center. Now I was filled with hope. The doctor had just settled down on his deck a few yards behind the accident site when he heard the crash. He had no idea that I was involved in the accident. Having been called via the emergency communications network, he had come at once in his car to the accident site. Now I was pleading with him: "Look, I got hit bad, but I can still move my toes! Please, save my leg, fix it so I can walk again, I don't care about anything else!" Werner was calmly reassuring me. "It will all work out in the end. For now, we'll get you to our clinic." Werner was just inserting an IV to prevent shock when a couple of policemen showed up. Thanks to my helmet and sunglasses I had remained anonymous thus far. That was just fine with me. The two custodians of the law were playing right along. They just called in "a traffic accident on the B99 at kilometer marker 23.4." Of course, they immediately recognized me and my motorbike. One of them briefly questioned me and radioed for additional help without mentioning my name. I am grateful to him to this day. It is unthinkable what would have happened if the press had gotten wind of the situation. This way, everyone could concentrate on the essentials. Maybe that's why everything went so smoothly.

In the meantime, quite a few people were standing around me. Up above, on the bridge that the red Mercedes should have taken, the usual crowd of onlookers was gathering. I kept hearing, "Unbelievable, it's Hermann . . . it's Maier. . . ." Luckily, there were still no reporters present, which is why there are no pictures of my rescue. In the midst of all this, I registered a flashing light, a gigantic ambulance. "Very nice," I thought. "I should fit into this thing!"

THE ACCIDENT
What Really Happened

The 73-year-old German pensioner Wolfgang S. was traveling with a female acquaintance and two friends in a red Mercedes C 180 along the Katschberg highway (B99). He was on his way to his vacation home in Mandling, which is two miles away. S. had already lost his way twice. After a U-turn on the B99 in the direction of Obertauern he was once again traveling toward Salzburg (and not toward Mandling). He made a right turn toward Radstadt East (which was in fact correct). However, he became confused by the road signs and turned around immediately beyond the traffic island, traversing a "crossing forbidden" line in the process. He returned to the B99, onto which he took a right turn. According to testimony about the accident, S. was traveling at this time (seven seconds before the accident) at a speed of 9 miles per hour (the speed limit is 50 mph). At 3.6 seconds before the collision, several cars behind S. had to slow down to a speed of 20 miles per hour.

Hermann Maier, on a Penz Performance motorcycle, was also traveling toward Salzburg at the time. He had approached the line of directional traffic, checked for oncoming traffic, put on his turn signal, and was overtaking three cars in succession. Right after Maier had overtaken the third car—1.2 seconds before impact—the red Mercedes turned to the left without checking for traffic, and Hermann Maier in particular, behind him. Even though Maier reacted quickly and attempted to make way for the vehicle, the collision was no longer avoidable. That is attested to by the witnesses: Maier reacted correctly and in a timely manner to the left-turn maneuver made by S. He had no further option to prevent the accident caused by the sudden left turn. If S. had glanced into his left side mirror only once after reaching the center line, he would have been able to see Maier's motorcycle. The motorcycle was clearly visible, particularly so because of the (attestable) fact that the headlight was on.

According to the police report, the motorcycle sailed through the air over a distance of twenty-six feet, hit the asphalt, and skidded another hundred feet. Hermann Maier came to rest in the adjacent ditch with severe injuries. In order for official duties to be executed, the Katschberg highway was closed down for forty-five minutes.

STATEMENT BY DR. KARL HEINZ KLEE, LEGAL COUNSEL OF HERMANN MAIER

Since the initial investigation at the county courthouse in Radstadt produced no indication whatsoever concerning any contributory negligence on the part of Hermann Maier, and neither did the report based on evidence gathered from witnesses, the Salzburg district attorney's office forwarded the case to the district court in Munich responsible for the driver at fault, namely Wolfgang S., for further prosecution.

Subsequently, the defense attorney for S. tried repeatedly to bring to a halt the court proceedings against his client based on a claim of exclusive responsibility or overwhelming fault of Maier. Against such allegations we were able to defend ourselves accordingly. The proceedings ended with a ruling on May 2, 2004, by the Munich district court, by which S. was sentenced to a monetary fine of 750 euros for negligent infliction of bodily injury. The negligence of S. was determined to be in the form of defendant's failure to look back and check for approaching traffic during his left turn maneuver on August 24, 2001, which caused him to fail to see Maier. That was the cause of the accident. This ruling subsequently became legally binding.

In the meantime, S. and his insurance company, HUK-Coburg, have brought suit against the province of Salzburg because of the claim for damages that S. has been held liable to pay to Maier, since according to them, the province of Salzburg holds partial liability for the accident due to their incorrect placement of traffic signs at the intersection where the accident took place.

Dr. Karl Heinz Klee
Attorney at Law

NOW I WILL WRITE A NEW CHAPTER IN MY CAREER

The emergency medical technicians—all of them familiar faces—removed the stretcher from the ambulance and began their struggle against the difficult terrain. They were going to have to carry me through the ditch. First, they tried to roll me onto the stretcher, but it didn't take long for them to realize that my 207-pound bulk was not to be taken lightly. It was then that I noticed that I was still sitting on my bike saddle, which had been drilled into the ground when I made my crash landing. They finally got me into the stretcher, and I gripped it with all my strength. If I hadn't been in such rough shape, I would have taken a moment to comment on this curious scene. The poor emergency aid crew was visibly nervous, since they knew who it was that they were dragging through the ditch. I was afraid I would fall off, and although I was strapped down on the stretcher, I was holding on for all I was worth.

We got to the ambulance, and now there was a problem with getting me inside, since my bulky leather jacket kept getting hooked on everything. What a relief when the door was shut at last! It had seemed like an eternity to me, though barely ten minutes had elapsed since the accident. My whole body was now enclosed in a vacuum splint, which felt like a body cast after the air had been sucked out of it. We drove the two hundred meters up to the Aufmesser clinic, where Werner's brother Harald was waiting with a worried what-have-you-done-now expression on his face. I called out to him while I was still in the ambulance: "Harald, it wasn't my fault!" Shortly thereafter, or so I have been told, I said to him, "Now we will write a completely new story about my career."

For years, the Aufmesser clinic in Radstadt had been an important address as far as my medical care was concerned: X-rays, blood samples, and similar routine stuff. In their emergency room, in which I had lain God knows how many times, the situation was grave. In the meantime, the injection of painkillers I had received was starting to take effect, and I perceived everything as if through a veil. I caught sight of my brother Alex and Andy Evers, who had made their way to the clinic. After waiting in vain at the soccer field, my brother had rushed here after my mother had called him. Alex ran over to me and started ranting about the driver of the Mercedes. "Just wait till I get hold of him . . . !" I had to calm him down: "That kind of talk is not going to help us now. Let's look to the future."

The first thing they did was put IV ports in veins in both forearms so they could start drip lines to counter the effects of shock. While Harald Aufmesser took over the logistics by notifying my surgeon, Artur Trost, at the trauma center forty-five miles away in Salzburg and requesting a helicopter, his brother Werner cut open the leg of my trousers. It is a strange feeling when someone cuts through your blue jeans with scissors and carefully pushes the remaining fabric to the side. I held my breath: Now the truth will be revealed. I carefully observed Werner's facial expression, and then my gaze went straight to what was left of my leg. Skin and tissue had been torn from my calf during my impact with the road. As I found out later, a small fragment of my shinbone must have gotten lost at the site of the accident. After the wound was bound up in a sterile bandage, they started to splint my leg. Full of trepidation, I asked, "Werner, can you do something so I don't lose my leg?"

"Yes, of course."

"And . . . when will I be able to ski again?" His straightforward answer immediately dampened my spirits: "You won't have to think about that for a long time."

At that moment I realized the true dimensions of my injury. Sports, which had been the main focus of my life thus far, suddenly became something of secondary importance. There were other things at stake now. "Okay, but will I at least be able to walk again?" "Yes, that will come, but it will take a while." With this devastating diagnosis, it was clear: The Olympic winter season is canceled! But as I said, that was now beside the point. Harald held his cell phone to my ear. "Hello, this is Artur. I heard what happened. We've got everything ready for you." I spoke urgently: "You've got to give your very best!"

Gudrun, my girlfriend at the time, was already on the way to Radstadt. She had just finished preparing her supper at her home in Flachau, but she left it on the table and was hurrying to see me. I wanted to warn her, to allay her fears. "Just a busted leg," I said, "nothing too terrible."

There was one more person with whom I simply had to speak: Heini, to whom I had just said good-bye a few minutes earlier. I made it brief and to the point: "I got shot down, and my foot is kaput!"

I don't know whether it was the medication or the surroundings, but at once I was no longer agitated. I grew very calm, almost apathetic. I understood: It's too late now, and at any rate, I'm getting help. I don't have to train and work out for a while now, so at least there are some advantages. Finally, I had an excuse that would brook no exception: no expectations, no pressure to perform. I don't have to measure up to anything. The only issue now is getting back on my feet.

I just had to get onto the operating table as quickly as possible. Am I glad that Harald arranged for the helicopter! While they were pushing me back into the ambulance, I registered my parents and Gudrun among the people outside. They were in each other's arms, and I felt very sorry for them. I just waved at them and called out, "It will all work out. Don't you worry!" Slowly, I could feel the pain creeping up inside me, and then Werner gave me a shot of piritamid, a strong opiate that I would get to know better in the weeks to come. While the rotor blades of the yellow Christophorus 6 helicopter were rippling my blanket in the evening twilight, I was pushed inside the chopper. I meekly greeted the emergency physician and his helpers and tried to relax. Because of the pain medication and the sound protection headphones you have to wear in the helicopter I felt as though I were being manipulated by remote control. I thought, "Such a skilled pilot, I can't even feel the liftoff." Then we were up and away. The computer display showed the time: 8:27 P.M. I was completely calm.

When we landed on the roof of the trauma center in Salzburg a few minutes later, it was already pitch dark. I took in everything happening around me with astounding clarity. There he was, my friend Artur, in his white coat, which he always wears when things get official. "What have you done now?" he asked me, as though I were a little boy who had skinned his knees on the playground. I was chiefly concerned that the doctors not keep anything from me at this point. "Artur, I know, it doesn't look good. But just promise you'll always tell it to me just like it is." I was so relieved to have Artur on my side. I like his pleasant demeanor, not to mention his professional expertise. In January 1997, before my career really took off, he performed surgery on my hand after my crash in Chamonix, and he was often present at the races in his function as an official doctor for the Austrian ski team, and at many victory celebrations as well.

THE OPERATION

A team of crack doctors saved Hermann Maier's right leg during a surgical intervention that lasted for more than seven hours. Alois Karlbauer, head of the trauma center in Salzburg, oversaw the operation. First, the wound had to be cleaned and a few paint fragments removed from the bone. Surgeon Artur Trost was responsible for setting the transverse fracture, during which the bones were moved aside 1 inch. He employed a fifteen-inch titanium rod, which was hammered through the bone marrow all the way from the top of the tibia down to the foot in order to piece the tibia back together. The rod was fixed in place with four lateral pins. The shattered fibula was left to grow back together on its own. The restorative surgeon Christoph Papp ventured a skin transplant during the initial surgery. A 2×5-inch patch of skin was removed from the left upper arm and transplanted to the portion of the lower leg that was missing skin and tissue. In precision microsurgical work, even small blood vessels were pieced back together. Usually, such intervention is carried out only weeks after an accident. But since time is a crucial factor for a professional athlete, the risk was taken in this case.

The injuries immediately after the accident
    Third-degree open lower leg fracture
    Pelvic contusion with pronounced hematoma
        in the area of the buttocks
    Lacerated pressure wound superior to right tibia
    Lacerated pressure wound superior to right heel bone
    Lacerated pressure wound superior to left tibia
    Right thigh contusion
    Abrasions in the right pelvic region
    Head contusion
    Lacerated pressure wound on the upper lip and
        bridge of the nose
    Injury to upper left and right incisors

Postoperative complications
    Thirteen hours after the accident: Signs of kidney failure

(continued)

Nineteen hours after the accident: Compartmental syndrome in the pelvic region. The pressure on the venous pathways in this region was so great that blood transfer back to the heart was failing. Because of massive internal swelling caused by the bruises, the nerve fibers responsible for leg movement were pinched off, which was causing signs of paralysis. The left leg, which had not been operated on, was more affected by this phenomenon than the right one.

In the operating room, Artur Trost had prepared the medical team for the surgical procedure they were about to perform. After X-rays of my leg had been taken, all eventualities had to be considered. Are there any internal injuries to be concerned about? Is the spinal column compromised? Will there be further complications to be reckoned with in the future? Then I heard the doctor say to the nurse, "Get some bandages, the biggest ones you can find!" The biggest ones—that sounds bad! Not exactly what you want to hear prior to slipping into an anesthetic coma. One of the nurses looked at me compassionately, and I pointed at my shattered leg: "This is going to stay on, right?" I wasn't so sure about that. Again and again I implored the doctors, "You have to tell me the truth, no matter how bad it is!" I wanted to know where I stood. Artur introduced me to chief surgeon Karlbauer, the head of the trauma center and an officer in the army reserves. He spoke with an authoritative voice: "No worries, young man. We'll handle this!" He struck me as one of those individuals who never makes a false move. I looked at him and said, "I'm scared shitless about my leg." The chief surgeon, with a hint of humor in his voice, replied, "I would be, too, if I were a skier standing at the top of the Streif racecourse."

If you've almost left your leg behind on the street, you're haunted by the worst kinds of fears. I quietly prayed that my leg would still be attached when I woke up. It was only nine in the evening, but to me it seemed like midnight. The strong medication I had been given was finally getting to me, and the anesthesiologist took care of the rest. All my thoughts were centered on my leg. "Hopefully, I'll see it again!" And with a dreadful feeling of uncertainty, I drifted off.

FLASHBACK

MY CRASH OF THE CENTURY
What really happened in Nagano 1998

My first Olympic downhill race lasted less than 20 seconds. To be exact, it lasted 17.7 seconds on the ground and 1.7 seconds in the air. Those last 1.7 seconds made me famous the world over.

Friday, February 13, 1998, Hakuba, Japan. Underneath my helmet, it is suddenly very quiet. That can mean only one thing: a tailwind! I'm already going fast, considerably faster than in my three training runs, during which I was always right among the leading contenders. Underneath my feet are sliding those rockets with which Markus Wasmaier already was twice triumphant in Lillehammer, 1994. Inside my head roars a boundless determination to win. Yes, sir, I'm on my way to solid gold! There's an "Alpen jump," which had been installed specifically at the request of environmentalists to protect fragile native flora. I like it. I've never jumped that well. Everything goes like clockwork, all the way down to that long, winding turn to the right, which I am approaching at breakneck speed.

The Olympic Games in Nagano had started like a nightmare for me. First, I was unable to decipher the Japanese instruction manual for the stationary bicycle that my coach, Heini Bergmüller, had ordered to my hotel room. That bike must have dated back to the time of Pearl Harbor. Once I was finally able to get going on a replacement bike, I was suddenly deaf, a total hearing crash. I had to rinse out my right ear until I felt halfway comfortable again. I didn't sleep well at night. Our hotel, the Weisser Hof, right in the center of Hakuba, was everything but conducive to high performance. Outside the room, which I shared with my teammate Andreas Schifferer, we could hear the snowplow thunder up and down the street night after night. We ended up moving, and were now living in true Japanese fashion. Sort of at the bottom of a shoe box. And all of this with Schiffi, who for all his good qualities manages to turn even the grandest master suite into a pigsty overnight. The real kicker was the weather, though. After three good training days, we sat and watched for six days while the Japanese weather ran amok. We went through a cornucopia of atmospheric conditions, starting with a spate of warm weather accompanied by fog and rain and ending with a polar freeze and a snowstorm. The weather generally changed every few minutes. One time, while we were once again returning from the mountain without having gotten our training runs in, a snowstorm unlike any I had ever witnessed began to rage. Such storms were to occur several times during the time I was there. Once, our press spokesman's four-wheel-drive BMW ended up stuck on the slope. He had gotten hopelessly lost and couldn't find any of the streets.

The downhill race had been scheduled for Sunday, February 8. It finally was held on Friday, the thirteenth, under completely new conditions. The sun was shining again, and the conditions were much faster than they had been six days earlier during the last training runs. One of the directional gates had obviously been moved. No wonder that not only I, but eleven other competitors as well, were shot down in the same area. I started the race as number four. Even though quite a few years have passed since then, I can still remember every detail of my epic crash.

That long, drawn-out curve to the right. I stick to my tight, superfast line. Total focus on the upcoming edge. First, I want to tie up the curve. I apply some pressure, but then I brush up against the snow with my boot, the outer ski slips away from below. I push against it. That triggers a trampoline effect. Just at this moment, I come up on the edge. Forces are released that no one can control! I take off like a bouncing ball. And now? Get your weight to the front! I am still accelerating as I struggle to redistribute my center of gravity forward. You can see me doing that in the famous pictures, where I am rowing with my arms like a ski jumper from the 1950s. I am straddling the air diagonally, and right then I see the directional gate below me. Shift weight! Nothing bad has happened yet. I had been in the air like that before and ended up back on my feet again. All right, I'll miss the gate. At least I'll have a decent landing. So I take my time in the air. There's nothing I can force here. I observe everything from above and want to adjust my descent to the terrain. I still believe in a happy landing and am thinking, "If I keep on flying, my skis will be pulled back down by gravity, and I can continue skiing." This is completely typical of my sense of self-confidence. During that season, I felt like I could do anything. My imagination was incapable of considering something like a crash. The high speed was no problem, I thought. After all, I have to be faster than the rest in order to win. But this time around, I am too fast. I simply underestimate the speed, probably because of the tailwind conditions.

My skis are pointing higher and higher up. Suddenly I realize, "Holy smoke, I'm looking down vertically! I am seeing everything upside down!" The flight seems endless to me at this point. By now, I realize that I am going to crash. Everything from here on out is a matter of damage control. Whatever you do, don't impact with your head! Like a ski jumper experiencing turbulence, I break up the flight in order to land earlier. I turn my head to the side as much as I can and blast into the Japanese snow with my shoulder and collarbone. A lightning-fast thought: "I think my head got ripped off." But I have to concentrate again in order to keep the crash under control. I put myself into an erect position and keep going downhill feet first. I see the orange border fence. Please, not like last year in Chamonix, where I broke my hand on the hard plastic pole. The higher you can clear the fence, the more the poles give. I don't even feel the first barrier. Flip. Straight into the second fence. The third one is left behind sideways. Rather elegant! A somersault across a dark all-weather coat. What is that thing doing here? I am hurled through the deep snow until my momentum is spent. I extend my arms and come to rest headfirst in the snow. Now the trick is to wait and see what comes down next. Usually, at least one ski detonates close to you. But that was it.

And now? I don't dare glance to the left. My collarbone should be sticking out, and I should bump up against it with my chin. But miraculously, everything is intact. Above me I see the "commander's hill" with the trainers and coaches. Down below, in the finish area, my support team is waiting. My parents are biting their nails in front of the television at home. This sort of thing is a horror for them. In order to calm everyone down, I wave at the TV camera.

In the meantime, my knee is making itself felt. Since I've never had a torn ligament or anything like it, I am bracing myself for the worst. There's our team physician, Toni Wicker, stumbling through the deep snow. He must have started running while I was still in the air. He is huffing and puffing and uttering incoherent sentences. I can only say over and over, "Unbelievable, crazy, this is too much!" Suddenly, the photographer is here; tall and skinny, pockmarked face, and a head full of curls. First, he dutifully inquires as to my well-being: "Are you okay?" I nod and he grins. "Great shot!" And indeed it was. Not only will I become world-famous because of this crash, but *Sports Illustrated* photographer Carl Yarbrough will make so much money from his shot of the century that he will be able to remodel his house in Boulder, Colorado. Even though he wasn't supposed to, he had hauled an aluminum ladder up onto the mountain, and slipped through all the barriers. He instinctively placed his podium so as to have the best view of the S-curve, in the very spot where originally the TV tower was supposed to go. For security reasons, the TV infrastructure couldn't

STAR PHOTOGRAPHER CARL YARBROUGH

Concerning the seconds that gave him world renown as well as considerable amounts of cash.

I was sitting on my ladder, waiting for the competitors. Every time I heard a scratching noise in the curve ahead of me, I brought my camera into position and had my finger on the shutter. Only with Maier there was no scratching sound; he was already in the air and was coming toward me at breakneck speed. I'm thinking, "Not a chance I'll have time to get off the ladder, so I might as well push the shutter. The pictures will be awesome, whether I survive this stunt or not." My Nikon takes twelve shots per second. I could feel a draft of air as Maier zoomed by me at close range, hit the ground, tumbled across my jacket, did a few somersaults, and came to rest in the snow. "No way could he have survived that," I thought. But suddenly, the guy starts moving. I couldn't believe it. A few seconds later, my cell phone rang. It was my boss on the other end of the line: "Well, do you have the picture?" "You better believe it. If the film makes it down in one piece, we have a cover shot!"

be placed there, which was lucky for me, considering what could have happened if instead of Carl's jacket, I had encountered a bulky metal scaffold.

After I was assured that nothing was seriously wrong with me, we started walking. I had one ski pole in my hand, and Wicker was walking ahead of me. We collected my lost pieces of equipment piece by piece: one ski, then the other ski and the other pole. Next to me was the press photographer, who was making his way backward through the deep snow without taking his lens off me. Then I could hear the voice of chief trainer Werner Margreiter through Dr. Wicker's walkie-talkie: "Get a move on! Schiffi is waiting to go up above!" I couldn't believe it and cursed under my breath, "He can just stifle himself and be thankful that I'm still alive after such a crash."

"A fine beginning!" I thought. Or was it rather the end of me and the Olympics? We marched back to the lift station that I had just skied past. Inside, the German women's ski team was waiting for their training runs. I stripped down to my underwear and stretched out on three tables that had been pushed together. Wicker was doctoring around on my knee. It still seemed relatively stable. We cooled it down with a water bottle. Then it was off to the hotel. I insisted on scooting down the rest of the mountain on my skis. Someone asked me if I would take part in the subsequent combination downhill race. I just shook my head. When we finally got back to the hotel, I called my parents right away. "Everything is okay, nothing's wrong." I could sense their relief.

Back in my room, I could hardly get any rest. First, Petra showed up. She was incredulous. "Are you really okay, don't you have any pain?" I just nodded. Shortly thereafter, my brother and Ernst and Schipi from my fan club stuck their heads inside my room. "Hermann, that takeoff really looked good," they grinned. "Did they give out any points for form?" I still remember that the Carrera serviceman wanted to exchange my red racing helmet. "Not a chance," I told him. "That's my victory helmet. I still need that for my next race."

As though in a trance, I stumbled down to the improvised press conference. The hotel lobby was jam-packed. A host of cameras, lights, flashguns, and a huge crowd of excited journalists all of whom wanted to know how I was able to survive such a crash. I was still pale, and my feet were wobbly. Slowly the true dimensions of my takeoff dawned on me. At one point during this conference, I made a statement that would be quoted over and over: "If I can still win a gold medal on top of everything, I must be immortal."

Deep down inside I feared, though, that my Olympic dream might already have come to an end. I disappeared into my room. I didn't want to see or hear anyone. My knee swelled up like a handball, and the pain slowly crept up inside of me. I tried to look forward, a simple psychological trick that has worked for me so far.

Once Heini showed up at my side, I knew what was next: stationary bicycle, three times ten minutes. "You have to move your knee, that's your only chance," my trainer told me with great urgency. Sure enough, things soon improved. The physical activity supported the effect of the anti-inflammatory medications I had been given. Then, alpine skiing director Hans Pum showed up in my room and started to negotiate the starting positions for the super-G in case I wasn't able to start the next day, with Pepi Strobl on standby as my replacement. After my accomplishments so far this season—four victories in four races—I didn't understand the whole discussion, and I said, "I do believe that I've earned the right to remain on the list." After all the logistical setbacks I had had to cope with in the course of my career thus far, I wanted to take my fate into my own hands at all costs. I felt like I had to be selfish and fight for my chance. If worse came to worst, I would stand up for my decision in front of the public.

That night, Petra moved into my room. Luckily, she was sharing quarters in Hakuba with Schiffi's girlfriend at the time, Marit, and thus my roommate didn't mind switching places with Petra. At any rate, I had bothered him during his daily afternoon naps with my exercise sessions on the stationary bicycle. And it wasn't exactly cozy in my room. I was being treated around the clock. My coaching team did everything humanly possible to get me back into shape. Next door, there was a battle among the physicians. "He's racing," one of them insists. "Of course he isn't," retorts the other. Finally, Andreas Lotz shows up and suctions blood from my knee with a long syringe. After that intervention, I was able to bend my knee. Then everything went like clockwork.

During lunch I ran into Olympic pastor Bernhard Maier, and I apologized for having missed Sunday's worship service because of my injury. He didn't let me get away with this excuse. "If you wish, we could make up for that privately in your room." After the remarkable protective services my guardian angels had provided for me, I felt that I couldn't turn down the offer. Petra did the reading, and both of us received Holy Communion. A church service in such a small setting seemed rather odd. Since I knew that there are rules to be followed during mass, I was as nervous as in a ski race. I didn't want to do anything wrong; in church you can orient yourself to those who know what they are doing.

Every now and then, Alex and my friends from the fan club dropped by at the hotel to cheer me up. They constantly thought of new antics for keeping up my spirits. Once, they took me to an ice-hockey match in the Olympic capital, Nagano, an hour and a half away. Another time they described the Olympic gold medal to me in precise detail. They had visited downhill Olympic champion Jean-Luc Crétier at his hotel and were allowed to touch his gold medal, two days before they would be allowed to admire my own.

The weather kept acting up and it became impossible to run the super-G the next day. Every time they had to postpone, my chances improved. When the super-G was finally held on the third day after my downhill takeoff, I actually was starting to feel fit again. The upper part of the racecourse was still fogged in, but they were able to hold the race.

I could hardly believe that I would be getting another chance at Olympic glory, and in my favorite event. I knew that if I could get across the finish line with both skis on my feet, nothing and no one could prevent my victory. I skied a very cautious race, and once I was at the finish, I ever so carefully looked at the display sign. My name was at the very top, and next to it "– 0.61." Over half a second ahead! I did it! I looked up toward heaven and thanked the good Lord that I was allowed to experience this. "Unbelievable," the thought coursed through my mind. "Now I've actually won the most important race of my career, in spite of all the things that have happened here."

When Heinz Prüller shook my hand during the victory interview, I had tears in my eyes. Today, when I look at the pictures from way back then, I get tears in my eyes once again, only this time from laughing. For heaven's sake, look at that bizarre hairdo and revolting felt cap! Hard to believe, the things that were fashionable back then. Oh well, after all, that was way back in the last century. Then I couldn't have cared less about my outward appearance: I was concerned most of all about the competition, and the victories.

NOW I AM IMMORTAL (NAGANO, 1998)

The legendary super-G gold interview with Austria's Heinz Prüller.

HEINZ PRÜLLER: It's been a while since a victory interview has pleased me so immensely. My sincere best wishes! An unbelievable race! Congratulations!

HERMANN MAIER: I don't even know what to say. I am a bit touched. I never thought that I would still be able to pull this off. After all this, my career could well have been over. Really unbelievable!

PRÜLLER: What went through your head during the three days since your crash?

MAIER: I haven't actually looked at my crash on tape, but I've analyzed it in my mind. I've tried to figure out why it happened. After that, I just concentrated on the upcoming race.

PRÜLLER: Millions of Austrians have put their hopes on you. Did you yourself believe that it would work out today?

MAIER: Somehow, I did believe in it, but I didn't want to create too much pressure for myself. I wanted gold, and I knew that I was the favorite by far. Apparently, a normal race is enough for the Olympics. It wasn't one of my best races, to be sure. After such a crash I thought, "If I can win gold now, I must be immortal!"

PRÜLLER: A bit more immortal, in any case. Hermann Maier, the man who can't be destroyed, who can't be wounded. Now a childhood dream has come true for you. After all, you said even as a child, "I'll become an Olympic champion!"

MAIER: Yes, when I was eight years old, I thought, "I'm going for it!" That it actually happened is incredible. I must say thank you to my doctors, and to my guardian angel. Such a great deal of good luck!

PRÜLLER: The race was sensational. Did you analyze it in retrospect, and did you have any qualms when the others, like Cuche and Stemmle, came down the mountain?

MAIER: Yes, I was afraid, of course. When it was our turn, it was still a bit foggy, but then it cleared up all of a sudden. I felt like I was going so slowly, and I thought, nothing is moving here in comparison to the downhill, where I took off at three times the speed.

PRÜLLER: The timing was right after all . . .

MAIER: Yes, but when I was at the finish, I wouldn't have thought that it was enough.

(continues)

(*continued*)

PRÜLLER: Now there's still the giant slalom . . .

MAIER: I've already got one gold; anything that came after this would be an encore. I can't possibly get more after this.

PRÜLLER: What is Arnold Schwarzenegger going to say during his next live broadcast to the United States?

MAIER: I don't know. Maybe he'll make a "Herminator" movie and throw the Terminator into the trash.

NOT EVEN ARNIE WAS PUT THROUGH

The media had turned me into a global superstar. I just wasn't aware of the scope at that time. The television images of the crash of the century had gone around the world and were delivered into every second U.S. household on an hourly basis. Even Arnold Schwarzenegger, whom I knew only from the movies, contacted me via telephone. But not even the Terminator was able to get through to me; that's how well I was being insulated from the outside world at that time. Arnie, in true Hollywood fashion, simply relayed a message that I should make a good comeback and destroy the competition. The rest is known to most people by now: three days after the super-G gold, a victory in the giant slalom as an encore. Advertising executives estimated my market value at an astronomical ten million dollars a year. The Americans liked the story of the "bricklayer turned millionaire." Even while the Olympics were still going on, I received offers from several big U.S. television talk shows.

Chapter 2

NURSE, DO I STILL HAVE A LEG?

I had lost all feeling for time. When I awoke, I thought that I had just barely fallen asleep. In fact, it was already 6 A.M., and my medical team had yet to learn how my body had coped with the demands of last night's seven-hour operation. Seven hours! I had no idea what could have taken so long. I didn't feel a thing. No pain. There didn't seem to be a connection between my brain and the various parts of my body. Then, a completely absurd thought: "Am I already cured?" Slowly, I was being pulled back out of my dream world.

I was lying in the recovery room, and the neon lights were shining in my face. The beeping of the monitors could be heard in the background. There were hoses and IV lines everywhere. Two nurses were fussing with drip bags and towels. I was interested in only one thing: my leg. I pointed toward the thick brown lump swathed in bandages and asked, "Well, is it still there?" That may sound like a "typical Maier" wisecrack, but I was dead serious. I wasn't sure I was getting the unvarnished truth. I was afraid that they had amputated my leg and put something into the bandage just to keep me calm.

My mouth was completely dry. It felt like I had swallowed a box of tissues. I begged the nurse, "A cola would sure hit the spot!" And in fact, they gave me not one but two cans of soda, which I gulped down greedily. They probably thought, "Nothing can kill Maier! After all he's gone through so far, a can of cola won't do much harm." Wrong! It wasn't long before I regurgitated the entire contents. I apologized a thousand times. After this strenuous and embarrassing interlude, I fell back onto my pillow completely drained.

I had been pumped full of medication. In contrast to my last operation, when I had felt as though I was in a drunken stupor upon awakening from the anesthesia, this time around I felt like I had been put through the wringer. I had never felt anything like this before in my life. It was as though all the blood had been drained from my body, and I just lay there, indifferent to what was going on.

I JUST WANT TO BE LEFT ALONE

Once I found myself lying in the intensive care unit (ICU) surrounded by other people with grave injuries, I realized how serious my condition was. It seems they had pushed tubes into every available orifice. My bodily functions were going berserk. It started to dawn on me that my leg had now become a secondary issue. I had completely lost my orientation and had no idea which part of the hospital I was in.

The trauma center was still under construction at the time, and the ICU was housed in a giant modular unit that had been docked to the end of the building. It was steaming hot outside, and inside our metal box you could scarcely breathe. Add to that the typical hospital smell, and it was enough to give me one overriding desire: Get well and get out of here!

There are no private rooms in the ICU. The six beds were divided by green hospital curtains. The patients to my immediate right and left were under anesthesia, but the old man diagonally across from me was wide awake. He kept begging his nurse to pull the curtain aside for just a moment so he "could just see Hermann Maier." My fan was worse off than I. He was paralyzed from the neck down after a bicycle crash.

The situation was oppressive. Suddenly, you are staring death in the face as though it's the most normal thing on earth. If someone dies, he dies. You don't think about it much after that, yet there is a strange connection among the fellow sufferers. It's almost like it's your family. We sure weren't a pretty sight with all our cables and hoses. Everyone felt sorry for the next guy. You think to yourself, "Wow, he sure is bad off!" Or, "Compared to that guy, you're doing pretty well after all." Of course, one wanted the best outcome for everyone. But in the end, one had to do battle for oneself to get out of there as soon as possible. Unfortunately, not everyone was going to make it. But I wasn't thinking even for an instant about giving up. Least of all here.

I didn't want to see a soul or speak to anyone. At least not yet, the day after the operation. I was too weak, and everything was too much for me. I had to be selfish just to protect myself. I know that this was unbelievably hard for my family and friends who were waiting outside and wanted to see for themselves how I was doing. I considered all that only later. Of course, I realized that they all meant well, that everybody wanted to help me and comfort me. But that was exactly what I didn't need in this situation. I didn't want to be lied to, especially by those who didn't have a clue as to my true medical condition. I knew all by myself that I was doing poorly and I wanted to avoid any exhausting conversations. My doctors weren't surprised by these sentiments. They spoke of a "postoperative depression." Furthermore, my mind was altered by all the drugs I had been given. As a performance athlete, you have an extraordinary awareness of your own body. You often can sense the minutest signs of illness long before the doctors discover what's going on. But because of all the medication I was on, my connection to my body had somehow been severed. It even seemed to paralyze my mind. I knew only that I had to get through this, and I had to do it all by myself! At some level, you use the same skills that help you cope in a sports-related situation: You experience a tough defeat, and still you have to get out of bed the next day. The deciding factor is that you must never lose your focus, never lose sight of your ultimate goal. It is this quality that makes a winner. In the ICU, my goal was quickly defined: Get the hell out of here!

SUDDENLY, MY LIFE IS IN DANGER

Just as I was about to succumb to my depression, a doctor came along who seemed to be in exceptionally good physical shape. I tried to start a conversation. "It's all uphill from here on out, right?" (I hadn't lost my odd sense of humor.) The doctor was surprisingly honest: "It doesn't look very good, I'm sorry to say." What is it now? The doctor explained to me that my liver as well as my kidneys would be causing me some problems. Those vital organs seemed to be stressed beyond their limits trying to process the enormous amounts of toxins that had to be eliminated as a result of the massive contusions I had suffered in my pelvic region. Right then, my gaze fell upon the transparent urine-collection bag that was hanging by my bedside. "What is that?" I asked with amazement. "That came out of you," explained the doctor. "But why is it so black?" The color could be blamed on myoglobin, an indication of destroyed muscle cells, which had been eliminated in great numbers by my body. The myoglobin level that was measured in my system was alarmingly high: Normally, if you have a value above 20,000 micrograms of myoglobin per liter, your blood needs to be sent through dialysis. My level was at 128,000! The kidneys, which basically function as a filtering system, were simply overtaxed. Artur tried to explain this to me. He said, "If we can't get this under control by giving you lots of fluids, you won't escape dialysis." An artificial kidney! The thought alone gave me the shivers. "Now I really am up a creek!" I was beginning to realize with startling clarity that this was no longer just about my leg. This was a matter of life and death.

Mortal danger. Just the sound of it! From a medical point of view, I was in dire straits. But not for an instant did I think that I might not make it. I was completely convinced that I could muster enough energy and will to fight against the odds. "Is there anything, and I mean anything, that I can do?" Artur was glad to see my fighting spirit. "Drink as much as you can. Drink, drink, drink!" That's all? I was used to drinking a lot anyway. If I had poured seven liters of fluid into my body in Chile because of the high altitude, eleven liters shouldn't be a problem now. Including the IV fluid drips I was on, I totaled 22.8 liters that day. That was the saving grace for my kidneys. I became completely swelled up with fluids in the process, but that was the lesser evil.

I was lying in bed like an empty sack. My right leg was elevated, my head down. We had to avoid blood pooling and circulation problems. The front of my leg was shattered; on its side rested the delicate transplant, which I wasn't allowed to touch under any circumstances. It was dreadful to have to stay in this uncomfortable position. And it would be for several weeks! I drank and drank, and still had IV drips hooked up to my body day and night. As soon as one bag was empty, it was replaced by a full one. And somehow, all those fluids had to exit my body again. My catheter certainly wasn't up to the job. I was lying in a puddle, and I felt like a wet rag. It was as though I had stayed in the bathtub too long and was becoming softer and softer, like a croissant left in your morning coffee. There was pain everywhere, and my various body parts no longer seemed to fit together.

I had barely recovered from the "kidney scare" as the next hammer blow was preparing to strike. One of the doctors asked me during a routine exam to move my legs. My shocked reply was, "I can't, I am unable to move anything!"

"Try again!" I tried with all my might. "I can't, there's no way!" Nothing! Neither my legs nor my toes were moving an inch. What's the trouble now? Am I paralyzed?

I caught snatches of conversation from the medical team that made me weak with fear. "We missed a transverse lesion of the spinal cord. . . ." I was completely stunned, and for the first time started to question my fate. "Paraplegia? No, that couldn't be! Everything worked just a little while ago!" Time to give up? No! I started to rub myself vigorously in my groin, the region through which the femoral nerve passes, which is responsible for initiating leg movement. Voilà! My leg was able to move again! Only a quarter of an inch, but that small motion almost elicited a shout of triumph. "Look, it still works!" The doctors weren't satisfied.

They had become uncertain. They all, from Artur to the department head, had come running by now. A few moments later they rolled me out of the modular unit. Artur notified the neurology department at the regional hospital, a few miles away. They were getting everything ready to do magnetic resonance imaging (MRI).

I didn't realize that I had been shuttled on a roundabout route through the heating room in the basement and out of the trauma center. I didn't even notice that I was suddenly inside an ambulance, which was slowly making its way through the crowd of reporters positioned outside the hospital. No way should they find out about this dramatic turn of events!

What I didn't know at the time was that since the first news of my accident hit the press agencies, there had been a media tornado surrounding my story. All the headlines seemed to be about one event: Maier's accident.

Dozens of journalists from all over the world had traveled to Salzburg to gather "exclusive" facts or quotations surrounding the story. Every day around noon the doctors spoke to the media in the big auditorium about my condition. Luckily, I knew as little about all that as I did about the daily "health bulletin" taking the form of a press release. The correspondents largely played by the rules, except for two reporters who were caught trying to make their way into the ICU dressed in scrubs. I was well guarded, though, and completely shielded from the outside world.

How well that worked could be seen in the previously described diversionary maneuver. While Artur Trost was chatting with the waiting horde of journalists in front of the ICU, the ambulance, with its lights off and me inside, started up and slinked past the photographers and the Austrian TV broadcasting vehicle. A few minutes later, Artur joined us at the regional hospital in his private car and said with a broad grin, "It didn't take much to fool them."

I didn't feel much like laughing at the time, though. There are no words to describe what I went through during my twenty minutes inside the MRI tube. My rear end was aching so badly that I could no longer lie still. It was as though I had been tied to a bed of nails. An MRI is nothing new to me. Normally, there is something soothing about it. A few times, I have even fallen asleep inside the tube. But this time around I felt like I had been stuffed inside a boiling hot microwave oven. The extremely confined space brought out beads of sweat on my forehead. The incessant beeping was driving me to distraction. Instinctively, I reached for the alarm button. I wanted out of there, but at the same time, I knew that this scan was incredibly important. After all, the doctors had to find out whether my symptoms really indicated a possible paralysis. With my thumb on the alarm button, I was trying to buy time. Just like after a dive, when you hold your breath and try to stay below the surface for just a few more seconds. Finally, I was gripped by pure panic. While I squeezed my eyes shut, I pushed the red button. The technicians didn't react to my pleading, though, and didn't pull me out of the tube. I felt like a suspect during an interrogation held under a blinding white light. Then the team of doctors showed up in the MRI room. They all looked at me seriously, and I was bracing myself for the worst. What had they found? But all they wanted to do was convince me to remain in the scanner until the MRI was complete. The scan wasn't done yet, and if I gave up now, the whole procedure thus far would have been worthless. I screamed, "Hurry! I can't stand it any longer!" Of course, my tormentors didn't want to stop until they had gathered enough evidence for a definitive picture, which was in my own best interest. Artur seems to have been the only one who realized the true state of my condition. He put a moist washcloth onto my forehead, and I began to calm down. Unbelievable, how much difference such a simple gesture can make. My heart rate went down, and I felt at least a little better in this miserable situation. I thanked him a thousand times and continued fighting.

When Artur held the MRI images in his hands a few minutes later, I could almost feel the lump falling from his chest. My spinal cord was okay! The temporary signs of paralysis had a different, if not pleasant, cause. But now things sounded a lot less threatening. The strong internal bleeding in the region of my lower back had pinched off the main nerve route that runs down to my legs. The pressure was so overwhelming that I might never regain total feeling in both legs. This symptom was going to cause me great problems in the future, mostly in my left, "good," leg.

The doctors could not believe the fact that my pelvis had not been shattered, considering the force with which I had slammed into the hillside. "Any other person would have suffered a pelvic fracture," they maintain to this day.

Either I had become acclimated to the painkillers or their effectiveness was lessening. At any rate, I could feel the massive contusions more and more. I was still lacking any sense of orientation. And no wonder. There were no windows in the modular ICU unit, only those glaring neon lights. So I constantly stared at the large clock hanging on the wall. It was even exhausting to try to decipher the time. I didn't know whether it was four in the afternoon or four in the morning. I closed my eyes for a few moments, or so it seemed, and when I opened them up again, it was several hours later. I was unspeakably tired and perceived everything as though in a trance. Real sleep was almost impossible due to the constant throbbing pain. The enormous blood loss caused by the accident and the internal bleeding in my pelvic region made my hematocrit, a reading that indicates the blood's ability to transport oxygen, sink to a critical 19.4 from the normal 50. Not even ten blood units of one-third liter each could prevent this alarming drop. In addition, I was given erythropoietin (EPO), a hormonal supplement that is a favorite blood-doping agent among endurance athletes. EPO stimulates the formation of red blood cells and is used in a medical context in cases of high blood loss or dialysis. I thought to myself, "Unbelievable. For once I'm getting the stuff that the professional bicyclists are always being doped up with. I'm curious to see if it really has such spectacular results!" Unfortunately, I wasn't granted that sort of peak experience in my present condition. In any case, I wasn't kept on it for long, since my doctors were worried that my body would subsequently have to work harder to produce hemoglobin on its own.

The monitors were still humming all around me, the hospital personnel were constantly bustling about, and they continued fiddling with oxygen masks next to me. I was glad to go without the oxygen. It reminded me too much of my monotonous training routine. Whenever I am sitting on my exercise bicycle at a World Cup location high above sea level, I am breathing oxygen from a tank. As an athlete I know exactly when I need extra air.

I had had enough of the cables and lines on my lower arms, my finger, and my upper torso, without which my body no longer seemed able to function. The most intrusive one was an entry port on my chest. From it a plastic hose went underneath my collarbone, directly nourishing my body with vital substances. I was receiving liquid nutrients, pain medication, antibiotics to prevent infection, diuretics to aid in urine excretion, electrolytes, and trace elements. A strange machine was dispensing the medications in exactly configured amounts. All in all I counted at least ten or fifteen drip bags hanging on a metal rod above my bed.

Everything was measured and strictly supervised. If one of the values, such as oxygen intake, was lagging, immediately a red light would flash. Although I could barely turn in my bed, I had to maneuver the whole mess of hoses with great care at even the slightest movement, since I was paranoid of ripping the venous catheter out of its port.

My upper arm, from which they had taken the tissue for the transplant and then sewed up again, looked to me like a large sausage. The lower leg that had been operated on was thickly bound, though the surgeon had left a small window at the site of the operation, which he was always opening up to see whether everything was okay with the transplanted skin flap.

August 26, 2001. In an irregular pattern of sleep and wakefulness I made it through the second night after the accident. I was beginning to feel that I was emotionally ready to have visitors. Even though I was doing miserably, I had a bad conscience. I knew that Gudrun and my mother had been waiting with a hundred questions in front of the ICU for a long night, a whole day, and then another night. It was certainly not a pleasant experience for them to enter the sticky, hot ICU closet with all the critical care patients inside.

But I was relieved. Finally, some familiar faces, but I almost had to laugh. You're only allowed to enter the ICU in the sterile green scrubs issued by the hospital, and there was something odd about those two walking in their little plastic slippers. The green gown fit Gudrun very well, and the face mask made her look like an oriental princess. I was glad to have her here; after all, we were very close. This first visit was good for my spirit. When you are doing so poorly, you normally collapse into the hands of your doctors and let them do all the work and make all the decisions. I was determined to have a part in my care, though. I knew that now that I was fully conscious again, I would have to struggle to gather up all my reserves and give my very best. It was important to mobilize my inner strength to speed up the healing process and to present a cheerful face. I even tried to be funny and crack a few jokes. We chatted about mundane matters. But I couldn't hold up for long, and I soon fell asleep again. But I could tell that my worried mother had become less anxious. Now she understood the situation and had firsthand evidence of how her boy was doing. Now no one could make things up as far as my condition was concerned. Nonetheless, I was relieved when the visit was over. In fact, I kicked them out kindly but decisively. "I'd kind of like to go back to sleep now!" After all, there were more people outside who really wanted to see me.

In the afternoon, my coaching team from the Olympic Training Center were allowed to visit. Heini, who put together my conditioning program on a daily basis, was already talking during his first visit about different possibilities of working out inside the hospital. Johannes Zeibig, our sports physician, gave me confidence and hope with his optimism. Moreover, he immediately established rapport with the trauma center doctors. He came and went freely in the ICU and started to work on me as though he were one of the staff here. Together with the intensive care physician, Sylvester Klaunzer, he instituted a policy of my being treated largely with conservative measures. As much as I was able to, I tried to have a say in my treatment. As it was, we had to improvise on a daily basis.

The biggest problem was lying down. We tried everything. We tried out different beds. I got seasick on the inflatable mattress. We tried soft mattress pads, then hard ones. Finally, we found a simple solution, one I could live with for better or for worse: a thick foam pad with a hole cut out in the place where my bottom should have come to rest. They hung me into that thing, but even so, the pain did not lessen. I must have looked terrible. My rear end was as wide as the hindquarters of a draft horse. And of course I was exclusively wearing one of those chic hospital gowns.

The next shock I suffered occurred the first time the dressing was changed. My lower leg, or rather what was left of it, was thicker than my thigh. "And I'm supposed to fit that into a ski boot? That will never, ever happen."

I was in a permanent state of semiconsciousness. Dazed phases of wakefulness were alternating with short episodes of leaden sleep. Remarkably, I was out of critical condition by now. Hoses and lines took over all my vital functions. I was taking in artificial nourishment, and had to use a catheter for excretion. I couldn't even think about getting up. The outside world didn't have a clue about all that, it seems. Indeed, one magazine couldn't seem to accept the fact that I wasn't giving any interviews out of the ICU. Instead, they were printing a "turbo-plan," according to which I would be back at the starting gate by December. The following statement was even attributed to a "source from among Maier's coaching staff": "I wouldn't be surprised if Hermann skips only the overseas races and is back in business by December 8 of this year." Honestly, I am glad to say that I had to read this rubbish only much later.

I MAKE A HORRIFYING DISCOVERY

I was much too involved with more immediate problems at the time. Like the frightening changes in my body. If I pushed down with my finger into the swollen tissue in my hip region, it created a hole. You could see the indentation for several minutes. And it made a dull thump, like when you push into snow or Styrofoam. When I showed my discovery to Heini, he was startled. And the whole thing was incredibly painful. This had to be treated as soon as possible! For this reason, I insisted that we start with physical therapy at once, even while I was still in intensive care. I implored the doctors, "This has got to go away! We have to somehow revive the tissue and get the hematomas to soften up!" There it was again, that sports mind-set, that burning desire to get back into shape, regardless of my busted leg, as quickly as possible. "Otherwise, this is all going to drag out over a period of weeks!" So they tried new variations of treatment: ultrasound and laser treatment as well as the so-called hot roll. In the process, my rump muscles were heated in the hopes that the elevated temperature would cause the toxins to be flushed out at an increased rate via my lymph system. By now, the Olympic Center training team was coming and going at the ICU: Vinzent, my physical therapist, worked together with Barbara Neureiter, the trauma center physical therapist, on getting the hematomas in my lower back region to clear up. Dr. Zeibig spent half the nights at my bedside, and Heini was here more than he was with his family. Each day that I was able to spend in any other than the stiff lying position should speed up the healing process considerably. Once we started the physical therapy, my hospital stay seemed to turn overnight into a full-time job. I wasn't bored for one second, which was a great advantage, since I didn't have a chance to succumb to depressive thoughts. But even that wasn't enough for me. On the fourth day, I began to nettle Artur on a constant basis. "Can we finally start with a real workout regimen, please?"

The more my thoughts cleared up, the more questions I started to ask. I was interested in everything: the daily routine at the hospital, the length of the operations that Artur was performing, and of course, every single one of my blood test results. Because of the closely monitored training at the Olympic Center over the years I probably know some of this stuff better than many sports physicians. I was expecting from the doctors who were supposed to make me well again the same level of professionalism with which I approached my own training. Every time I had a problem, Artur was there, except when he happened to be in surgery. So I was once again calling for my doctor. "Unavailable," they said. "Then get me Zeibig instead!"

"He is at the press conference!" I lost my cool and yelled, "Maybe they should worry more about my leg and less about giving interviews all the time!" Not a day went by without bad surprises. I might have been spared one of them had they listened to my request for a meal from McDonald's. I was receiving liquid nourishment, which meant that the next fiasco was just around the corner. I was given an enema—a nightmare even for a healthy person—but in my miserable condition, it was unbearable. They squeeze in the fluid, and at some point you can no longer keep it in. I imagine that a rocket feels this way just before it is about to blast off. It seemed to me like I was levitating fifteen feet above the bed. In addition, I was pouring sweat, and the machines I was hooked up to were now emitting a single crescendo of beep, beep, beep! Just dreadful!

But it would become worse. The terrible pain was getting stronger and stronger, and I could think about little else. The daily washing ritual was the only thing that gave me a sensation of normalcy. Brush your teeth, or what was left of them, a few seconds. Sponge down with the washcloth. The nurse holds a mirror close to my face and I comb my hair. For whom? I was startled when I saw my reflection. My features had changed, like an extreme bicyclist who is sitting on his bike day and night and becomes completely emaciated. The medications had also taken their toll on my appearance. My face had turned a dreadful yellow, which was a sign that my liver had been seriously affected.

When the pain became more than I could bear, only one thing helped: a dose of morphine or piritamid. My body was completely poisoned for sure. And no wonder, considering the amount of pharmaceuticals I was subjected to. There were pustules erupting everywhere, veritable little volcanoes growing out of my skin. But I knew that it had to be like that. This way, I was spared the worst-case scenario, an infected leg or an inflamed transplant, and then everything would have to start over from the beginning. Even though the healing process was moving forward, the pain continued to increase. Because I couldn't even think of sleeping normally in this situation, I constantly had to increase the amount of painkillers I was taking, the administration of which had been left up to me. There was a hand control that made three milligrams of medication available to me every ten minutes. During the worst phase, I was counting the seconds before I was allowed to pull the trigger again.

F L A S H B A C K

MY FATHER, THE HERO

A sticky, hot, early summer day, 1988. The racket of the machines drowned out my father's cries for help. Only three hundred yards away from our house he was desperately clinging to a beam. The scaffold had broken away, and the ladder on which my father had been standing had fallen down. He was hanging twenty-five feet above the concrete floor, and no one could hear him. He had been working on the glass dome of a timber-processing building in Reitdorf when this happened. Then help arrived. A colleague appeared with a ladder. But it was too short. "Move aside!" my father yelled, "I can't hold on any longer!" Moments later, he hit the ground. Both heels were shattered, ankles, fibula, complex pelvic fracture. Even some of his vertebrae were cracked, and a slight skull fracture was diagnosed as a result of the impact on the back of his head. A tragic event that would prove to have a lasting influence on me.

While my father was in the hospital and my mother, her nerves shot, had started smoking again, I was drawn to the accident site. I desperately wanted to know why this had to happen, and was hoping to find some answers at the site. I climbed up onto the scaffold at the construction site. I looked down and saw how incredibly high twenty-five feet really is. Anyone who has ever stood on the ten-meter diving tower at a swimming pool knows what I'm talking about. I had just turned fifteen and was at the first turning point of my life. I did not at all feel comfortable at the school I was attending in Schladming. It was a combination vocational and skiing school. It just didn't work out for me. While my classmates were collecting trophies on the slopes, I was spending a lot of time in doctors' waiting rooms. The terrible knee pain that kept me from pursuing my favorite pastime was caused by growth problems. The doctors called it "Osgood–Schlatter disease" and tried to reassure me. It was supposed to be only a passing disturbance of the growth plate in my shinbone.

All that was going through my head as I was standing at the top of the rickety scaffold. That's when I made a decision that would influence the rest of my life: "I have no interest in business; I'm going to become a bricklayer." My family needed every extra penny, so the timing was fortuitous. We had no idea whether my father would ever be able to work again. We especially didn't know what would happen to the ski school that my parents had opened just the winter before. Thus, I terminated my schooling after the first year of the three-year program and began an apprenticeship as a bricklayer. This decision was especially difficult for me toward the beginning of my apprenticeship. My father, by the way, was able to get back on his feet remarkably quickly as a result of his tremendous determination, and he and my mother together turned the ski school into what it is today. Later on, when I was lying in the hospital with severe injuries, I often thought of my father. My father the hero.

My first memorable experience as a bricklayer's apprentice occurred on my first day, August 16, 1988. While we were constructing the valley relay station of the Achterjet gondola in Flachau, I was smacked on the head by a huge aluminum panel. I remember its dimensions to this day: ten feet long, fourteen inches wide. I also remember the ensuing dialogue: "Anything happen?" my fellow construction worker wanted to know. My stunned answer: "Everything's busted!" I got a huge bump on my head, and a crease in my forehead reminds me even today of this incident.

I had an even more significant experience at the end of my first week, when I was helping the foreman take down a scaffold. While he was handing down the yellow panels from above, I thought, "Pretty unstable, the whole affair." Right then, the whole scaffold collapsed. I squeezed myself into a corner in order not to be struck by the long support poles with iron brackets at the end. The foreman got off with a complex lower-arm fracture. "I don't know," I was thinking while they were pushing the injured man into the ambulance, "maybe I would be better off in school after all." Moreover, I wasn't at all used to the hard physical labor or the rough work environment. When I wanted to sit down to rest for a moment, one of the foremen yelled at me, "Don't even think about sitting down!" I was relieved every afternoon when I was allowed to pedal home on my bicycle, with a bricklayer's level sticking out of my backpack.

Once I realized how dangerous a bricklayer's existence can be, I spent part of my time in business, so to speak. Every morning, I grabbed my wheelbarrow and went to the supermarket, which was about half a mile away. There, I grabbed a twelve-pack of beer, mineral water, sausage rolls (with and without pickles), cigarettes, and so on. Because I collected a hundred-schilling bill from each of my twenty or so bricklayer colleagues, I was always out and about with two or three thousand schillings. When I returned the change, I always rounded it up to my advantage, which meant there was enough left to get my own lunch at least. The more I earned from this side business, the better care I took of my customers.

Now I knew exactly what such everyday items cost at the store. While the other apprentices who went to run such errands were sloppy in carrying out their business, I was always the one most in demand.

I was starting to enjoy the work I was doing. I was earning my first money, and I learned how to get by on my own. I was well liked at the construction site because I wasn't afraid to work hard, and at home I made myself useful by helping out wherever I could. I was about to become an adult, and along with me, my brother Alex, who is one and a half years younger than I.

We were both concerned about being independent, and we financed all the bigger purchases ourselves: the first motorcycle, the driver's license, and the first car, a 1978 GM Star Kadett. Even though we were a very close-knit family, my brother and I developed a sort of independence that we are still proud of today.

The true impetus behind everything I did was the dream of a career as a ski racer. Thus, I started the coursework to become a state-certified ski instructor. This was an ideal combination for me: bricklaying work in the summer, ski instructor in the winter. I got to spend the whole day on skis, and after I had finished with my students, I went off skiing by myself, or I hauled the gates for a race-course up to the top of the gondola in the early morning light and put up my own training run. In a way, my rhythm is very similar today. In the wintertime, I am on my skis in every type of weather, and during the snowless months I am hard at work conditioning, with the slight difference that the staging areas today are no longer Flachauwinkl and Kaprun, but Kitzbühel, St. Moritz, Vail, and Bormio.

I took my training to become a ski instructor very seriously. While my colleagues went out on the town in the evenings, I sat in my room and studied theory. I read everything I could get my hands on as long as the topic was skiing. I got an A on every single theoretical exam, and sometimes it even seemed to me that I knew more than my teachers. A few times I even felt like a straight-A nerd, which also applied to the practical aspects of my training. Of course, much of my skiing ability can be classified as natural talent. But I did lay the basic foundation for a big portion of my carefully developed technique way back then.

Later, when I should have been competing in the Europe Cup rather than fighting for a spot on my state team, I had to organize my entire infrastructure myself. A typical Sunday looked something like this: In the darkness, I drove alone up to the Kitzsteinhorn in our ski school VW van. I drilled the gates into the hard snowpack, and then took off. Or else I just skied without a predetermined course. Always I waited until the very last second before I packed up my stuff at the end of a day of skiing and tore back down the mountain to put on my soccer jersey for the Flachau team just before kickoff.

Unfortunately, my soccer coach had little understanding of my tight timetable. Once, when I arrived for a game ten minutes late, he made me sit out the entire game, which is not the position preferred by a goal-hungry center.

A ski instructor's existence was quite practical, since I was able to make optimal use of the time before and after instruction. They opened up the lift in Flachauwinkl early just for me, and they even let me use the timing system.

My ski training was the absolutely most important thing for me. I was the first one on the slope, worked between instruction hours, and continued my workout afterward. This was a time I grew both as a skier and personally. My workouts were somewhat disorderly and often dangerous. I placed the gates myself. The course often led over passages that I couldn't possibly see as I was coming down. It goes without saying that at times some risky situations developed when someone was skiing into my racecourse. Time and again I had to scold skiers, especially when they skied over my markers. I skied one run, then I put all the markers back up and skied the next one. If I didn't have enough time to mark out a course, I skied off-slope in heavy snow, in deep powder, or on mogul runs. Not only was it a lot of fun, this helped me enormously during my first few FIS (International Ski Federation) races. I put together the different aspects of the training all by myself. I often rode my bike, sometimes into the darkness if that was the only way to get it done, since I could get started only after work. I had my power lifting and muscle development on the construction site, and the rest of a balanced workout came from bike riding and running. I built coordination units into my running workouts, and even back then I was quite creative in this regard. For instance, I would add an additional handicap to my two-mile route home from soccer practice. I fastened ten-pound bags to my calves and spent the entire bike ride with flexed feet. Or I put up a rope in my backyard and played circus performer. As soon as my job allowed, I started to prioritize all other things as secondary to skiing, even regarding my nutrition. For three years, I tried to eat an almost exclusively vegetarian diet, which if anything, however, had a negative effect on my performance.

In the evenings, I would study old tapes of World Cup racers. Double world champion Rudi Nierlich was my only true example. Unfortunately, he had a fatal accident in 1991. When my mother came into my room, she always encouraged me. "Hermann, the things those guys can do, you can do as well." After all, it was my mother who had taught me to ski. My father had imagined the whole thing to be much easier. My mother likes to recall the scene that took place at Christmas 1975, a few days after my third birthday.

My first pair of Atomic skis is lying underneath the Christmas tree, and the very next morning my ambitious dad marches me up to the Griessenkar lift. My mom protests severely, but my father is as stubborn as I am. "You and I are both ski instructors," he says to my mother. "Why on earth should our boy not be able to ski?" Three hours later we're back, and my father tosses me like a young, disobedient puppy at my mother's feet: "Here, you can try." My mother was much more patient, and a few days later I was able to navigate the slopes on my own. The only thing I couldn't do by myself was get up onto the chairlift. The lift attendant still had to do that for me, and he usually did it anything but gently.

Back then, I was too little, and now I was too old. No one seemed to take me seriously. There was no room for a 21-year-old on any ski team. In order to live my dream of a ski racer, I had to continue working as a bricklayer and ski instructor, and for most of the races I had to pay the entrance fee myself. I will always remember some important stations on my rocky road to the top:

First close contact with the stars: Rudi Nierlich remembrance race, a giant slalom on the Postalm near Wolfgangsee, end of December 1993. Sixth place behind World Cup racers Sigi Voglreiter, Heli Mayer, Thomas Sykora, Conny Walk, and Mike Tritscher. For the first time, the local media take notice of Hermann Maier. I am standing in the finish area and fuming: "If I can keep up with these folks, why can't I get a chance in the Europe Cup?"

Excursion into the pro league: The day after the Nierlich race I pay the five-hundred-schilling fee for a pro race in Schladming and get back seventeen thousand schillings in prize money, and that after eleventh place in the qualification. I think, "Hey, I am becoming a pro!" However, as a real pro I would have to take off with the professional tour to the United States within the next few days, and that seems too hurried for me. After skiing in that race, I am punished with a two-month race prohibition for having competed professionally.

State championships, 1994–1995: I am able to win titles in three Austrian states: Carinthian state champion in slalom, Tyrolean RTL champion, and three-time champion in Salzburg, where I was ahead by nine seconds in the slalom. The Vorarlberg Ski Federation is starting to show an interest in me. And even Liechtenstein is encouraging me to become a citizen. Salzburg's ski federation president Alex Reiner takes the hint.

My first appearance at the Austrian championships, March 25, 1995, at Semmering: I race as number 130 in the giant slalom, and the indentations around the gates are so deep that the gate referees can't see me in some of the turns. I still make the best of my chance and end up in eighteenth place.

The breakthrough: I am able to compete in the FIS giant slalom in Château-d'Oex, in western Switzerland. Because I am unaware of my real standing, I arrive at one o'clock at night and still have to prep my skis. The next morning, I am standing at the starting line in my off-the-shelf orange Technica ski boots and am envious of the awesome ski equipment of the Senegalese competitor next to me. Yet I am able to score seventh place, and the next day, in the second round (less sleep-deprived), I come in sixth. This earns me so many FIS points that I will be granted a halfway-decent starting number for next season.

My first three FIS downhills: In Altenmarkt-Zauchensee, I first strap on the seven-foot planks with the shallow tips. In three races I am able to improve incrementally, progressing from twenty-fourth to nineteenth and finally to sixth place. Now I can call myself a downhill racer.

My last day as a bricklayer, October 25, 1995: I have become a young foreman myself by now, and I bid farewell to my colleagues on the evening before our national holiday with the following words: "I am going to give skiing a try one last time. If it doesn't work out, we will see each other again in the spring." I arrive home and toss my backpack with the trowel and the level into a corner of the garage. It will remain there until Christmas 2002, when its contents are auctioned off for a considerable sum at a charitable event. I will hear from my bricklayer crew, a fun bunch of Englishmen, in 1998. Even before the Olympic Games they have somehow heard about my World Cup victory in Wengen, and they send me a congratulatory greeting card: "Congratulations to the fastest bricklayer on earth!"

3

I MUST BE CRAZY

August 30, 2001.   On day six after the accident I received unexpected visitors. Two local policeman apparently thought I must be ready to talk about the details of the accident. I recalled their faces from the scene of the crash. But their uniforms were different this time around, since they, too, had to don the sterile ICU scrubs. I could tell how uncomfortable they were, but after all, they had to do their job. The trauma center's chief physician, Karlbauer, impressed on them that they could not talk to me for more than ten to fifteen minutes in my present state. I was still so drowsy under the influence of the pain medication that the officers quickly abandoned their inquiry and decided to try again in a few weeks.

Others were more persistent. Although I had been at the trauma center for almost a week, there still was no picture of me, let alone an interview. The Austrian Broadcasting Corporation (ORF) had given up and withdrawn their silver satellite van and team of reporters from the entrance to the trauma center. The print media were more tenacious. Their correspondents roamed the hospital corridors morning to night, hoping to glean some "exclusive" bit of news in addition to the official noonday bulletins. A strange mood reigned at the ICU. Immediately beyond the glass door that separates the ICU from the rest of the hospital, my entourage were sitting almost around the clock. Further back, the visitors of other injured patients were waiting, as well as patients waiting to be admitted to the emergency room. Even farther back, at a respectful distance, the reporters were lying in wait, time and again attempting to sidle up to my family and friends. "Please, show some understanding!" My mother tried to nip any sort of conversation in the bud. Because the media were running out of things to say, the photographers took out their zoom lenses and took close-up shots of my mother and Gudrun, both with faces swollen from crying. Was it really necessary to publish those pictures? At any rate, my mother gave in after days of silence, granting a single television interview, which was broadcast time and again in the days to come. The next logical step for the media was to get me in front of their lenses.

To the chagrin of the paparazzi, there was not a single window looking into the ICU modular unit. Through the electronically guarded door came only the closest relatives and friends. I registered them all as through a curtain of fog. To be honest, I can remember only a few visits from nonrelatives. Peter Schröcksnadel, president of the Austrian Ski Federation and my most important adviser in business matters, made an appearance. He had interrupted a fishing vacation in Canada. "Well, you have looked better," he joked in his Tyrolean accent, and tried to cheer me up with his characteristic optimism. "Look, you've won everything that can be won. You don't have to become an Olympic champion yet again. Now the primary concern is your health, and with your constitution, you'll get back on your feet again!" The president was deeply convinced of the feasibility of his own advice. What I didn't know at the time was that Schröcksi had already been negotiating with agents and directors about a proposed documentary film. Even the title had been set: "Hermann Maier: The Journey Back." Which was more proof that he truly believed in my comeback from the beginning. As did our men's head coach, Toni Giger, who on his return from Chile had rushed directly from the airport to my hospital bed.

DIVERSIONARY MANEUVER
FOR PATIENT TRANSFER

My blood count had stabilized, and the coaching team was hard at work trying to figure out how to protect my privacy once I was moved out of the ICU. For the move itself, another diversionary trick would be necessary. My team placed a press bulletin onto my homepage on Thursday night, which read, "Depending on the further upward trend in his recuperation, Hermann Maier will be moved from the ICU to the regular wing of the hospital over the weekend." A few minutes later, this same news was reported over the radio worldwide, as well as on ORF's main news show, *Zeit im Bild*. My handlers' phones were ringing off the hook. While the photographers were working out all the best angles for taking pictures during the move, the actual relocation had already taken place quietly and unobserved. Shortly before, one of the nurses had herded together the entire medical team of the ICU for a farewell picture. It was truly a sentimental moment. Unbelievable, how close we had all become during the past six days. After all, I had shared some horrific days suspended between life and death with these helpful and caring people.

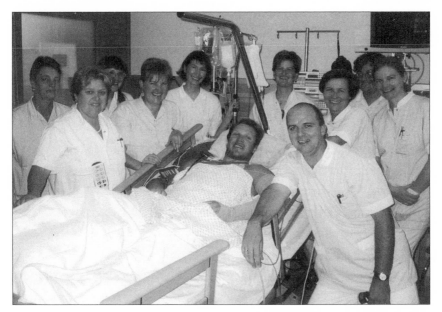

August 30, 2001. I am on the mend and allowed to leave the intensive care unit.

Once I had escaped from the oppressive, sticky ICU container, I felt like I was on a magnificent outing. On my bed, I rolled past healthy people; in front of the hospital newsstand I saw newspapers and magazines. I soaked up everything around me like a dry sponge. Once out of the elevator, we traversed an endless hallway, at the end of which a stately man in blue with a gun strapped to a holster welcomed me with, "I will be here to ensure your safety." Sure enough, the Austrian Ski Federation had engaged my very own bodyguard! I had what seemed like an elegant suite, consisting of two adjoining rooms. It was brand new and tastefully furnished with wooden decor. I had a balcony with a view out into the country (albeit constricted by a scaffold), a TV next to my bed, a bathroom, and nice nurses who made me feel that they were there just for me. I felt so good that I even forgot for a few moments how poorly I was really doing. I closed my eyes and savored complete quiet for the first time since my accident. Through the open balcony door I could hear the soft sound of the late summer rain, and I was breathing the fresh air. No beeping from the monitors, no red alarm lights, no oxygen mask. At last, I was starting to live again. I had a feeling that things were heading in the right direction.

And I was allowed to sleep as long as I wanted! The pain medication made possible my first halfway restful night since the accident. When I woke up, I could see daylight. It was as though I had been sleeping forever. Gudrun and my mother had brought baskets of fan mail, personal items, and other diversions from home and positioned them all on my nightstand: my "Good Luck Hermann Maier" piglet, which had brought me luck during my crash in Nagano; DVDs to distract me (including *Gladiator*); the new Lance Armstrong best-seller, *It's Not About the Bike*, seven copies of which my mother had found in my fan mail; as well as herbal teas and homemade fruit juices from none other than Arnold Schwarzenegger himself. A handwritten motivational letter in English from my friend accompanied the healing juices from his own store of magic potions.

For the first time, I felt something akin to hunger. The fresh-baked rolls at breakfast tasted delicious. Lunch was a salmon filet with steamed potatoes. In contrast to the ICU, where my nourishment was almost exclusively intravenous, I was able to eat in peace. How wonderful! Unfortunately, I still couldn't savor things. My hemoglobin count, which indicates the blood's ability to transport oxygen and thus is a benchmark of the body's endurance level, was on the rocks. Or even further down. A healthy person has an "HB" count of fourteen to eighteen. Bicycle ace Lance Armstrong complains in *It's Not About the Bike* that his HB count, hampered by chemotherapy, had dropped to seven. Mine was below six! It sucks all the energy out of your body. You really feel completely devoid of blood. In medical jargon, it's called anemia. I was so exhausted that even the act of eating soup was a physical exertion. Reading and talking were too exhausting. I lay in bed like a wet rag.

At least my thumb was in working order, and the sport I was able to actively engage in is called "channel surfing." With Gudrun sitting next to me studying for her final exams, I was zapping through the TV programs on my little bed monitor.

We didn't get much time alone, just the two of us. The pressure from the media had become unbearable for those around me who had successfully protected me thus far. In addition to all the big Austrian media outlets, several large German TV stations as well as a dozen international broadcasters were standing in front of my door. Even the U.S. TV giant CNN, which at the time was playing a promotional Olympic spot that included my Nagano crash (*Celebrate Humanity*) several times a day, wanted to air an original "Herminator" statement. Since there simply wasn't anything new in my case, more and more misinformation started to circulate about my condition. So I huddled with my spokesman, who is very savvy about such matters, to prepare my first official press report. The whole world seemed to be waiting for my appearance. No matter how badly you are doing, when you're in the public spotlight, there is no mercy!

Outside my room, ORF and the print media were arguing over who would get the first interview. A sensitive issue. We didn't want to favor anyone, but someone had to go first. It was a matter of reaching as many interested members of the public as possible in the shortest time span, without letting me suffer too much in the process. Finally, President Schröcksnadel laid down the law and issued the following judgment: ORF senior sports correspondent Elmar Oberhauser will be allowed to talk to me for ten minutes for the show *Sport am Sonntag* (Sunday Sports News). The interview will be broadcast to the hospital auditorium two floors below, where the rest of the reporters are waiting. They will be allowed to ask questions via a live broadcast following the interview.

September 2, 2001. After a quiet Saturday with my family, the interview hysteria came upon us with full force. ORF showed up with their star producer, Lucky Schmidtleitner, two cameramen, and a handful of technicians, who wanted to transform my beautiful, quiet convalescence room into a television studio. They started to unpack their huge lighting tripods and were in the process of discussing camera angles when my doctors arrived and intervened. The hallway in front of my room would have to serve as "sick room," which no one would notice during the broadcast. Elmar Oberhauser came alone to my bedside an hour before the showdown and joined me in watching the end of the Formula 1 race in Spa-Francorchamps. We talked about the horrible crash of the Italian Prost driver Luciano Burti, who had veered to the right, crashed into a tire barricade at 200 mph, and miraculously suffered almost no injury. Now it was time to get going. To make me presentable on television, I asked the doctors to remove the IV lines from my chest. The narrow plastic tube underneath my right collarbone, through which medications and electrolytes were entering my body, was taped up for the short duration of the interview. The same for the venous port on my lower arm. With my hair haphazardly combed, without makeup, pale, and bare-chested, I was pushed into the "interview room." I didn't have any reason to pretend to anyone. The gap in my teeth that had appeared when the two incisors were knocked out had already gotten a temporary fix.

The following minutes were more tedious than an eight-hour training session in the conditioning torture chamber. Kalle Törnström, from

Sweden, the former personal photographer of the great Ingmar Sten-mark, was the only one allowed to take a few photographs. Those would be wired around the world within a few minutes, and would grace the front pages of numerous daily papers the next day.

When I saw the sports journalists on the little monitor next to my bed, I felt like crying. Some of them I had last seen during my World Cup victory at Aare, as a triumphant winner. Now the miserable state I was in became overwhelmingly obvious to me.

The spotlights came on, Lucky gave the sign for camera number 1, the red lamp glowed, and I was jolted by a rush of adrenaline like I get only at the starting gate. I knew that I looked like shit, but there was no going back. The technician shoved the microphone in my direction, and Oberhauser started out slowly, for him almost hesitantly. He clearly wanted to go easy on me. Nevertheless, the interrogation was an effort for me; but I pulled myself together as best I could. I said to myself, "Go ahead, pull yourself out of this pit and show that there will be no surren-der!" And so this sentence, which would be quoted again and again later on, crossed my lips: "I *shall* return. And certainly not weaker. I'm betting as strong or even stronger." The interview lasted all of ten minutes, but I was exhausted. Just the act of speaking was harder than ever before. I felt like crying. Eight-hundred thousand people were watching me on their television sets fighting back tears. I could read the shock in the faces of the reporters down in the auditorium. Am I really that down-and-out? Hesitantly, politely, and with restraint they posed questions that had remained open after Oberhauser's interview. They obviously were em-pathizing with me. Except for one guy who was brash enough to ask a provocative question regarding my accident: "Mr. Maier, weren't you traveling a bit fast?" At that point, Austrian Ski Federation press chief Josef Schmid broke up the press conference, and I was allowed to go back to my room. I was incredibly relieved.

I closed my eyes and let the past half hour go through my head once more. It hadn't been too bad. Nevertheless, for the first time—except for the brief interrogation by the police—I was confronted with the accident. Did I bear responsibility? Was there really someone who felt that I was at least partially at fault? For me it was always totally obvious that I was not at fault in the least. It's like when you're sitting in an airplane and it crashes. Of course, you could have stayed home and not gotten on the plane. Come to think of it, I wonder what happened to the guy in the Mercedes. Why hasn't he contacted me? Should I be mad at him? No, I guess the situation was too much for him to deal with. It was an accident, and tragically, there were dire consequences for me. I felt that fate had certain plans for me, though I didn't know what at the time. At any rate, I was confronted with the future for the first time. To talk about the present wasn't a problem, but the future? In my state?

At 6:30 P.M. I had a strange experience. I saw a man on TV who previously had been seen only as a triumphant victor on the winner's platform. Now he was just lying there. The delayed broadcast of the interview was showing on *Sport am Sonntag*, and I tried to put myself in the shoes of the viewers. I think they could tell how I was really doing.

The interview triggered reactions all over the world. The pictures were broadcast on different channels until late at night. I even found myself on the CNN Sports broadcast. For me it was incomprehensible that to the media, my calamity seemed to be worth more than my most glorious skiing triumphs. Of course, the newspapers were filled with quotations the next day. Even though I could tell from the reactions that most had underestimated the gravity of my condition and were almost shocked after the TV pictures, the public continued to believe in me. That was demonstrated among other things by an opinion poll among Austrian sports fans.

"Will Hermann Maier ever compete in ski races again?" The astounding result: 93 percent of Austrians believed in my comeback to the race circuit at this early point in time. I have two explanations for this phenomenon: Either my team of medical experts had not managed (or not wanted) to convey the true scope of my grave injuries to the public, or the people in the outside world thought I could do the seemingly impossible. Even I started to be affected by this euphoria. In my brain, still in an altered state due to the medication, the first visions of Olympic glory started to take root. My coaching team was beginning to put together concrete training plans for my comeback while I was still hooked to a catheter and tied to my bed.

My days were stuffed with appointments and therapy. One wellmeaning visitor after another came and went, even though my handlers had prevented most visits to begin with. I needed my strength for more important tasks. Despite three daily sessions of physical therapy, Heini was champing at the bit to start my training in earnest. Before I could say anything, a white scaffold with a hand-cranked ergometer was erected next to my bed. Heini's eyes were shining when he demonstrated his new acquisition to me. The ergometer, which had been secretly imported from Germany, worked in principle just like my bicycle ergometer in Obertauern. Instead of my injured legs, my arms had to do the work. But not even that was without pain at first. The twelve-inch scar on my left upper arm where the skin transplant had been harvested was not even close to being healed. But such "minor aches and pains" don't even start to count as a valid excuse with Heini. As an avid fan of technology, I took some interest in my new roommate. I was able to guide everything electronically: watt resistance, rotations per minute, different levels of exertion, constant heart-rate monitoring, countdown, and so on. Despite all that, I didn't quite know what to think of the thing. "At least it's a diversion," I thought and started cranking. At the beginning, I really took off. Ten minutes twice at a whopping ten watts. Heini got out his lactateanalysis kit, pricked my ear, and determined the level of exertion according to my blood levels. At least I was in the moderate region, at lactate 1.5. And because the reporters would otherwise have sucked stories out of their fingers, we once again allowed Kalle Törnström into the room to take a picture that he was to distribute to the media. "Hermann is back on the bike," was reported euphorically in bold letters.

In actuality, what we were doing was madness. My pulse skyrocketed as though I were running high-altitude time trials. After just a few minutes, I was pouring sweat. My body was completely beaten and was fighting against this sort of exertion, but I persisted in what passed for training. I talked myself into it. "You've got to get through this if you want to come back!" Every child has this experience. The first steps are the hardest. Heini was completely convinced of the benefits of his unconventional method. "We have to stimulate your metabolism," he said. "Besides, this will get your cardiac and circulatory systems back into motion." In the process, further toxins were eliminated from my body, and it took my mind off my current situation. Nevertheless, I quickly grew tired of my new workout regimen. I must have been crazy to go through with this torture. My sheets became soaked with sweat, and then came the cumbersome procedure of washing and changing the sheets. I was always completely dependent on others' help. Every day, my team had to motivate me anew. I was sort of at their mercy anyway. What else could I do when they took my bed and shoved it underneath the hand ergometer with me in it! So, I started to crank away again, as though I were on remote control. Naturally, I was interested in my lactate levels and my accomplishments on the ergometer. And sure enough, my values were improving. After a few days, I was able to go against thirty watts' resistance and keep it up for half an hour. Nevertheless, the better my values became, the worse I felt!

MUSCLE MOUNTAINS OF STYROFOAM

I think that everyone underestimated how much my body had been undermined as a result of the accident, the surgery, the medications, and the intensive treatment I was receiving at the time. The misleading factor was that at 207 pounds, I weighed almost as much now as I had weighed during the peak of my performance. When I was helped onto a scale for the first time after ten days, to my pleasant surprise I still weighed in at 198. My thighs were larger than ever. I thought, "Well, I must be in great shape!" In truth, though, I was distended from top to bottom due to water retention. Water and destroyed cells had taken the place of muscle mass, something I did not realize at the time. Everything felt strange, tense, and hard. My left knee was like a rubber doll. When it was bent, it bounced back into a straight position all by itself. Already in the ICU I had the scary experience with the indentions that had remained behind after I had pushed into my muscles with a finger. Despite the intensive physical therapy I was receiving, not much had changed for the better in this regard. Heini was the first to objectively give a name to the problem: "I've never seen such mountains of muscles made of Styrofoam," he said, not exactly adding to my cheer. "As far as strength is concerned, we have now reached the bottom of the cycle, which is not surprising, considering everything you've been through." But that's one of the things I love about Heini; he doesn't leave a stone unturned when there is a problem to overcome. And so during his next visit, he brought a special apparatus with him designed to provide electromyostimulation. You attach electrodes to your skin and the muscles are stimulated with small electric shocks. This was the only method of strength training remaining to me at that point. Unfortunately, it yielded no tangible results. So I clung to the physical therapy and begged Vinzent, "Please help me, no matter how difficult it may get!" I let them do everything to me: activation, ultrasound, lymph system drainage, and the burning hot "roll."

Outside, it continued to rain without end, and it seemed to me like nothing was happening. I was on an emotional roller coaster. Even though I was making progress from a medical point of view, it seemed to me like I was moving one step forward, then two steps backward. The moment I saw some measurable, tangible improvement, there was another setback.

At last it was time to think about starting to walk again. I could hardly wait. Professor Papp, the restorative surgeon, had warned me again and again not to stress the transplanted flap of skin too soon, and so I had to remain in my uncomfortable position longer than I would have liked. Finally, he gave me the green light for my first attempt at walking. My right lower leg was provided with an extra-stiff bandage. Then the moment came when I was allowed to get up. Because I had been lying horizontally around the clock, my circulation was at rock bottom. Even the act of standing up caused the blood to drain from my head, and I was pale as a ghost. The first time I put weight on my leg, it felt like hell. Like a bolt of lightning, the pain coursed through my entire body into every last nerve ending. But the transplant held tight. With all my force I leaned into my crutches in order to relieve pressure on my injured leg. The exertion made me sweat like crazy, and after a few moments I gave up and let myself fall back onto the bed.

I celebrated my next big victory in the third week after the accident. I was allowed to go to the toilet all by myself! An incredibly difficult task, but with my strong upper arms I lifted myself up into the wheelchair and managed the few yards to the bathroom, and then to the toilet. And without anyone's help! My bad leg was sticking out, and Gudrun pushed the stand with the IV bags alongside me (okay, I guess I did have *some* help). The whole scene seemed like right out of a movie. When I sat down on the toilet seat, I thought, "It's going to rip my butt off and I'll shoot right up to the ceiling!" Because of the hematomas, my buttocks were so tight that I could not wipe myself properly. I wanted to cry out, but instead I clenched my teeth. "Everything all right?" asked the nurse from outside the door. "Yes, just fine," I lied. I didn't want to reveal my incapacity. Completely drenched from exertion, I rolled back out on my wheelchair and paused, thoroughly exhausted. A madcap performance!

But the whole process of recuperation was anything but fun. The constant pain was numbing my mind, not allowing me to think clearly. Considering the circumstances, it is no wonder I griped at the people around me most of the time, which I regret in retrospect. Artur was the only one who knew how to handle me. He could tell by my body language when it was better not to speak to me. He made the best of the few moments I was in a good mood by using them for small talk, which I needed sorely at the time. During those moments, he told me about his weekend hikes in the mountains around Salzburg, or his sailing, which he cut down to half-day excursions because of me.

I thought constantly about one thing: "I will get out of here, and I will be able to do all the things that normal people can do, even if it's on one leg at first." I felt like a genuine overachiever just by virtue of being able to hop around my room on one leg with my crutches. And then, out of the blue, even here there was a nasty surprise. Suddenly, my left leg, the apparently healthy one, gave out! By a stroke of good luck, Heini happened to be in the room at the time. He reacted with lightning speed to at least partially cushion my fall. I cried out in pain, "Oh, no! Now I've torn my cruciate ligament on top of everything!" Heini, too, cried out, "Ouch! My Achilles tendon!" Only a few weeks before, he had had surgery on his heel. The misfiring of nerves in my left thigh would burden me for a long time to come.

September 9, 2001. After ten days in the recuperation ward of the hospital, I was about ready to lose it. I was tortured by the worst kinds of nightmares. Time and again I was startled out of my sleep in the middle of the night. At four in the morning, I was done sleeping for good. Bathed in sweat, I dug out my cell phone and dialed the number of my trainer.

"Heini, I can't stand this any longer, I'm going berserk!"

Heini, half asleep: "What's the matter?"

"The pain! I can't lie still anymore. My strength, it's all gone! I'll never get it back."

"Hermann, calm down and try to relax. I'll be right over."

Forty-five minutes later, my fatherly trainer was sitting at my bedside and giving me new courage. "Starting as of now, someone has to spend the night with you! Either Gudrun, your mother, or I!" The choice was not difficult. Shortly after dawn, Gudrun moved into my hospital suite, bringing along all her odds and ends. For days at a time, she didn't take one step outside. I am grateful to her to this day for this act of selflessness. From this point on I was really on the mend. If I was in danger of falling back into a deep depression, someone was there to catch me. My mother, too, was very concerned about making my hospital stay as pleasant as possible. That afternoon she brought me fresh flowers, a Bundt cake, and steaming hot coffee in a thermos. With the aroma of the coffee, the familiar voices of my family, and a folk-music CD from Austria's Pongau region in the background, I almost felt like I was home. But after everyone had left in the evening and I was alone with Gudrun, I once again realized how miserable my condition still was.

My body seemed to be fighting against everything. When I was sweating, my skin burned, and it hurt to dry off. Because of the medications, my back was covered with pustules. Every night was a horror, and I began to grow frightened once it got dark. Only the piritamid shot that a stout nurse plunged into my stomach every evening promised a few restful hours.

If my morning program allowed it, I began to do more and more walking laps. Or else I rescheduled my walking exercise to midnight, when no one could see me. Then I would limp down the hallway as far as I could with the aid of my crutches. After every such excursion I returned to my bed completely exhausted. I can't remember any training session taking this much out of me. But I continued working at it until I reached exhaustion. Every time I put pressure on my injured leg, pain coursed through my entire system, putting a great deal of stress on my body. My hematocrit was still extremely low. I divided my walk into stages. The first was from my bed to the door, where I gripped the door handle and took a break. Then, I wobbled along the hallway about twenty yards until I got to a group of chairs, where I sat down and caught my breath. It felt like a break in one of my intense training sessions. I sat there drenched in sweat and everything hurt like crazy, with the skin transplant all puffed up. I asked myself later what had compelled me to such insane actions. It was pure ambition, the obsessive drive to be able to walk again normally. At the time, that was more important to me than anything else.

It seemed, though, that I wanted too much at once. Time and again I approached my absolute pain threshold. It was unbelievable what kind of force my cobbled-together tibia and my not-even-close-to-mended fibula had to withstand such a short time after surgery. Now that I can think clearly again, I realize what an enormous risk I took back then. As a complicating factor, the nerve connections to my left leg still didn't work properly. Thus, the next mishap during one of my little workout excursions was practically scripted ahead of time. Once again, the supposed healthy leg gave way, one of the crutches slipped, and again I was down on the floor.

From then on, my physical therapist, Vinzent, insisted on accompanying me during my longer walking excursions. That worked so well after a while that I grew a bit cocky and started to leave one of the crutches by my bed. I really went to the limit every time. But for Heini, even that was too little. He was ready to put me back on my stationary bicycle. Since he received only angry or shocked looks from the doctors when he brought up the idea, he had a "compromise ergometer" delivered to the trauma center, one where you step into the pedals from a reclining position, almost lying down. At some point, Heini could see that this was not a good idea, and he had it removed.

September 11, 2001. In the meantime, just about everything was getting on my nerves at the hospital. I started to count the hours to my possible release. Although I had no real reason to complain about the food, every meal seemed like torture to me. Between lunch and my afternoon training, I had two hours to rest. Since I couldn't sleep, I usually distracted myself by watching television. While I was flipping through the channels, I was struck by a CNN broadcast from New York. There was smoke coming from one of the twin towers, and I thought, "It's an airplane accident." In the meantime, Vinzent had arrived and was ready to start with my physical therapy. Together we were glancing at the screen to see what was going on when a second airplane appeared above the skyscrapers. I have flown over New York many times, so I was surprised and said to Vinzent, "Strange that they're flying so low." Right then, the plane took a turn to the left and crashed into the second tower. Horrendous!

Both of us were absolutely speechless. My training became completely secondary on that day. I felt like I was paralyzed, and switched from one channel to the next. The terrible pictures of desperate people jumping to their deaths from the buildings haunted me deep into the night. I saw that there were many people who needed much more help than I, and I thought, "I wonder how their loved ones are doing." At that moment, my own problems seemed almost laughable. How unimportant my motorcycle accident was compared to this!

September 12, 2001.   Before breakfast, Artur showed up in my room and gave me hope. "Hermann, how would you feel about spending the coming weekend at home?" When I heard these words, I felt almost well for just a moment. That same evening, the press bulletin announced, "Provided there are continuing advances in his convalescence, Hermann Maier will be released this weekend." I became almost giddy. At a late hour, a friend of mine showed up and dug around in her bag for contraband: two bottles of beer, which we downed during the Champions League match pitting Feyenoord Rotterdam against Bayern München. Granted, alcohol is strictly prohibited at the hospital. But I thought, "Considering all the poison that has been pumped into my body during the past few weeks, this shouldn't do too much harm."

September 13, 2001.   The countdown for my release continued. Final checkups, X-rays, ultrasound, blood work, and a range of motion tests of my ankles, knees, and hips. At the end, the doctors had me walk with crutches once more and checked whether my gait was halfway acceptable. I received detailed instructions on what to do at home for my continuing rehabilitation. Since my hemoglobin count was still below ten, there was no way my rehabilitation could be continued at the Olympic Training Center in Obertauern as had originally been planned. The altitude of just below six thousand feet would have exhausted my last reserves of strength. Moreover, I still was in need of the medical advice available at a top-notch clinic. And so even I was convinced that it would be best to bide my time another two weeks at the Aufmesser clinic in Radstadt, with the option of spending the weekends in Flachau, only a few miles away. So I had to be transported from the trauma center in Salzburg to the clinic in Radstadt. Each of the following steps was planned as though this were a major military campaign. Final parting shot? Press conference or small talk with the journalists? Wheelchair or crutches? Ambulance or private car? One thing was certain as far as I was concerned: I will leave this building on two legs, and certainly not in an ambulance!

At the end of my stay there, I wanted to take a walk with the trauma center chief physician, Karlbauer, and the physical therapist up to the new balcony. Dr. Karlbauer pushed the button for the elevator, but I insisted on walking up the stairs. I wanted to show everyone how well I was doing already. On arriving on the platform, I was overwhelmed by the sensational view. But my first glance was cast toward the helicopter landing pad, where I had touched down only nineteen days earlier. "My leg is still attached," I thought, full of contentment. "Actually, a lot of progress has been made in a short time."

After weeks and weeks of rain, the clouds had finally parted, and the old fortress of Salzburg seemed close enough to touch. It was gleaming in the bright sunlight. Then I admired the remodeled hospital complex and asked about the innovations and plans. "This is where we will put the new ICU," said Karlbauer, and I thought, "Thank God, I'm through with that! Hopefully, I won't have to go back there anytime soon." I inhaled deeply. The fresh fall air smelled lovely and lifted my spirits. I even had visions for the future. "Yes, now it's time to get out. If the weather stays this nice, things are going to keep moving ahead in my life." I couldn't have dreamed at that moment that everything would turn out differently. The worst days since the accident were yet to come.

Chapter 4

BETWEEN HOPE
AND DESPAIR

September 14, 2001. Day twenty-one. I am preparing as though for a race. The evening before, I had assembled my equipment: my favorite gray, tattered jogging pants; the gray-green sweater with the Austrian Ski Federation's sponsor patches; the dark blue cap with the Raiffeisen logo; and my silver, extra-large Adidas sneakers. Gudrun and my mother had already taken over the rest of my stuff, and Heini had taken down the hand-operated ergometer and transported it to Radstadt. That gave me at least one workout-free evening.

The last night at the trauma center was short. I was as excited as a prisoner about to be released. I was glad, but I couldn't quite imagine the freedom that was lying before me. Too many questions remained. Will I ever find the way back to my old life? Will my foot fit into a ski boot again? Will I once again earn my living through competitive skiing? And the Olympic Games, which were to take place in Salt Lake City in four and a half months, seemed to be a serious topic for my medical team. Should such a miracle be possible, at least in theory?

During my good-bye rounds I was truly moved. I was amazed at how much I had become accustomed to the hospital routine. With a strange feeling in the pit of my stomach I took care of the remaining paperwork, posed for a memento picture with everyone who wanted one, and gave autographs with personal remarks to members of the hospital staff as well as their children, grandchildren, nieces, and nephews. Then I limped into the chief physician's room for a farewell coffee and a final meeting. Everything went surprisingly smoothly. It happened so fast that I ended up being early, something that almost never happens in my life.

Outside, it was pouring again. In front of the trauma center, underneath the overhang of the portico, waited a drove of reporters. Only the ORF people were still missing. I had fooled them with my uncharacteristic punctuality. Or else they had gotten stuck in Salzburg's Friday afternoon traffic. They telephoned to beg us to hang on a few more minutes so that they could get the moment of my release recorded in full authenticity. I know what it feels like to be late, so I obliged them.

When the elevator door finally opened, I was surprised by the barrage of flashes from the photographers' cameras. I clenched my teeth and strolled out into the open with my crutches, as though walking were the most normal thing on earth. Instead of the usual press conference, there was a stand-up game of question-and-answer. For three weeks now we had been putting the reporters on an "information diet," and with the exception of the one television interview from my sickbed, we had fed them parsimoniously on official press statements in the form of daily bulletins. Finally, they were allowed to ask me personal questions. I have never experienced such a hungry horde of journalists.

The ORF reporter held the microphone under my nose and had at it: *Hermann, there's so much we have heard and read. How are you really doing?*

I pulled myself together and tried to make a completely relaxed impression. "Really, I'm doing very, very well, especially when I think back to the first interview. Actually, I couldn't be better." No one guessed what gruesome pain I had to bear during those few minutes. But I did not want to burden anyone with that. To whine and complain, no, that was not an option! My focus was on the future. I tried to exude an air of optimism. After all, I did not want my competitors to start rubbing their hands in anticipation too soon. During the past three weeks, they had nobly kept back their comments and visits. Now I was back on my feet and wanted to show with my rapid steps toward a comeback that I could do without any displays of pity.

With a last sentimental look behind me, I thanked my rescuers. "Everything worked out very, very well. The healing process has gone forward so quickly that we are even a bit ahead in our schedule." Then, I lied. "I'm not even thinking about sports right now; that just seems too far away."

Okay, there really were other priorities during these next few weeks: "The main thing at this time is that I learn to walk normally again, that my pain subsides, and that I be able to do without painkillers soon."

How does it feel to be allowed out of doors again? a reporter wanted to know.

"Well, I must say that I had wonderful accommodations here. Everyone worked very, very hard. But a change of scenery is the best thing that can happen to me at this point. Even the rain doesn't bother me. I can truly savor it."

A few words concerning your leg. How much pain are you still in?

I bit my lips so hard that when I later watched the interview on TV, it was really noticeable. "The pain is being kept in check. My Achilles tendon is still a bit sore, since there are still circulation problems there. But the physical therapists right here as well as the ones from the Olympic Training Center have worked tirelessly, and a lot of progress has been made, even from yesterday to today. If my progress continues like that, then I may even be able to put away my crutches before too long."

We hear that with regard to his motivational level, Hermann is still his old self. How far is he still away from that?

"Yes, right now it's a matter of making strides in my quality of life."

What has changed since the first TV interview from two weeks ago?

"A lot. My self-confidence, which was already there back then, has returned to an even greater degree."

Whom do you credit with your healing besides yourself?

That was my chance to once again thank everyone officially. I tried to mention all of them: the Aufmessers and the rescuers who had picked me out of the ditch; the helicopter team; Artur Trost; chief physician Karl-bauer; Professor Papp, the restorative surgeon; Barbara Neureiter, the physical therapist; and of course my daily companions from the Olympic Training Center, including my intrepid press spokesman. "The most important aspect was that everyone worked together so smoothly, that no one was selfish, and everyone focused on the patient. The chief physician and his team deserve great respect." The topic "hospital" was now finished for me. Then they wanted to know how I had coped with the accident. I wasn't able to hold back a little grin at that point. "I'm sure I'll get back on my motorcycle as quickly as possible. I just can't do without it!"

I patiently answered more questions from the rest of the reporters until Andy Evers, who is very familiar with my body language, noticed that it was getting to be too much for me. He made his way through the crowd in the ski federation BMW and I lifted myself, somewhat awkwardly but with the greatest care, onto the passenger seat. Flanked by three other cars, we disappeared into the rain.

I can't say that I completely enjoyed my regained freedom. In front of the journalists, I bluffed in order to appear as convincing as possible. But in the car I didn't have to pretend. My agony was so great that I clenched my teeth and cut short any sort of conversation. Just sitting down was extremely painful, and I didn't know what to do with my right leg. After only a few miles, we made a stop. In the parking lot of the Point Hotel in Anif I transferred to a minivan. At least now I was able to stretch out on the backseat and take the pressure off my demolished lower leg. Instead, my butt started hurting.

Even though it was great to know we were heading home, my physical agony became unbearable. I kept shifting around, but I couldn't find a satisfactory position. Because I had to elevate my right leg, my blood ran down and I felt like my rear end was about to burst. I didn't know how I should place myself, and once again I was sweating like crazy. I was becoming claustrophobic. I felt like a dog that had been forgotten in the car and was being roasted by the sun.

Forty minutes later we passed the site of the accident in Radstadt. You couldn't miss the traces of the tragic events of three weeks ago. The many orange marks on the road, plus the images in my head—it was a strange feeling indeed. I noticed that a veritable path had been worn out around the site of my accident. Kind of like a pilgrims' shrine. I heard that not only Austrian fans were showing up. My mother told me about a young French couple who parked their car on the side of the road, went down into the ditch, and cried. And the old man who lives right beyond the ditch and was the first one to get to me after the accident was seen time and again tramping around the meadow with his head down. Perhaps he was looking for the bone fragment that is missing from my tibia to this day. An acquaintance from Flachau found my watch, but even now, I haven't gotten it back.

Rehabilitation at the Olympic Training Center in Obertauern was out of the question. My hemoglobin count was still miserably low three weeks after the accident, and the endurance sessions that I had included in my daily schedule for the past two weeks seemed to make little difference in boosting it. Even though Heini kept trying to convince me otherwise, it felt as though the workouts were sucking the last bit of energy from my body. I can't tell you how exhausting it was just to walk on my crutches. Every short distance, every trip to the toilet, caused me to perspire profusely. And that was way down in Radstadt! At the elevation of Obertauern, where your physical performance potential goes down by 15 to 20 percent because of the decrease in oxygen, I would probably have keeled off my bike in neutral. When Alex, who had just gotten back from his workout in Obertauern, told me that the first few cars were beginning to get stuck in the snow as they crossed the Tauern Pass, I felt somewhat melancholy. I still rejoice like a small boy every year when the first snow falls. When I see that the mountaintops are sprinkled with snow, I march up into the higher regions in order to hike in the snowy woods. However, this time around I was as far from undertaking such an excursion as New Zealand is from Austria.

I took my first steps back into normal life at the clinic in Radstadt. The private hospital, which belongs to my friends the Aufmessers, was reconfigured into a Hermann Maier Training and Rehabilitation Center for two weeks. I occupied almost an entire floor, in which three rooms had been furnished and equipped lavishly, one to live in and one with pads and exercise balls for physical therapy; the biggest room was turned into a small torture chamber. My Technogym stationary bicycle from Obertauern, the hated sit-down ergometer, the by-now-notorious yellow hand-crank ergometer setup, plus a few light weights—none of this let me forget for a moment that I was actually in a hospital.

On my first day in Radstadt I was pampered and allowed to take it easy. Barbara Aufmesser tried to keep my spirits up with her culinary delights. As a welcome treat she served a plum cake, there were fresh grapes on my nightstand, and I was offered two different dinner menus from which to choose. Even though the food was delicious, my normally hearty appetite had not yet returned.

I wanted to spend the first night after my release in freedom. After twenty-one involuntary nights somewhere else, I got one weekend of "home leave." When Andreas drove me home, I had an unbelievable encounter that was like fate knocking at the door. We were driving by the accident site when immediately in front of us, a car made an illegal left turn at the very spot where the red Mercedes had taken me down. It was a bizarre déjà-vu experience, as though fate were trying to tell me something. We looked at each other, stammered something like "Outrageous!" and "That's unbelievable!" and then fell silent. Each of us had his own thoughts. Although I pass this intersection at least twice a day, I have never again witnessed such a maneuver.

At home, the next horror awaited me. For days I had yearned for nothing other than to snuggle beneath my down comforter and fall asleep at least somewhat free of pain, and in my new bed, which I had exchanged for the water bed after my return from Chile. When I am away from October until March with the World Cup, I sleep on normal hotel mattresses, which isn't so bad, so I had decided to switch back to the tried-and-true at home as well. Sometimes, the simplest things work best. The day after the arrival of my new bed, the mishap occurred.

As I was saying, I had been looking forward to sleeping in my new bed. Gudrun had prepared everything lovingly in order to make my return home as comfortable as possible. But as soon as I was in the bedroom, it started. The strange smell of a new mattress made me feel unwell. It had almost been nicer at the hospital! The air, it seemed, was full of textile fibers. Suddenly, my whole body was itching violently. I scratched myself, rubbed a towel all over, and was practically beating myself to get rid of that itchy feeling. I spent a good twenty minutes thus engaged, and wanted to crawl out of my skin, in the truest sense of the word. I yelled at Gudrun, "What's going on? What did you do with the sheets? What is all this fiber fuzz in the air?" Only later did I realize the cause of my discomfort. The aggressive chemicals that my body had been pumped full of had triggered an allergic reaction. I was sweating the poison out of my body, and I was covered in a sheath of perspiration. I was familiar with this itching from my days as a bricklayer, when we had to handle fiberglass insulating material. I was desperate. I couldn't really wash because I had to be careful not to get my scar wet. I couldn't simply climb into the shower. Gudrun, too, was puzzled. It was not easy for her, dealing with me back then. I felt helpless and was constantly grouchy and combative. But it wasn't my girlfriend's fault that my homecoming hadn't lived up to my expectations.

The truth is, I had lived under the illusion that I would only have to walk out of the trauma center and everything would be fine. In fact, the opposite was the case. My difficulties had only just begun. The worst was those first few nights. As soon as it got dark, panic would start to rise within me. I sweated through one set of sheets after another. Each time I woke up completely drenched, I tore off the wet sheets and screamed in desperation. My bedding had barely been changed when the next wave of perspiration hit me.

Then, there was the difficult task of lying down. Since I was still paranoid about my skin transplant, I wanted to avoid moving my right leg. A useless struggle! At some point, I didn't care anymore. I just puffed up my pillow as best I could and wanted nothing but to be able to sleep. Finally, my eyes would close. But only for a short time, until the intense pain caught up with me again.

And so I turned into a junkie. I couldn't stand it any longer and gave myself a piritamid shot through my abdominal wall. I had experience in these matters because I give myself antithrombolytic shots before long-distance flights. Except that the needle was longer this time. I couldn't make it through more than three hours at night without pain medication. At the hospital, no matter how much I begged, they had never granted me more than two. Somehow, I made it through those hours, and through the day on Saturday. At night came again the cruel cycle of sweat attacks, piritamid shots, and despair.

On Sunday, the bright sunshine helped me briefly to forget my pain. Gudrun drove me up to the Rossbrand, a lovely walking path above Radstadt, and although I was limping along with my crutches, just being out in nature gave me a feeling of great joy. I fought my way forward step by step, and every foot gained was a small victory, even though the leisurely Sunday strollers were overtaking me and Gudrun joked, "At least you can't run away from me now!"

I was completely exhausted when I checked back into the Aufmesser clinic after the weekend. For the next two weeks I had no further desire for a home leave.

My team had put together a round-the-clock rehabilitation and training program. But it didn't go exactly as they had imagined. The sit-down ergometer was a total joke. At the first turn of the pedals, I yelled out in pain. My knee was still locking up, so it was impossible for me to complete a full rotation. Besides, my contusions still caused untold pain while I was seated. So Heini tried to switch over to his old favorite, the hand-crank ergometer. But that was getting old for me by now. I was itching to get back onto my high-performance ergometer, on which I had spent hundreds of hours in Obertauern. I couldn't do it. My compromised rear end wouldn't let me remain in the saddle for more than ten minutes at a time.

The only thing that really worked were the attempts at unaided walking with Vinzent. Under his instruction and with Heini's, as well as Doc Zeibig's, help, I was able to take my first few steps without crutches only twenty-five days after I had almost lost my leg. Thus, I had achieved my goal for the first stage of my long way back: I was able to walk again. At least somewhat. Right away, I keyed in on my next goal: Yes, I was very much thinking about skiing at the time. In my euphoria, I hadn't even quite ruled out the impossible: the Olympic Games, which were to take place in February 2002 in the United States.

September 19, 2001. Mentally, I was ready to start with serious training. But my body was still far away from such exertion. The doctors were still worried about my transplant. The sobering numbers did the rest to fetch me quickly back to reality. Normally, I was able to work out on the high-performance trainer at the Olympic Center in my lower pulse-rate zone (the so-called KB region) at the 330-watt resistance setting. Now I could barely handle 70 watts at the same pulse rate. A catastrophe! I felt like I was making no progress at all. My daily exercises seemed to be completely perfunctory. Suddenly, everything seemed to be going much too slowly. I tried again and again to tell myself that I had to do this one step at a time: "First, you have to learn to walk again; then to bike halfway normally; then, at some point, maybe you can run." My problem was always the time constraint. To tell the truth, I was thinking about the Olympics on a more and more frequent basis, though to talk about it with anyone was completely taboo. Then an ORF journalist hit right on that sensitive point and asked what all of Austria had been discussing for the past four weeks: "Are you secretly thinking about a miracle so you can take part in the Olympics?" I started stammering out an answer, searching for the right words. "We hear about medical miracles on a frequent basis. Let's see what we can do . . ." I answered diplomatically, and tried to remain realistic. "To make up for my deficit in such a short amount of time is a bit unrealistic."

After the almost unreal high last summer in Chile, when it all seemed like child's play, I was now confronted with the greatest challenge of my life. While I was leafing through the *Kronen Zeitung*, I happened across a report that completely bummed me out. In it was a photo of our Alpine skiing director Hans Pum inspecting the Olympics accommodations in Salt Lake City. Before I fell asleep, I counted how many weeks I still had left until the momentous occasion. And that was only the beginning. I still would have to qualify. Even though the public was clamoring for a "wild card for Hermann Maier," it was unthinkable that the strongest ski team in the world would keep a spot open for someone without proven top-flight results. The elite trainers of the Austrian ski team were having weekly conferences with my coaching team at the Olympic Training Center in Obertauern. Heini and Andreas kept me informed about the deliberations and let me in on their plans. My only realistic chance was a start at the super-G in Garmisch. On the very same slope where I had celebrated my first World Cup victory in 1997, there would be two super-G races on January 26 and 27. I had four months till then.

As time went by, I started feeling quite at home with the Aufmessers, almost like part of the family. In the evenings, I might have a beer with Harald as we took in the Champion League games. Sometimes, Doc Johnny Zeibig and Heini joined us, and told anecdotes from their eventful lives. That helped me at least to delay a bit the lows that I suffered every evening before falling asleep.

Nevertheless, the training wasn't getting any easier. Johnny, Vinzent, and Heini did all they could to teach me how to walk again without the aid of crutches. You might say that I was enrolled in "walking school." I had to perform balancing exercises and deliberate, slow steps, with Vinzent concerned that I carry out every movement in a graceful style. Because I wanted to stop limping as soon as possible, I constantly went to the limits of my pain threshold during those walking exercises, as though I had to stress my ankle every time to the point of torment. It was a drawn-out and agonizing process.

To be sure, there were some alarming setbacks. Once, when I tried to lift my right leg up onto a railing to stretch between two walking sessions, my left leg failed me and I was on the ground. Once again I had suffered the sudden loss of nerve function in my left leg. Again, the same awful feeling came over me that I remembered from the hospital. "Did I tear my cruciate ligament?" But once again I had been lucky.

In the meantime, requests for interviews and visits were piling up. On the one hand, I needed every minute of rest and recuperation the way a baby needs its mother's milk; on the other hand, I realized that I had to face the public at some point. After all, I was still a professional athlete, and such appearances are part of my job. Thus, my PR man came up with a "meet the press" hour on my first Wednesday off from training for five important media outlets: Each of ORF, *Kronen Zeitung*, *Bunte*, and one *Standard* reporter, who also wrote for the *Frankfurter Allgemeine*, was granted a brief thirty minutes. They were also allowed to film and photograph me doing my training and physical therapy. After being thus on display, I was completely worn out; little did I know that this sort of regimen was going to be in store for me every Wednesday from now on. And that was not the only weekly appointment I would have with the media.

September 22, 2001. My program included underwater training at the Sporthotel Radstadt. Just reading about it on my daily schedule gave me the shivers. "At least it's something new," I thought. By then I was thoroughly sick of my two old friends, the hand-crank ergometer and the stationary bicycle. On the other hand, I was plenty cold already. As I was climbing up the ladder out of the pool, suddenly the water's buoyancy was gone and with the full effect of gravity bearing down on me, I was overcome by a terrible feeling: "Don't bump into the edge of the ladder with your skin transplant, or it might end up floating in the water!" Naturally, the physical therapist wanted to help me, but I insisted on getting out all by myself.

I didn't begin to have my body under control. It was incapable of self-regulating its normal temperature. The lower the temperature, the more miserable I felt. I knew this feeling from my sleepless nights. First I sweated like crazy, then I froze in the soaked sheets. It was horrible!

In the afternoon, DJ Ötzi, alias Gerry Friedle, paid me a surprise visit with his wife Sonja. They had a *News* reporter in tow who had arranged the meeting, plus a photographer. At that time, Ötzi's pop song was being played the length and breadth of Europe. "Hey Baby" was a hit single in sixty countries, and the rough-voiced bard had even knocked U2 from the top of the charts in England. When he saw my stationary bicycle on the deck of the Aufmesser clinic, he insisted on biking away right next to me for a photo op and announced, "I'll come up here and let you all get me into shape for the Olympics." That prospect filled me with a certain apprehension. Might this chain-smoking king of the charts have better ergometer numbers than mine?

Once the show was over, I continued to struggle along on the bike by myself. The visit had given me pause. I made a mental accounting of the events since my motorcycle accident four weeks ago. The term "healthy," let alone "fit," did not come close to describing my current state. I still wasn't able to sleep, and I awoke soaked with sweat several times a night. Because I was afraid of becoming addicted to pain medication, I insisted on going off my analgesics. It was horrific. The massive pain was far from gone. However, now that I was able to think clearly, I was much more aware of everything: the accident, my terrible condition, the waning chance of competing in the Olympics. The one aspect of my physical condition that really set off an internal alarm was my drastic weight loss. I was startled when I looked into the mirror: "There's not much left of me!" I had shrunk down to a low of 172 pounds from my previous weight of 207. For weeks, they had been pumping liquids into me. I had been puffed up like the Michelin man and had not noticed what was happening to my muscle mass. Now all the excess water had left my system. Suddenly, 35 pounds was missing. Thirty-five pounds of muscle mass that had been added during years of focused training had vanished. I could have wept. My hemoglobin count had slowly climbed up to a value that hovered around eleven, but there was still plenty of room between that and a normal value, which begins at fourteen. No wonder everything was so exhausting.

During my last week in Radstadt, the physical therapist who worked with me the most was Barbara, who had been assigned exclusively to me by the Olympic Training Center. In addition to the "hot roll," which I already knew from the hospital, I had to endure long laser treatments. As for the leg on which I had had surgery, I couldn't complain about the progress. The healing process was progressing wonderfully, and the skin flap had grown in faster than expected. That was the most important aspect, since the danger of infection was now essentially nil. The work of Professor Papp, the restorative surgeon, and his team had been perfect.

September 24, 2001. Exactly one month after my accident, Johnny and Vinzent wanted me to "run" in the yard of the Aufmesser clinic during one of the last beautiful autumn days. You couldn't really call it running, though. I tried to pry my feet off the ground quickly. And sure enough, I managed several somewhat short, wobbly steps. It's called "skipping" in track-and-field jargon. You always see it on television when sprint stars are preparing for a race. In retrospect, it was sheer madness to let me perform this exercise in my condition. I hunkered down and waited for the pain to subside.

Heini constantly had new ideas. Like one time, when he showed up with a small ball and wanted to play soccer with me. That didn't work out at all. I couldn't even step across the ball with my left leg. The leg's range of motion was completely inhibited. There was a tension as though I was being held back by an invisible hand. To be sure, nothing more could surprise me in the condition I was in. But for Heini, these symptoms triggered an alarm. Finally, he too realized the unbelievable truth: My right leg, which I had come within an ace of losing a month ago, was in better working order than my left! The better things were starting to work on the right side, the bigger the muscular problems were becoming on the left. My left thigh was as thin as when I was a teenager, when a growth disturbance had seemed to put an end to my plans as a ski racer. At times, I even had symptoms of impending paralysis. Time and again the memories of my accident coursed through my head: how I had pressed my thighs together so hard that I had dented the gas tank on my motorcycle. "These are the consequences," I thought. Furthermore, my adductors, the muscles on the inside of my thighs that I had over-stretched in the act of squeezing, still hurt.

Heini was trying to increase the number of ergometer sessions. This was possible only in shockingly small steps. Three times ten minutes on the ergometer turned into three times fifteen, and even this seemed to be too exhausting for me. The thing I hated most was the hand-crank ergometer. I started to negotiate: "What can I do so I don't have to lie down under that thing anymore?" I was disgusted with everything: limp-ing on crutches, climbing onto the bike, getting going on it, and the physical therapy. Only the walking trials in the hallway were a chal-lenge. But even there, the characteristic hospital smell haunted me.

Finally, I was allowed to start working on my lower body. I had insisted on it, since I was alarmed by what I saw in the mirror. Because of the con-stant pulling, lifting, and heaving that were necessary during each trip to the toilet, I had kept myself fit "upstairs." Now, the real training could start. I could hardly wait. We began with dynamic strength exercises: The physical therapist threw the medicine ball toward me, and I had to volley it back while I raised up my upper body. Or I lay on one of the big gymnas-tics balls on my stomach and balanced two medicine balls on my extended arms. There were problems with my knees and whenever I needed my left leg, which was completely numb. With each session, my body contours be-came more discernible. Since I had lost so much weight, every muscle fiber was visible. Despite the pain that accompanied each exercise, I enjoyed this type of training enormously.

I can't say the same about bicycling, which was my monotonous mainstay. It was truly boring. The hematomas in my buttocks turned the simple act of sitting on the bike seat into torture. My right ankle was locked up, the lower leg was without sensation on the outside, and the area of the fracture hurt like hell. There was no use complaining, though. Heini and Doc Johnny had a medical justification for everything. And it was certainly clear to me that if I wanted to make a comeback this winter, I was going to have to get through this. So I gloomily kept pumping the pedals.

The constant pain almost robbed me of reason. In this state, I couldn't think of distracting myself while pedaling with reading or watching TV, so I stared at the irregular, pastel pattern of the long curtains. My skin excreted a kind of disgusting, sticky liquid. If I'm in good shape, I like to sweat during my workouts. But here, the opposite was the case. I could well have done without the sticky goo that instantly triggered an impulse to scratch myself. On top of that, it was like working out in a minefield. Once I was pumping away, a brutal, flashing pain suddenly drove through me as though I had been seared by an electric shock. I cried out and Heini asked, "What's the matter now?" I looked at him accusingly. "Do you guys want to *kill* me?" Heini didn't know what to do, and we broke off the training session. I don't know to this day what exactly caused this odd phenomenon; perhaps a blocked nerve pathway in my left leg had cleared up. At any rate, for several days I felt like both legs were fighting against the workouts.

My backside hurt so badly that I had to interrupt my pedaling time and again to change position. Nevertheless, I continued my workout, like a complete moron who insists on continuing to ride on his rims after his tires have gone flat.

FLASHBACK

THE BEGINNING: THE TRUE STORY

How often do I have to read the story about Hermann Maier the forerunner? About the bricklayer who was discovered by complete coincidence on his own stomping grounds in Flachau, because he had skied right into the world-class ranks in twelfth place, based on his time, which had been recorded only by accident? Who jumped the Europe Cup freight train at the last second because of this lucky strike? I must admit that at some point I played along with this distorted portrayal of events. It made for a great story. It is now time, however, for some demystification.

Since I knew how many important ski federation trainers would be at the slope that day, I was highly motivated and gave my very best. Even back then, I worked up to my optimal performance under pressure, and put down two good runs. However, I had a good starting number and thus an accordingly good slope. If I had had to attack toward the end of the race, things would probably have looked a bit different. Nevertheless, people were talking about me.

In truth, though, people had already started to notice me earlier in the season, when I had made a good showing in several races, such as during the FIS giant slalom in Stubaital, where I made third place, and in Predazzo, where I came in fourth. On December 26, I had started against several World Cup competitors in Abtenau. I was all ready to triumph over them when I was eliminated in the second round. Immediately after that I received the call from Europe Cup trainer Reini Eberl: "Hermann, you're on your way to France to the Europe Cup." They had begun to take me seriously!

As preparation for my first staging in the Europe Cup, the chance to appear as a forerunner in Flachau two days ahead of the big race seemed perfect. "You will ski with the helmet camera," I was informed by an official from Union Ski Club (USC) Flachau. "That doesn't interest me at all," I answered brashly. "If I'm going to ski, I want to ski at my best."

I got into the starting booth just ahead of Alberto Tomba, who had starting number 1. Of course, I knew that the clock was running for me, too (albeit unofficially), and I registered with great satisfaction that I would have come in twelfth during the race.

The day after, I got into the car with Andreas Evers, who was a Europe Cup trainer at the time, and we took off for France. Andy had been a skier himself way back when. I knew him as a neighbor from Flachau. Besides, he had been my soccer coach when I was trying my luck as center with USC Flachau, and later we met every now and then at courses for skiing instructors. In the car, Andy told me that he had witnessed my performance during the trial run the day before. "You really skied a strong race. The ski federation folks were quite impressed."

Full of self-confidence, I planned to get through both giant slaloms with a respectable result. As fate would have it, I came in second, behind Steve Locher, the fourth competitor from Flachau, which gave me an enormous emotional boost. The next day, I won ahead of the strongman from Switzerland.

Finally, I could do what I had always wanted: compete in ski races, sometimes as often as every other day. Two days later I started in Serre Chevalier and won again. During that race, a certain Stephan Eberharter had skied past a gate shortly before the finish. During the next season, Steff wanted to stay in the Europe Cup, while I had a fixed starting position in the World Cup. I carried out a monstrous schedule: Between January 8 and March 9, 1996, I was at the starting line twenty-one times in two months, which was twice as exhausting back then. Since I was responsible for all my equipment with no assistance, I spent most of my time off the slope in the ski prep room. Thus, it is not surprising that I ranked only twenty-sixth in my first World Cup giant slalom in Hinterstoder. I had run myself dry, but I had done it to myself. At some point, you have to give your body a chance to recuperate.

During the 1996/1997 season, the fierce World Cup wind was blowing in my face. During the overseas preseason in Park City, I was able to rank sixth. As a lone ranger, I first had to get used to the team dynamics. Hans Knauss was the first to invite me to join him for a beer in the evening. I think I made an unfavorable impression in the gym, where I worked so hard during the training kicks that everyone had to watch out for their safety.

In addition to seven giant slaloms and one super-G in the World Cup, I got my chance at a downhill race in Chamonix. I was incredibly motivated. During the training runs, I had gotten the best time in the upper portion, and had gotten third and fourth places. When I entered the race with number 54, the slope, which had been covered in new snow, already had holes in it. Nonetheless, I constantly skied to my limit, and it was only a matter of time before the slope bucked me off. I sailed through the air and crashed into the safety fence. I must have twisted my wrist in the process. Two days later, I was lying on the surgeon's table at the trauma center in Salzburg and got to know Dr. Artur Trost.

While my team colleagues were fighting for their positions in the world championships in Sestriere, I sat at home with my hand in a cast and thought seriously about my career. "If there was any sense in this crash, then it must be to give me the time to really work out," I decided. I had had a permanent cold in December and felt weak and worn down. Thus, I drove to the closest training center, which happened to be the Olympic Training Center in Obertauern. I had already noticed earlier that the athletes coached by Heini Bergmüller, who was in charge up there, trained differently. While I was lifting weights like a bodybuilder in the weight room, Mario Reiter, Heinz Schilchegger, and Christian Mayer were sitting on the bicycle ergometer reading the paper. Every thirty minutes, they were pricked in the ear. "That's how guided training works," Heini explained to me. He and medical supervisor Bernd Pansold made for a congenial duo at the Olympic Training Center. "You should give it a try."

"Okay," I said, and jumped onto the ergometer, only to have to listen to Heini thirty minutes later as he explained to me how poor my conditioning really was. Starting right then, my stationary bicycle was my daily companion, and Heini registered with enthusiasm how my values got better and better every week. While I was pumping the pedals, a small pool of sweat formed underneath me, and a bright spotlight was burning onto my forehead from above, which made me start to worry seriously about my hairline.

But the new regime at the Olympic Training Center was effective. After only a few weeks, my batteries were recharged, and I was doing better all around. For the first time in a long while I felt completely healthy. After five Europe Cup races I returned to the World Cup in Garmisch. And what a return! In the first of two super-G races I came in second behind the budding overall World Cup champion, Luc Alphand. In the finish area, the now-famous "good luck Hermann Maier" pig was waiting for the first time. That was the final boost I had needed. The next day, I won ahead of Kristian Ghedina. I was celebrated as a skiing sensation.

I knew that this would not be my last victory, and I decided to train harder than anyone else. Thus, I drove up to Obertauern day after day even after season's end and biked and biked. In the training room underneath Heini's office I got to know every single tile on the wall.

With such a monotonous workout regimen, you sometimes have to stir things up. So one warm summer night I met with my friends in Flachau to play beach volleyball after a hard day of training. (Where's the beach? you might ask.

Well, there are sand pits even in a landlocked country.) After the first round, we had a few beers. Then, shortly before midnight, we felt like playing another round. We got so hot during our game that competitor after competitor began shedding their clothing. Nude volleyball in the middle of Flachau—that was a first! The prudish tourist girls from the city could hardly believe their eyes when they saw all these (well built, one and all) physiques and took flight. We hadn't been playing long when we were disturbed by flashing blue lights. "Run, it's the cops," yelled a friend, and at once eight streakers were on the loose in Flachau. Breathlessly, we ran across the meadows and took the barbed-wire fences in elegant hurdle strides (which is not altogether without risk when you're devoid of cover). The blue lights of the police cars were illuminating the mild summer night. The police had taken up the chase! Finally, an officer confronted us with drawn pistol: "*Halt*, stop where you are! Hands up!" I didn't know whether I should lift up both hands, or just one and use the other as a fig leaf. At last, the dutiful keeper of the peace started laughing once he recognized the culprit who was causing a public spectacle here. "How would you like me to take a picture and send it to the papers?" "Is that really necessary?" I asked with trepidation. Finally, the officers took down our names. The next day, we assembled, fully clothed, at the local police station, where we paid the fine.

Chapter | 5

BLIND AMBITION

A ll I wanted was to get well again, and to do so as fast as possible. I was ready to do anything to achieve my goal. My body was rebelling, but my spirit was driving me onward. Then, there were the Olympic Games, in which I desperately wanted to take part. "I can make it," I still thought. In retrospect, that was a complete illusion. Perhaps I just could not admit to myself at the time how poorly I was really doing. The Olympics were my motivation to get well, beginning with learning how to walk properly.

September 26, 2001. As nice as it had been with the Aufmessers, it was time for me to move back into my familiar training environment. My hemoglobin count had risen to 12.4, so it was not too far below a lowest normal value of 14. My hematocrit, at 35.2, was still far below my normal value (47 to 49), but at any rate my blood counts had gotten back within a range where we could (at least carefully) start thinking about high-altitude training. And so I was released from the Aufmesser clinic.

After the first team meeting, the question arose as to who would take care of the shuttle service between Flachau and Obertauern. "I will," I heard myself say, as though that were the most normal thing on earth. Yes, I really wanted to drive my own car again. That additional bit of independence was incredibly important to me. I also wanted to spare my team the cumbersome taxi service.

And so, only thirty-four days after the accident I was back behind the wheel of my BMW. Fortunately, my car had an automatic transmission, as well as cruise control. That was a decisive advantage, since I had zero sensation in my right leg. Yet, it took an enormous amount of determination to cover the twenty miles up to the Tauern range. On the winding road there is no room for any lapse in concentration; you can't relax for an instant. My fibula, which was far from healed, made its presence felt at every curve. It might sound strange to hear someone who is used to bending into a curve at sixty miles an hour on skis complain about centrifugal force while driving an automobile. But in fact, my injured leg reacted very sensitively to the swaying motion induced by the curves. The biggest problem was trying to accelerate using my right ankle, which was necessary time and again, the cruise control notwithstanding. It somehow reminded me of my time as a ski instructor, or my career in the Europe Cup. If I was late, I would drive short distances with my ski boots on. It's just a matter of practice.

When I arrived in front of the Olympic Training Center at one o'clock in the afternoon, a television crew was supposed to meet me. "Thank goodness there are no reporters here yet," I thought. We made do with reenacting my "homecoming scene," with training center director Heini Bergmüller welcoming me, hours after my first training session. I marched toward the entrance full of confidence, and without crutches. "Long time no see," I joked while the camera was running, and I forced myself to smile, even though I didn't feel like it. I felt like an outsider up there. I felt that I didn't fit in with my colleagues, all in top form, who were preparing for the World Cup preseason. To top it off, I wasn't allowed to return to my familiar surroundings. My bicycle ergometer had been brought down two floors to the physical therapy department, and the room had been remodeled just for me. The area that was usually used for giving massages to athletes and treating rehabilitation patients was now the new "Hermann Maier Training Center." Next to the ergometer stood a heavy metal oxygen tank, and behind it an exercise ball, foam pads, free weights, and equipment for balancing exercises.

Screened from the other athletes, I started pedaling behind a curtain. Heini, who knows my physical condition better than anyone else, had me start out with a regime of fifteen minutes at 70 watts' resistance at only 65 revolutions per minute. A pretty lame beginning! Such an assignment was almost an insult. On the day of my accident, I had easily biked for one hour at 75 revolutions per minute and 250 watts' resistance. The bicycle ergometer, on which I used to spend several hours a day, is an important parameter. In conjunction with your lactate count, which is determined after each training session with a prick in your ear, you know exactly where you are. Seventy watts! My training was a joke. The piece of paper on Heini's desk said three times thirty minutes at 80 watts. But alas, that wasn't my workout schedule, but that of a hotel guest in Obertauern. I was allowed to bike only once for fifteen minutes, and at a lower resistance.

Bare-chested, I fought against the resistance. The oxygen mask made an indentation around my mouth and nose. I wanted to joke around with Bettina, the nurse who had taken care of me during those monotonous sessions in "the good old days," but that was impossible now. The bubbles were dancing around in the transparent container. I observed the dial on the oxygen tank. It is to prevent hypoxia, a natural consequence of the lowered oxygen content in the atmosphere at this elevation. In front of me on the wall were the typical glossy display posters that you can't avoid seeing in any physical therapy or doctor's office: skeletons and diagrams of human musculature, with explanations of every anatomical detail. I stared at those nameless creatures and counted the minutes and seconds until the timer finally ran down to zero. I was cold. The mountain air was coming in through the poorly insulated windows. Sweat, cold, and a draft: a combination that conspired to make me even sicker. Bettina could tell how I was suffering. She hung towels carefully in front of the windows, but that helped precious little.

Even before the accident, my training at the center had often been monotonous and boring. But that was no comparison to what was awaiting me now, especially with fall at its most lovely. I complained constantly, at least to the extent possible with the oxygen mask on. After a few days, Bettina and the fitness trainer had the glorious idea of putting the ergometer outside. I have no idea how they managed to convince Heini. He was strictly against it, since an ergometer outdoors did not at all fit with his idea of sterile laboratory conditions. In the end, though, my bike ended up outside the training center complex, and I was breathing fresh air. I looked out onto the beautiful mountain scenery and rejoiced at being back in natural surroundings. For a few training sessions I was at peace with the world. Then, the rainy autumn weather returned, and I was forced back into my torture chamber.

And every day is Groundhog Day. I felt like I was stuck in the Bill Murray film *Groundhog Day*, where he has to live through the same day over and over again. My Groundhog Day looked like this:

7:30 A.M. Get out of bed. Breakfast. Twenty-mile drive to Obertauern.

9:30 A.M. Lab check at the training center. The nurse pricks my finger, the blood climbs up into the thin glass capillary tubes all by itself. It is applied to the test strip, which is inserted into the analyzer. The suspenseful wait for my readings: creatine kinase, urea, blood gas, which provide an indication of my physical condition and the effects of the training. In the meantime, I can interpret each value by myself like a medical professional. If you undergo this procedure on a daily basis, you learn a lot about your own body and the way it functions. On the day after my strength training, my creatine kinase value rises, while if I pedal for too long in the lower endurance range, it sinks. Creatine kinase is a muscle enzyme that shows in retrospect how much exertion your muscles have undergone. The urea value helps determine how intense the training of the past few days really was, and whether my carbohydrate reserves are full. The blood gas value shows the hematocrit and hemoglobin count, as well as the acid-base balance. Even though I have gotten to know my body very well, it is always interesting to observe the extent to which these values align with my subjective feelings. They determine my training routine and help me recognize an incipient infection before I even feel ill. When I work out by myself at home, I sometimes take my own blood. For Heini, these values are the alpha and omega. Only after he has them on his desk does he put together my day's program.

10:00 A.M. Physical therapy. The therapist mobilizes my stiff right ankle. Since the accident, this has been necessary every day before actual training can begin.

10:30 A.M. I am sitting on my bicycle. Three times twenty minutes. After each unit, an attendant pokes into my (already perforated!) earlobe in order to draw blood for the lactate check. The lactate value indicates the level of exertion. The lower the reading, the less intensive the subjective stress on your body. If it is too high, I reduce the watt resistance, and vice versa.

12:30 P.M. Walking class. The treadmill is humming beneath my feet, and Heini meticulously monitors the sequence of movements that I originally acquired twenty-eight years ago when I first learned to walk. I am learning to walk again. "You have to develop a rounded step again," Heini warns. "If you get used to limping, you'll never get rid of it." I try to endure the difficult session with humor. "I feel like an old draft horse," I complain. Heini reassures me. "Soon you'll be able to run again." My ironic response is, "Yes, and no doubt just in time for the Vienna Marathon of 2010!"

1:15 P.M. Stretching and loosening-up exercises. At the end of each training session, the muscles are stretched with active and passive exercises.

2:00 P.M. Lunch at the training center restaurant. Afterward, I rest in Heini's apartment.

4:30 P.M. Back on the ergometer, two times thirty minutes.

6:00 P.M. Balancing exercises. I am sitting on an air cushion balancing medicine balls or practicing with a tilt board, or on wooden blocks, a tipped-over gymnastics bench, or some other equipment. Alternately, there is a series of step tests on special diagnostic equipment, where contact and lift times are measured to thousandths of a second. A sports scientist observes every step.

7:00 P.M. Physical therapy. The last, often painful, highlight of the day. Once again, my ankles are mobilized. Then there is lymph drainage, and magnetic as well as laser treatment of my scars.

7:45 P.M. Massage. Finally, it is time for relaxation. Blockages are cleared, or else I am treated with acupuncture and other methods of traditional Chinese medicine.

8:45 P.M. Finally, end of shift! After a twelve-hour day, the drive home in the dark is yet ahead of me. Usually, I stop in to see my mother, who provides me with an ample supper.

Except for small deviations, this was my itinerary from Monday through Friday. Wednesday afternoons were off, but on those days, I had exhausting press and PR sessions on my schedule. Saturday was a half-day workout, and Sundays were free, unless I was scheduled for an advertisement appearance. Gudrun, who was off studying in Linz, visited me on the weekends.

If I didn't want to develop a traumatic inhibition, I would have to get back onto a motorcycle as quickly as possible. Whoever has once been infected by the motorcycle virus remains infected all his life. It was unthinkable that I would consider depriving myself of the joys of biking just because of an accident. I have always picked myself up after a serious crash on the slopes, dusted myself off, put on my skis, and faced the challenge once again. I crept into my parents' garage. There they were, my prized toys: the Ducati Monster, the Trial Gasgas, and the BMW GS.

The bike on which I had crashed was not among them. That was being stored at the manufacturer in Upper Austria. Not one of my bikes was currently registered. What to do? I picked up the phone and called one of my motorcycle buddies: "Will you lend me your machine?"

A few minutes later, I was cranking the gas and rejoicing. "Now, that's progress!" I hadn't a shred of fear. I just wanted to get going, feel the wind in my face, the freedom you can feel only on a motorcycle. I wasn't going to have many opportunities for biking this close to the start of winter anyway. So I put it in first gear, let out the clutch, and off I went. My path led me directly to the accident site, but I quickly left it behind. I was heading for the winding road up to Obertauern! Alas, I made it only as far as Untertauern. The agonizing pain from sitting forced me to turn back.

I gained an important insight from my brief trip: I had not lost my feeling for the road. On the contrary, the curves, accelerating—everything worked just as before. Except that I needed help to dismount; I don't think I could have made it off the bike by myself. At any rate, another important step back to normalcy had been taken. The newspaper *Bild*, which had caught wind of my motorcycling attempt, proclaimed euphorically, "Monster Maier—secretly back on his bike."

No matter if it was motorcycle or ergometer, the problem concerning the act of sitting followed me always and everywhere. Thus, I often couldn't find a position in which I could eat my meal without pain after a rigorous day of training. I couldn't even sit on the well-cushioned corner bench in my parents' kitchen. The pain was enough to drive me crazy. Everything felt much too hard! I lay down clear across the bench and was close to collapse. It was sucking the last bit of energy out of my body. I tried to kill the time until I could go to bed. Since I could fall asleep only in a state of complete exhaustion, I usually stayed awake until long after midnight, sometimes even until four o'clock in the morning.

Once in bed, the too-warm-too-cold problem kicked in. Usually, I was much too cold. But once the thermostat was turned up, I was too hot. I started sweating, and then freezing in the wet bedding. In the morning I was a wreck and tried to get one or two additional hours of sleep. On such days, I showed up late for my training.

It was actually an act of madness to presume that I was fit to train in the condition I was in. Not only I, but also my coaching team, seemed to be completely over their heads with the situation. I could not believe it, but I was still losing muscle mass.

I finally hit bottom. My body weight had sunk to 168 pounds. I never would have thought that this would happen so quickly. Doc Zeibig tried to use the stomachic liqueur Averna as an appetite-promoting agent. "Before you eat, take a fourth of a liter," he instructed me. I had doubts concerning this prescription. "If I follow this regime, I'll be constantly tipsy." Heinz Schilchegger, my training colleague, offered himself as a guinea pig. A little later I was able to witness from my window as he staggered back to his apartment. Thus, I decided to be a bit more careful with the dosage. When that didn't help, Heini took more drastic measures. He decided to pump me up with massive infusions. Thus, I was attached to an IV for two hours while ten thousand calories dripped into my veins. That comes to about ten Wiener schnitzels, with fries! I had heard about such methods from cycling pros. After especially taxing legs on the Tour de France, this is how they fill up their energy stores.

October 6, 2001. My inner fight was becoming more and more dramatic. My tortured body was demanding analgesics, but the athlete in me yelled, "Stop taking them!" Drugs and training—that's an ill-fated combination. Thus, I decided to wean myself off the medicines from one day to the next. It was an attempt that I had to abandon in desperation. The pain became so unbearable that I started behaving like a junkie. Desperate, I was searching for the redeeming syringe at home, in order to inject myself with trembling hands. Thus I was assured at least a few hours of sleep. During the day, I continued using painkillers. They started tasting really good to me. At that point I hadn't fully realized that I had become dependent on them. Once the stuff no longer had an effect, I had to increase the dosage. Otherwise, I simply wouldn't have made it.

DOUBLE VISION

I probably would have been on drugs for many more months had I not had a shocking experience that finally shook me awake. On my way home from training one night, I suddenly had double vision, and the cars ahead of me appeared to have two rear license plates. I thought in desperation, "This is the last straw. I can't even drive a car by myself anymore." Until then, I had felt that even in my current condition, I was still a better driver than most. But now what choice did I have? I called Heini and presented him with the alternatives: "Either I start to work out at home, or I quit altogether!" I was reduced to a shadow of my former self, and I was terrified to lose even more weight from the endurance training. Psychologically, I had reached my absolute nadir.

Should I have defied my coaching team at that point and simply taken a break? From today's vantage point, that would probably have been the most sensible course of action. On the other hand, I still felt I had a realistic chance of making a comeback by the Olympics, and I believed that I could accomplish this goal only by continuing to train rigorously. For Heini and the team at the Olympic Training Center, the situation was incredibly difficult. No one could really put himself in my place. They all seemed to believe that I was fully capable of performing miraculous feats. Their motto seemed to be "If something terrible happens to Hermann Maier, he just bounces right back."

Even my team of doctors seemed to be overwhelmed. An open fracture in conjunction with a tissue transplant is not without risk even for a nonathlete. But with someone who tears down an icy slope at ninety miles per hour, completely different problems arise. How will the transplant withstand the pressure in an extremely constricting ski boot? How will the fracture heal? How will the surgically treated bone react to the enormous forces released during a ski race?

The mending of the fracture was the least of my worries. When I stroked the bulge on my right calf, I could feel the callus, the new bone growth, at the fracture site. The other injuries caused me considerably more trouble. Since the nerve pathways on my left side were thoroughly compromised, my thighs were becoming thinner and weaker daily. I could no longer move correctly and had to concentrate with every step while climbing a staircase in order not to tumble down backward. I was desperate. "Why isn't my left leg working? How can I resolve this difficulty?" But the doctors still didn't realize the full implications of the problem. At any rate, no one was able to tell me if and when the pinched nerve pathway would open up.

No wonder my training was suffering from all these complications. Time and again, I had to pull the emergency brake. For Heini, a conflict of interest arose every time that happened. On the one hand, he wanted to get me back into shape by winter, but on the other, he knew me better than anyone else and understood that he must not overtax me. Today I realize that I let myself be pushed into something that my body wasn't nearly ready for. I simply should have listened to my body and let it rest.

October 10, 2001. Seven weeks after surgery, I had to go back under the knife. But this time, it was nothing that should cause me much concern. The fifteen-inch titanium rod in my lower right leg was fastened in place with the help of four lateral bolts. In order to speed up the healing of the fracture and stimulate my leg, the pressure at the fracture had had to be increased. To accomplish this, the two screws that attached the rod to the bone would be removed. As silly as it may sound, this operation was by far the most wonderful experience of that time. I still remember vividly my feelings at the moment the anesthetic took effect. For the first time in many weeks, I felt not an inkling of pain. "Don't fall asleep! Whatever you do, don't fall asleep!" I kept thinking. I had an indescribable feeling of happiness and fought against drifting away. But it didn't take long, and I was gone.

When I opened my eyes, there was a microphone in my face. I was thoroughly confused. But then I remembered, "That's right, they're filming my documentary!" I had expressly agreed to the film crew's presence, since I wanted to have an honest and seamless account of "the journey back."

In an anesthetic fog, I tried to follow the questions. "Hermann, how are you doing?" Artur wanted to know. I stammered some total nonsense: "Like the morning after a party. Like in Nagano . . . with the white velvet gloves . . ." While Artur was fumbling about with a demonstration rod in front of the camera and explaining the surgical intervention, I tried to listen to the elaborations of the surgeon. I desperately fought against my heavy eyelids, and finally wanted to know, "Am I healed now?"

"At least you've taken another step forward," was the answer. We had expected more from this intervention, to be sure. Even though a callus had already grown around the fracture zone and the bone had partially grown back together, it failed to shift into place quite properly even after the removal of the lateral bolt. This would cause me considerable trouble for months to come.

October 20, 2001. Once a week my medical team, the Austrian Ski Federation bosses, and my ski trainer from the Olympic Training Center held a powwow to discuss in every possible variation my theoretical chances for participation in the Olympics and the necessary measures for such a scenario. To be sure, these meetings took place behind closed doors and under the strictest secrecy. But time and again, bits and pieces trickled out to the public at least in the form of rumors. With the same regularity, the media speculated about the possible date of my comeback. One thing was striking. Every journalist who actually visited me in Obertauern during this time and saw how poor my condition truly was ended up with a similar prognostication concerning my pending Olympic participation: "Probably not." But no one dared to make a categorical statement.

No one, that is, except the *Salzburger Nachrichten*, which came charging forward with a "secret plan" on October 20: "This is how Maier will still make it to the Olympics," was proclaimed in bold letters. In the story I read that "during weekly meetings under the leadership of Austrian Ski Federation chief trainer Toni Giger, a secret plan for Maier's Olympic comeback is being worked out." They thought they knew everything, for example that my ski boot company at the time, Lange, was working on a special boot, and that Atomic was keeping an especially soft ski at the ready for a possible Herminator comeback. As a scenario, they proposed the ski federation qualification trials in January, or as a final option, my participation in the two super-G races in Garmisch. I was speechless.

Chapter | **6**

BACK IN THE LIMELIGHT

It was time for me finally to show my face in public. At least that's what my team was thinking. After all, it had been more than two months since the accident, and I wanted to begin my comeback in three months. Sports Night, the gala at which Austria's top athletes are honored, seemed like the perfect venue. Officially, the result of the vote was kept secret until the festive evening itself, but I had already been informed that the sports journalists of our country had, just as in the past three years, elected me "athlete of the year." It was important to me that I accept the trophy in person. With this gesture I wanted to signal, "I have returned!" And so I was preparing diligently for the event. My thoughts were focused less on the acceptance speech than on when I would be taking which painkiller. One Tramal pill before the event, one during, and one after. No one, least of all my competitors, should know what miserable condition I was in.

October 25, 2001. Of course I was in no condition to undertake the 220-mile drive from Obertauern to Vienna with my injured leg, and so Toni Schutti, head of the Austrian Sports Association and chief organizer of the gala, had arranged a helicopter to ferry me to the capital. As seems generally to happen when I resort to this time-saving mode of transportation, half of Austria was shrouded in fog. We couldn't even think about flying. So we started driving, with Knut, my press spokesman, at the wheel and Heini sitting next to him. I was lying in the backseat, writhing in pain. Since Toni Schutti's nerves were already strung tight enough, we wanted to keep the slight change in mode of transportation a secret from him as long as possible. But one thing was certain: There was no way we would be able to make the 6:30 P.M. press conference. We would have to drive through the Lungau region on the heavily traveled state highway toward the Semmering pass. Shortly before we were out of Obertauern, we heard a traffic report on the radio about an accident near Judenburg. A few minutes later, we were stalled in traffic. It was high time we were calling Schutti. He first thought we were teasing him. Once he realized how serious things really were, he suggested that we telephone the local police and request an escort. But our friends from law enforcement apparently concluded that someone was pulling a prank and left us stuck in the jam. Long before the gala had even started, I'd had enough and felt like turning back. We arrived at the Hofburg, Vienna's imperial palace, only after 8 P.M., when the evening's program had already gotten under way. "What do you expect? Maier is late as usual!" Once again, I had to take the blame, and it wasn't even my fault.

After the monotonous months at the hospital and in Obertauern, the hustle and bustle at the gala was quite a culture shock. I felt out of place, surrounded by athletes everywhere, all of them colleagues of mine, walking about in top shape. But I didn't belong to the fit set this time around. In the big changing room I ran into my brother. Alex had dyed his hair bright red and was getting ready for the fashion show. Since I had missed the press conference, I had a few minutes left to catch my breath. That's when ski federation press spokesman Robert Brunner showed up and fixed me a wakeup concoction toward whose contents I immediately adopted a don't ask–don't tell policy. That's what I needed at the time! The pain! The nerve-wracking, exhausting journey! I couldn't even guess what was still in store for me that evening. It was to be a run through the gauntlet such as I hadn't seen even during the Olympics. The organizers had provided me with two bodyguards, something that I normally feel uncomfortable about. But this time around I was grateful to be professionally shielded from the horde of reporters that followed me every-where. Herbert Garr, Austria's Hugo Boss CEO, personally saw to my out-fit, which, thank goodness, I would be wearing only on that evening. I had become incredibly skinny. I had shrunk from a size 42 down to a 38. And the shoes! Just thinking about them makes my feet hurt. Inside the designer sock was my swollen right foot, which the four-and-a-half-hour drive had caused to become even bigger. What I needed here was moon boots, not these super-tight, stiff designer shoes that I had to squeeze into. While I was fighting against my footwear with a pain-wracked face, Gud-run finally showed up. She could tell with one glance how miserable I was. My girlfriend had traveled by car from Linz and had been waiting at the wrong entrance, a mishap that seemed oddly in step with this price-less evening. Once I was finally inside my festive attire, I was shepherded through the endless Hofburg hallways among a cascade of flashlights to an opulent reception room for the television interview. When the cam-eras were running, I would pull myself together and present a cheerful façade, even though I was seething inside. An Austrian actress who was present that night could tell right away that I was only playing a role. Doris Schretzmayer, well-known from the television series *The New Girl*, took me aside and told me about a horrendous accident she had suffered when someone driving on the wrong side of the road crashed into her. She had been bedridden for half a year. "The journey here by car must have been a horror for you," she said. "Since my accident, I can no longer bear to ride in the passenger seat." She was not wide of the mark, even though I had not suffered any lasting psychological trauma. Otherwise, I would not have been able to stand the odyssey from Obertauern to Vi-enna, which was my first long drive since the accident.

The gala ended up being a very well-planned event, but I wasn't able to enjoy it much. I certainly did not have any time to get in the proper mood. I was shuffled behind the stage, where I waited together with ski jumper Andreas Goldberger for my appearance. On stage, I acted the vic-torious golden boy. When I was holding the glass trophy and the big hall was filled with minute-long standing ovations, I was filled with joy. For a moment, I again felt like a champion and thought about the Olympics. A few seconds later, as I limped off the stage, a surge of pain ripped me back out of my daydream. I fought my way back to my table and wanted nothing but to be left alone. I could not even enjoy the food. People were constantly shoving scraps of paper, napkins, cell phones, menus, and such at me to be autographed. Here a picture, there a picture. And everyone was talking at me and wanting impossible assurances:

"Are you coming to our party?"

"Will we be training together?"

"Do you have time for the next sports gala?"

"Are you in favor of bone marrow donation?"

Reporters were constantly crowding around my table. My head was spinning, and I wanted nothing but to get out of there. It was midnight when the event's press officer had the brilliant idea of making up for the press conference that I had missed earlier in the evening. Again, we marched off into a grand reception room. I was almost blown away when I saw what was going on in there, even though I am normally inured to such events: The room was packed with reporters and camera teams. Since with the exception of selected interview appointments on Wednesday afternoons I had been essentially unavailable for two months, their thirst for information had collected like water behind a dam. When the floodgates were finally opened, a rush of curious and bizarre questions cascaded down on me:

"What do you do on weekends?"

"Is this your new gala look?"

"How important are good looks to you?"

"Are you thinking of starting a family?"

"Do you believe in miracles?"

"Who will be your successor?"

I returned to my table, downed the beer that had gotten warm in the meantime, and ordered another one right away. "In one end, out the other," I thought. With the pain cocktail I had taken earlier, I was in my own world at any rate, which made the whole thing bearable. Even though it was a kind of forced happiness, the event was actually beginning to be fun for me. When there were only a few guests left inside the Hofburg, Gudrun and I strolled outside. The tanks for next day's parade celebrating Austria's national holiday had already been parked on the Heldenplatz. We were making a beeline for the Volksgarten pavilion, where several friends had assembled, including Artur, along with his beautiful daughter Julia, Heini, and Raika marketing chief Leo Pruschak (who had stuck by me, and not only as a sponsor, during the worst of times). It ended up being a lot of fun. By the time we got back to the hotel, the birds were already singing. For the first time since August 24, I felt like I was really living again. Maybe that cocktail of drugs and alcohol could have sustained me for the whole next day. At any rate, I talked myself into believing that I had taken another small step forward.

Whether the trip to Vienna helped my physical recovery is another question altogether. Today, I see things differently. I would probably hide away, keep everything far away from me, invest all my energy in my health, and send a video message. Just as the racing driver Michael "Schumi" Schumacher does for every honor he receives.

October 28, 2001.   I was a couch potato on Gudrun's sofa at her apartment in Linz. Images from the World Cup prelude came across the television screen from Sölden. I watched Frederic Covili give his very best, and thought, "Damn, I can do better!" I had dominated the previous giant slaloms in Sölden according to my whim. Now I was suffering like a dog. At every turn I knew exactly how to save precious split seconds. I had everything stored in my head, but I couldn't transpose it into action. I would experience that same feeling of hopelessness with a soccer ball a few days later in Dubai. It was damned painful, but there was nothing I could do to change that. I had to learn to deal with it. I would have to watch several more times this winter how my races were being divvied up among others. It was some consolation that the season before, I had decided thirteen World Cup races in my favor.

November 7, 2001.   The first snowflakes of early winter were falling in Obertauern. They were calling me to put on a sweater and come outside. The idyllic Alpine landscape around Lake Grünschnabel, normally enveloped in quiet, had been transformed into a set for an advertisement. I was doing overtime. Unlike my previous advertisements, which could be boisterous and flashy, we were now aiming at something more understated and thoughtful. The creative minds at Sabotage Film Productions had come up with a simple and modest comeback spot.

With a musical backdrop from the Oscar-winning motion picture *Platoon*, images from my previous triumphs at the 1998 Olympics in Nagano, the 1999 World Cup in Vail, and the overall 2000 world championships victory in Bormio flashed across the screen. Cut. Then the insert: "Obertauern 2001. Rehabilitation." I pull up my trouser leg and thoughtfully stroke the scars on my right calf. The Tauern range, sprinkled with snow, rises in the background. A small mountain lake shimmers in the distance. The sky is shrouded in a melancholy cloud cover. I get up and run toward the water, in the direction of the mountain peaks. Then the slogan: "The true victories are the quiet ones." No spot could have better expressed my feelings at the time: my gratitude over having survived, over being able to walk again, even starting to run.

I thought the day of shooting would never end. At the Olympic Training Center, "radio lady" Claudia Stöckl was waiting to record her Sunday morning show. So we "breakfasted" on cold pancakes and coffee from a thermos long after it had become dark outside. When I heard the show three days later on the radio, I was surprised at how many personal feelings I had been willing to reveal even back then.

November 19, 2001.   Outside, the snow was piling up, and I read daily reports in the newspapers about my ski-racing colleagues who were getting ready for the overseas competitions in Colorado. I, alas, was lashed to my stationary bicycle in Obertauern.

I was treading water. Even worse, I was asking myself for the first time why I was doing this to myself. Luckily, Heini knows me so well that he could quickly tell how dire my state was. He looked me in the eyes and said, "You have to get to a warmer climate as soon as possible!" Which was easier said than done. A long flight would be poison for my transplant, and a large time zone change was not feasible for my overall physical rhythm. Heini got on the Internet and stashed piles of information onto the reading rack of my ergometer. We quickly agreed on the destination of our journey: Dubai. Dry heat, sandy beaches, and all that with only three and a half hours of flight with no time change to speak of. Ski federation alpine director Hans Pum made use of his connections with the opulent Jumeirah Beach Hotel. Before I was allowed to escape the November blues, I still had to endure a media tour.

IN MUNICH WITH ANASTACIA, JENNIFER LOPEZ, AND COMPANY

November 23, 2001.   My first appearance outside Austria since the accident. The German television channel ARD has invited me as one of their star guests at the Victoria Gala in Munich. Five million viewers would be watching it live on their televisions. It was an evening teeming with superstars. There was Jennifer Lopez, as well as Anastacia, Mariah Carey, the Lighthouse Family, Sasha, etcetera, etcetera. The great decorated athletes such as Michael Schumacher and Lance Armstrong were missing, though, as is often the case with such events. That's because the likes of us actually have to work out. We don't exist by media hype but by virtue of our accomplishments on the slope, on the track, on the soccer field, or on the racecourse. But I was there, even though (or maybe because) I was in a lot of pain. Otherwise, I would have been at the overseas races. Besides, the date was easily combined with another errand. Together with Gudrun I was picked up directly from my training in Obertauern by the ARD helicopter, and we made a stop at Ried im Innkreis to fit my new ski boots with a special kind of tongue. The stop was a complete success. I stood inside my specially constructed boot and for the first time, it felt right. It just fit. For the first time since the accident I could imagine skiing again. Unfortunately, there was no time to savor this feeling of happiness. The rotor blades outside were spinning, and a few minutes later we took off.

At the Munich exhibit hall, the mood was tense. Mariah Carey, Jennifer Lopez, and Anastasia were having one of those infantile power struggles that you constantly read about in the papers. The point of contention was the order of their appearances, and the live show was in danger of being canceled. I was hardly interested in such childish antics, and Gudrun as well was rather worn down. We had hopelessly gotten lost in the chaos of hallways, helpers, and celebrity guests. Luckily, the former ski racer Tobias Barnerssoi—I had looked up to him during my Europe Cup beginnings—was present. He showed us the way through the catacombs. Tobi was working as a sports reporter for ARD, and he wanted to accompany me backstage throughout the evening. When I was called onto the stage amid thunderous applause, I clenched my teeth and put on a show. Breezily, sort of in a half jog, I swept onto the stage and gave a short speech thanking everyone for the honor afforded me. The newspaper *Bild* began their comeback speculations the very next day.

CLINIC BENEATH THE PALMS

In truth, I was far away from a comeback. My weight loss, the monotonous forced training, and the large quantities of medications had left me high and dry. The only thing that could save me now was a change of pace. I was yearning for a quiet place far away, for the sounds of the ocean and the warmth of summer. Dubai, which I already knew from an invitation after the world championships of 1999, seemed like the ideal place.

On the morning after the Victoria Gala I met Heini at the Munich airport, and from there we flew directly to the United Arab Emirates. The journey had an ominous beginning: One hour after takeoff one of the engines failed and we had to turn back. One more night in Munich. The second time around, all went well, and I was thrilled to be breathing warm ocean air.

The hotel lacked nothing: fitness studio, perfectly manicured green lawns in the middle of the desert, a gorgeous sandy beach, a sensational poolscape with the ocean surf booming in the background.

However, this was not looking to me like a holiday. My patched-up transplant bulge was squeezed into a tight "grandmother beige" support stocking. That, in combination with the foot-long scar on my left upper arm, did not exactly make me feel attractive next to the bathing beauties at the pool. I was disabled, worn-out, washed up, finished. Will I ever be allowed to feel like a top athlete again? With the sticky film of sweat that covered my whole body I constantly felt like I was stuck inside a scratchy sweater. It is still hard for me today to put into words my emotional state of that time. I constantly felt a yearning to climb out of my own body to escape the pain.

One evening, I sat down on a big boulder that was sticking out of the water, looked across the endless horizon, and sought to enjoy the unique, picture-perfect sunset over the ocean. Right then, a deep depression came over me. The pain that was my constant companion took care of the rest. I was yearning for contentment, for the ability to be happy without reservation once again. But I was moving further from such a state with each passing day.

An experience on the second day shocked me in such a brutal way that I would not be able to get it out of my mind for the next weeks and months. I decided to kick a soccer ball around on the lawn of the resort. I used to be really good at that, maneuvering the ball from one foot to the other, to the knee, the shoulder, the head; I could carry on forever. But in Dubai, I couldn't shuffle it more than two or three times. The balancing part wasn't the problem. My feet were simply too slow. I did not have the reflexes necessary to switch from my right to my left foot in time. I could see the ball at chest height, but I couldn't get my leg up. My brain was giving the order all right, but my leg reacted only once the ball had hit the ground again. I was in total despair. Close to tears. Maybe I really cried. I only know that I felt completely helpless at that moment. If you want to play and you can't, when the simplest things don't function, then you really ask yourself whether you're ever going to get well again. It felt like the end of the world.

"HEINI, IT'S ALL OVER!"

The next setback came when I tried to run along the beach. I had gotten permission for this attempt from Artur. Two and a half months after the surgery, Artur had declared the bone "sufficiently mended" to withstand this relatively mild force. What should keep me from making use of this beautiful white-sand beach for the first real runs since my accident? After a few steps, I knew. A sharp pain forced me to break off my attempt at running immediately. Heini tried to encourage me. "Walk for a few minutes, and then try again!" All right. I took off again. After thirty or forty seconds I had to give it up again and walk for a few minutes. I was desperate. Will I ever be able to run again? I couldn't push off and thus carry out the necessary motion for running. My right leg was hurting and the blood was pooling around the transplant region. My left leg seemed to be somewhat detached, as though it weren't part of my body. It was constantly under tension. I couldn't even properly flex my left leg. Every step required supreme concentration. Furthermore, my Achilles tendon hurt like crazy. Thus I ambled awkwardly along the beach, with Heini in tow. Finally, I lost my patience: "Heini, it's all over!"

"Rubbish!" he replied. "That's just the callus that has formed at the site of the fracture." Sure enough, when I touched the area, I could feel the bony bump. I launched a second attempt at running, but I lasted for only about two minutes at the most. Time and again I encountered fellow tourists jogging along the beach. Fat people who jog only when they're on vacation. But they were trotting nicely along. I thought, "Boy, are they lucky! How I would love to run right now, no matter how exhausting, even if my belly were bouncing up and down like theirs!"

The simplest movements turned into a serious challenge. For instance, I wanted to climb across a jetty made up of loose boulders alongside a little marina. But I had to think about every step and look carefully. "Where am I stepping? Will I get over that rock? Will I get hung up on something?" I had to make do with long, relaxed walks in the morning and evening. That had little to do with the usual training of a Hermann Maier!

On my third day, Franz Pammer, who is with the Graz sports photo agency Gepa Pictures, showed up in the Persian Gulf. He had been attempting to document the progress of my recuperation since my release from the hospital on an almost weekly basis. His order this time around was to shoot pictures of me "savoring my vacation." Since he had come such a long way, I indulged him. But there was little savoring involved. When I see those pictures today, I am still alarmed when I take a closer look at the (superficially beautiful) images: my face caved in like that of a bicycling pro after a 150-mile heat, my thighs thin as pretzel sticks. It was hard to believe that the man who is sitting there on the beach in loose shorts was once the strongest ski racer in the world.

Even though it was 85 degrees Fahrenheit in the shade, I was always cold. Inside the air-conditioned buildings, I felt like I was in a refrigerator. In my room, I turned off the climate control, and still I couldn't get warm.

At least in the ocean I felt halfway human. The relaxing act of floating in the water was good for me; there was something playful about it. On the other hand, I dreaded coming out every time. I was embarrassed. I, the athlete, stumbled across every uneven spot on the ocean floor. I constantly had to fit in extra steps, and I fought against the waves. But the most difficult hurdle came shortly before the actual beach area. The tide had dug a two-foot trench into the sand, which became an almost insurmountable obstacle for me. I looked for the lowest spot along the shoreline, and awkwardly clambered across. When I went in, I felt like a penguin. Since I couldn't jump the few inches, I just slid clumsily into the water.

On the second-to-last day of our Dubai adventure, we finally had some action. We discovered an amusement park with an enormous water slide. I watched as the park guests slid down toward the pool on inflated inner tubes. Should I risk that? A bit later, I stood on top of the tower. The lifeguard gave my transplant bulge a skeptical look, and the next thing I knew, I had pushed off. Unbelievable, how quickly you accelerate on one of those things! Then came a moment of sheer terror. The slide turned into a dark tunnel, and for a moment I was terrified that I would bump against something with my leg. Suddenly, the accident was right there in my mind's eye. An unbelievable feeling. At any rate, I was glad when I slid into the pool. I immediately got in line for the next trip.

A year and a half later I returned to Dubai, this time a healthy man. I enjoyed the pleasant climate, dined in beach restaurants, and explored the surroundings. Everything was perfectly lovely.

This time around, after my return from Dubai I still was not able to walk properly. Almost every day, the physical therapists and sports scientists were practicing with me. I have a hard time saying which I hated more, "walking lessons" or the endless sessions on the ergometer. It was snowing outside, and I became more and more aggressive toward my surroundings every day. Maybe that gave my coaches an additional incentive. They had one thing in mind: to bring Hermann Maier back to the slopes in time for the Olympic qualifiers.

How did I imagine my comeback at the time? I really can't say. Time and time again, I did the math and asked myself, "How is this supposed to work?" I couldn't even walk up the stairs normally. How was I supposed to ski in a race by the end of January? An impossible feat. But I simply did not want to face the truth, and so I kept chasing an illusion. Giving up was not in my vocabulary.

December 5, 2001.   Once again, it was one of those Wednesday afternoons when I would have much preferred my monotonous training. But I had to be available to the journalists and my sponsors. Although up to fifty requests for interviews came in weekly, I could meet with only a small fraction of them. I took time to talk to three journalists on that day: A dark-haired Asian woman interviewed me for the Japanese paper *Asahi Shimbun*, a mass-circulation publication that has the largest number of readers worldwide. Then came a question-and-answer session with the Moscow daily *Isvestia*, and a German television station was filming "a day of training with Hermann Maier" on the side. Once the press theater was over, the real action began. We were already way behind with the photo shootings for my equipment sponsors. After the first session with flash-guns, I wanted nothing but to get away. I fled into the training center garage and slammed my car door behind me. After long negotiations, I was finally talked into continuing the session. It was drawn out until late at night: change, put on makeup, smile. Over and over. Was there any-one who thought about my constant pain on that day?

Barely a day went by without new speculations in the media about my comeback. Once, they even talked about my special boots ("Maier's shoe is still bothering him"); then they found a Shaolin monk who sup-posedly was preparing me mentally for my return to the racing circuit with weekly qigong sessions. New "secret plans" for the Olympics con-tinually appeared. In order to show my fans how I was really doing, I flew to Vienna on December 9 and appeared next to Niki Lauda and Hans Krankl as a guest on *Sport am Sonntag*. Live, which I prefer. That way, no one can take my statements out of context, manipulate them, or pur-posely squeeze them into a mold.

THE FIRST TIME ON SNOW

December 11, 2001. In the idyllic landscape at the Gnadenalm, near Ober-tauern, where everything was covered with a thick blanket of snow, I un-packed my cross-country skis. My first attempt at skiing! I was glad to be back in nature. But my usual close connection to the snow was gone. When I was young, I had been a pretty good cross-country skier. But the short, diagonal steps I was taking now did not really have much to do with the sport of cross-country skiing. Once again I was fighting against myself. My right lower leg was swollen and almost bigger than my meager thighs. While I was laboring away with a pulse of 160, tourists easily over-took me. At this snail's pace, I felt sorry for Andy Evers, who was dutifully ambling along behind me. I asked myself, "What on earth am I doing here?" But in any case, I was finally back in fresh air. But this feeling of joy lasted only a few moments. The experience was too painful, and I ended the session after a mere thirty-five minutes.

During further trips to the cross-country track, photographer Pammer and the documentary camera team were among the party. Thus, the obligatory sponsor stickers had to be fastened onto my hat and on the tight ski suit. They kept falling off into the snow because of the frigid five-below-zero temperature. It was getting dark, and I was laughing silently as my coaching team kept having to search for the stickers along the frozen tracks.

Each morning I sat on the ergometer, and no one knew how monotonous that was for me. To be sure, I had established my strong skiing career on the basis of serious bicycle workouts. But before the accident, it had always been an ideal mixture between ergometer and skiing weeks. Moreover, I had often biked outside in the spring and summer. I need variety and speed. But to bike on an ergometer is about the most boring thing a person can imagine. Since it is very effective, though, I always haul my ergometer along, even to the World Cup races. But now, it was beginning to get on my nerves to the nth degree. Since the middle of September I had stepped into the pedals day by day. Without interruption! How I was yearning for the World Cup routine that my colleagues were blessed to enjoy at the time. After that feeling of weightlessness when you plunge into virgin powder, after the fight against the elements, after the challenges of an icy slope, if you are able to find your path and make tighter and tighter turns, yes, that was my world, and the ergometer workouts in between had been a means to an end. Now, it seemed to have become the focal point of my life.

At that time I closely clung to my blood values, which had improved week by week. My training is set up in a way that most of it takes place in the aerobic region, that is, at lactate two. There I can bike forever in a moderate pulse region. In Heini's "sports speak," it is called the compensation region. More intense training sessions are built into the training at crucial intervals. On November 5 we established our first few benchmarks when I biked for four times six minutes at 245 watts and lactate between two and three.

When I started with the strength training, I finally felt ready for the slopes. Edi Unterberger, my serviceman with Atomic, was waiting in the wings. For weeks he had been testing various ski models for me and had prepared for every conceivable snow condition. But a bigger problem was my boots. They had to be reconstructed in a weeks-long cooperative effort between my equipment firm and a cobbler in Upper Austria. I was skeptical about the whole deal from the beginning. I was assuming that my old, time-tested shoes would fit me again before long. But I was dead wrong. As much as Gerhard, my shoe service tech, tried, my foot did not fit into any of the available racing models. And that despite the fact that I had been uninjured below the calf. Gerhard was pushing, grinding, extending, but all in vain. I was lacking all sensation in my calf. Each time I squeezed my foot into the shoe, I was greeted with outrageous pain. But I did not want to complain. "I've got to get through this. After all, I want to continue skiing!" So we kept experimenting.

December 19, 2001. It was time. The first—secret—day on alpine skis. I still had Artur's words "Ski carefully" in my ear, but I had decided, if I'm going to ski, I'll do it right! I fetched from my closet my racing suit and the short outer pants that ski racers wear during training and showed up at the Olympic Training Center shortly after eight o'clock. Gerhard was already waiting for me with my shoes. I still get goose bumps when I think of the whole thing. Not only was the transplant swollen, my foot itself was all puffed up. I squeezed into the ski boot. It seemed to be at least two sizes too small. I fiddled with the buckles and tried to snap them shut. The metal parts went flying through the air. Everything was aching. "Nope, we can just forget about that," I cursed. "I can go without this!" I am used to my ski boot pinching me in all kinds of places. But the pain exceeded my worst fears. Everything inside me was resisting.

Andy talked to me like a sick horse and started his minivan. Without a word, he parked his car behind the Hotel Seekarhaus and got the skis out of the trunk. "What the heck," I thought. "Let's do it!" Of course I realized that I was not allowed to take any risks. The foot was still broken, the callus formation much too fragile.

I should have started off slowly, but that goes against my nature. After three, four turns, I was carving my way through the snow. There wasn't much style in it, but my speed was such that the few tourists out already on this Wednesday morning rapidly disappeared behind me. It really wasn't too bad. However, I had to ski in a rather upright position. Every time I bent my knees too much, my left leg gave way under me. I was already familiar with this extreme muscle weakness from the hospital and my dry workouts, when I had fallen down unexpectedly a few times. The right calf was without sensation and rather busted up, but despite the fracture, the stabilization rod on the inside, and the sensitive transplant, it was more useful to me than my left leg. I was incapable of bending at the knee and sustaining any kind of pressure with my left leg. All in all, though, the attempt at skiing was a positive experience. Finally I was being allowed to do the thing I loved. Even beyond that, I was pleasantly surprised and thought, "Not bad! Check it out, folks! I can ski!"

Of course at that point, everyone around me immediately began thinking about the Olympics. They all wanted to get me ready for a racing situation as quickly as possible, and I played right along. In retrospect, the mere thought of a quick return to racing was completely idiotic. You have to imagine a slope of blank ice, with sudden drops and many transitions, such as would have been waiting for me in Garmisch at the secretly planned comeback. Impossible! I would have fallen down. I would have lacked the conditioning. I would have placed myself in mortal danger. It would have been a colossal failure. But while I was removing my skis, I felt optimistic and thought, "Maybe something could really work out by the time the Olympics take place." With that sort of confidence in the back of my mind, we dared to have a first "official" attempt at skiing for the newspapers. It would become a day of skiing that I shall never forget! At the first hint, which I dropped in an interview, the photojournalists began to announce themselves. We tried to stay ahead of the game and offered the photographers the opportunity to ski down the mountain along with me. The Flachau ski lift company even made free lift passes available. What happened on that bitter-cold Friday morning was incredible. As I drove up to the valley lift station, I could hardly believe my eyes. Objective lenses, TV cameras, microphones, and scores of reporters everywhere. No World Cup race in my hometown had ever drawn so much media attention! A curious detail: They all had their skis with them! "What? They all know how to ski?" I marveled at this and was curious to see what would await me on the slope. I already had a bad feeling in the pit of my stomach. In front of us was the Griessenkar, the mountain on which I had made my very first attempts at skiing almost twenty-six years ago to the day. The fifty free lift tickets that lift operations supervisor Ernst Brandstätter had left behind at the ticket counter were gone in an instant. Everyone wanted to ski with me. Inside the gondola, which is licensed for eight skiers, ten reporters had squeezed in next to my camera team.

What came next was sheer pandemonium. A communal endangerment for myself and everyone else who was hustling and bustling about me. I wanted to start up with a few nice, easy turns and then briefly confer with Andy. But the horde of journalists seemed glued to me. "All right, then, I'll set the rules," I thought, and vanished down the mountain so quickly that no one was able to keep up with me. From the corner of my eye I could see how everyone was plunging down the mountain far beyond their true skiing ability. A few moments later, a cameraman was rattling right across my ski. He missed my injured leg by mere inches. Everything could have come to an end just like that. "Are you mad?" cursed Andy, who had taken over the function of bodyguard. It wouldn't have taken much more for him to have gotten physical. The pain in my right leg was now so severe that I had to open the upper two buckles of my ski boot. Then I took the initiative. "I'll ski down at a single go." I pushed off with two, three powerful shoves of my ski poles and skied away in long, slow turns. In my condition, I wasn't able to make tight turns. The risk I was taking back then was really sheer madness. If I had had a real crash, my leg would have been off again! After that one run, I gave it up. I never wanted to have such a horrific ski day again.

I had to walk the two hundred yards to our ski-school hut. I limped off in my ski boots, and the pain got worse and worse with each step. I could feel the bone fragments of the operated leg grind against one another, and I knew that there wasn't a chance that they had grown back together. It was torture! Since a dozen lenses were pointing my way, I pulled myself together, but my legs would not cooperate. I was under constant scrutiny, but my body no longer played along. That is the worst thing that can happen to an athlete who is trying to make a comeback.

I just wanted to get away, to see no one. But I couldn't vanish into thin air. At least I was able to escape into the hut at my parents' skiing school. I slammed the door behind me and cursed and cursed. At that moment I was done with skiing. "Done, my friends! I am no longer interested. Once and for all! Get me out of this damned tight ski boot!" I hurled the boot into a corner and slipped into a training shoe. At least that felt good. My father knows me so well that he needed no explanations. I was whining, "It hurts too much. It just doesn't make sense anymore! I am done with skiing for now!"

But what to do with the pack of reporters who were lying in wait in front of the hut and wanting an explanation? I tried to gain a few minutes. Once I was able to settle down a bit, I stepped in front of the door and in a flash became the media pro they all knew, and politely answered every question.

"There's not yet enough here for the true racing speed. My body still has to contribute a great deal in order to let things become again what they once were. . . ."

"I felt halfway secure. If I can keep my speed in check, it'll be all right."

One sentence wasn't taken very seriously, it seems. "The Olympic Games are coming up a bit too quickly. But maybe it'll work out a year from now."

Comment of an ORF reporter: "Maybe this was a story for the psyche in the first place."

My quick answer: "Yes, and a story for the media. I wanted to feel the pressure behind me. I'll really get going in the coming weeks!" In truth, deep inside, I was done with skiing. At least for a while.

Christmas was different than usual. Somehow more introspective. During years past, I had come home burned-out on Christmas Eve, and three or four days later I was off to Bormio. This time I had found an inner peace despite my bad condition. I could tell how happy my family was when I sat by the Christmas tree halfway healthy exactly four months after the accident.

December 28–29, 2001.   While the Austrians were winning on "my" race-course in Bormio, I continued my program at the Olympic Training Center. Heini put a TV in front of my ergometer so that I could follow the races. I skied along in my mind and went half crazy because I knew exactly which passages could be skied more efficiently. I looked at the electronic reading on my ergometer and watched as my pulse went up time and again without my changing frequency or resistance.

January 4, 2002.   I made yet another attempt at skiing. It was in Flachau, and I did it without telling anyone. After a few turns I could tell it was no use. I skied down the mountain on one leg and took off my skis. Until May. I had finally given up.

F L A S H B A C K

RULES ARE THERE TO BE BROKEN

To work as a bricklayer is not a bad life, but to be a ski racer is a dream come true. I was starting to prioritize everything according to this dream. In 1997, during the summer after my first World Cup victory, I trained harder than ever before in my life. While my friends were tanning themselves at the swimming hole, I drove the twenty miles from Flachau to the Olympic Training Center in Obertauern day after day. My ergometer was in the basement, where there was no daylight. I felt like I was in a dungeon. But every day I stepped into the pedals. I soaked up all the knowledge I could glean from Heini and his mentor, Bernd Pansold. Because of his past work as a physician in the Pansold was not without controversy. But in Obertauern he convinced me with his streamlined, honest work. Heini had given him a chance to start a new life. Thus, Bernd conveyed his medical philosophy to us in his Berlin accent, while I answered in the true Pongau region vernacular. Because he could tell how much I was willing to invest in my training and how much I respected him, we were quickly on the same wavelength.

My life consisted of training, eating, and sleeping. When the season finally started, there were races on top of training, eating, and sleeping. Everything else was secondary. Clothes? Doesn't matter, we got everything we need during the season's clothing issue. Haircut? Who cares? I could comb my hair behind my ears in a pinch, and during the race I was wearing a helmet, and afterward the sponsor's hat. Car? Didn't need my own, since I was being driven from race to race in ski federation vehicles.

During my World Cup beginnings, I stood out because of three things: The experts could tell that I was standing on my skis better than others. The trainers didn't miss my ambition. And my team colleagues noticed that I related to them with the necessary self-confidence. Thus, Patrick Ortlieb, who then was number one on the team as the Olympic downhill winner and downhill world champion, greeted me with a Maier quotation at the start of my first World Cup season: "Weaknesses? None!" I had made an impression on him with this statement during an ORF preview of the up-and-coming talents. Since I had not ascended to the World Cup along the typical route, I was never a typical Austrian Ski Team racer. If their plan said warm-up runs three times, I thought, "What the heck? I'll warm up the way I've always warmed up. That's how I got to where I am today." I never wanted to give up the freedom that is so important to me, and always remained self-sufficient. That also went for the course inspection (in fact, it is still the case), which happens ahead of every race. I always put great emphasis on getting to do this by myself. I wait until the last of my colleagues is ahead by a few gates, and then I study the course carefully at my leisure. Of course, I run into time constraints toward the end, but with one exception, I always got done on time.

I never wanted to submit to some of the stiff and senseless rules of the FIS. I tried to push everything to its limits. That had a very unfair result at the beginning of the 1997/1998 season. Because Andi Schifferer and I showed up on time, but not as requested five minutes ahead, at the drawing for the giant slalom in Tegnes we had to pay a ten-thousand-schilling fine into the ski federation coffers. I am still mad to this day about such insolence.

Schiffi and I were the perfect roommates at any rate. We brought out the best in each other. He made some improvements by copying my moves during the giant slalom, and I profited from the very beginning from his downhill technique. During the ski federation's snow training in Chile, I impressed my team colleagues to such a degree that Patrick Ortlieb, who had to give the most interviews back then, pointed me out time and again: "Pay attention to Maier, he will become big in the downhill as well." None of the journalists took him seriously. That would change rapidly, however.

There was a problem, to be sure. Even though I had won my first giant slalom in Park City and was in the lead in the overall World Cup ratings, the federation did not want to grant me a fixed starting position during the 1997/1998 season's first downhill in Beaver Creek. Finally, Toni Giger, the leader of my super-G/giant slalom group (WC3) at the time, came through and managed to get me a sure spot. That was the key to the first Austrian overall World Cup victory in twenty-eight years.

I started out completely unburdened that season. There was lots of joking around, and almost every race was fun. The success came almost by itself. I always had my stationary bike along, which earned me a few somewhat sympathetic glances from my teammates. Only by paying close attention to the necessary regeneration measures did I manage to recharge my batteries in the short time periods between races. Only once, in the middle of January, was there a critical moment. I had won five races in a row and could sense the first signs of fatigue. My shins were hurting right at the top of my boots, and the symptoms got worse with each passing race. "Heini, it's getting serious," I said on my return to the training center after my World Cup victory in Wengen. "We have to do something!"

"Okay, then you'll have to skip Kitzbühel," Heini replied wryly. Leave out the most important World Cup race of the season as a brand-new star and consecutive victor? It was sacrilege to even think about it. In order to appease the media, I was talked into the most exhausting press day of my life. After a quick press conference, my PR spokesman at the time, Manfred Kimmel, lined up individual back-to-back interviews for many hours. Until then, I had not realized what kind of demand there was for me. Shortly before midnight I finally stumbled out of the Austrian team quarters and drove home in a trance. I felt like I had been put through the wringer, as though I had fought all the Kitzbühel competitions in a single day. Afterward, I watched the races on TV. By the time the Olympics came around, I had gathered my strength again. Had I not left out several more races (downhill and super-G in Norway's Kvitfjell and the World Cup final in Crans, Montana, seven races in all), I would have easily broken Paul Accola's point record (1,699) during that first season; I might even have exceeded my subsequent record of the century of 2,000 points.

After these enormous successes it was obvious to me that the coming season would be the hardest. I was proud of the new Raiffeisen sponsor emblem on my helmet, and I wanted to prove to everyone that I could do even better. But suddenly, the ease with which I was able to ski before was no longer there for me. On top of that, I struggled with terrible back problems. After the two world championships gold medals in Vail, I still had a theoretical chance of defending my overall World Cup title. But nothing worked anymore. During the last giant slalom in the Sierra Nevada, my body no longer knew what my skis were doing. I fell on account of exhaustion. When I was lying in the snow in pain, I had serious qualms. That season had taught me a lesson.

In the summer of 1999, Andreas Evers came to the WC3 group as a cotrainer. For the first time I had a real partner in conversation. Until then, I had always been the one being chased. Andy worked a lot on skiing technique with me. He had been a good downhill racer himself in the past, but he ended his racing career after a severe motorcycle accident. He conveyed to me the right feeling for long, gliding curves. For the first time, I was testing my own material. Even though I was still a beginner, I suddenly felt like an old-timer and won the downhill World Cup for the first time. That small crystal trophy meant more to me than the record lead: 2,000 points in the year 2000. After I had started the 2000/2001 season with a convincing victory in Sölden, everything turned on the world championships in St. Anton. Two weeks before the opening ceremonies, I triumphed (this was my third try) on the classic Hahnenkamm downhill course, after I had already won two super-Gs that season. There was no stopping the Maiermania now.

As nice as it is to have a world championships in your own country, it is very difficult for a top contender to pull off. For me it ended in disaster. It had started two days before the grand opening, when the mechanism holding my bindings in place broke out of its hinges. During the crash, the cartilage in my right knee was damaged. But no one was listening to me. I had been primed for "three times gold" and was living in my own special quarters in Pettneu, which was four miles away from the site of the competition. I didn't have a minute to relax. The constant back-and-forth driving made everything especially bothersome. There was one appointment after the other: a sponsor presentation on a crane in the pedestrian mall, autographs, Austria House, TV studio, press conference . . . I was constantly under stress, and I awoke with a headache every morning. I started to tense up, just like during the 1998/1999 season. Right from the beginning, the super-G went wrong. Third place. In the downhill, I missed gold by one tenth of a second, and in the giant slalom, bronze by one hundredth. If I had been 0.82 second faster all in all, I would have won all three. Eighty-two hundredths of a second! That's how much I was usually ahead in a single race!

Once the championships was over, I relaxed again. With a simple trick I demolished the competition in Japan's Shigakogen. Because it doesn't make much sense to adapt your whole organism to the time change for a single race, I traveled there the day before the race, went skiing at 4 P.M., kept my normal sleep cycle, won the giant slalom with a lead of 1.74 seconds ahead of Marco Buechel, and flew back to Europe. I won four of the five remaining races in the season and won four crystal trophies, like the year before. I took the downhill overall victory from Stephan Eberharter; my eternal rival Michael von Grünigen had to yield the giant slalom victory. The more pressure I was under, the better I raced. Before the big victory party, I grabbed the telephone and called Heini, my conditioning trainer. "If I work out consistently over the summer, I'll be unbeatable."

"I'm starting to have an uncanny feeling about you," Heini told me after he extended his congratulations. He later told me that even back then, he had a somewhat disquieting premonition. Less than six months after my strongest World Cup final, I would have to start over from scratch.

7

THE OLYMPICS

January 7, 2002. The day of reckoning. It was already dark in Radstadt when I crept into the Aufmesser clinic through the back door under cover of darkness and met in the examination room with Artur Trost. While I uncovered my leg for the X-rays, the leading figures of the Austrian Ski Federation were arriving to attend the "Hermann Maier Summit." They sat down on the leather couch in Werner Aufmesser's living room and waited in suspense for the verdict. President Peter Schröcksnadel and alpine director Hans Pum wanted to hear in person how far I had progressed toward being able to ski again. Of course, my personal coaches Heini Bergmüller, Andy Evers, and Harald Aufmesser were also present. In front of the clinic, the usual reporters were lying in wait. Artur had accidentally mentioned the date during an interview a few days before. And since there is no such thing as a routine checkup one month before the Olympics, they were able to put one plus one together. They were certain: This meeting concerns the Olympics!

To be honest, I had already concluded at Christmastime that I would not be able to compete in the Olympics. I no longer behaved like an athlete who more than anything is working to be able to participate in the Olympics. In Obertauern, the "après ski" season was in full swing. I continued my workouts like a good boy, but it was important to me to feel alive again, and so I treated myself to a few detours on the way home from my base camp in Obertauern and let the day come to a pleasant close while celebrating with friends.

At any rate, it was with a rather relaxed attitude that I showed up for my examination in Radstadt. When the digital X-rays appeared on the monitor and I observed Artur's troubled facial expression, I already knew what would come next. Artur, always in keeping with his pleasant demeanor, started out in a very diplomatic manner. "Well, the flap of skin has grown in very well. The callus formation is making progress. Better, really, than you can expect with such an injury, but . . ." and now came the kicker, "the bone is really not sufficiently healed for such a risk." At that point, the deal was sealed. At least for me.

I struggled up the stairs into the Aufmesser living room and plopped into an armchair. All eyes were on me, but I said only, "Let's wait for Artur." They sipped their mineral water impatiently and nibbled on leftover Christmas cookies. Finally, Artur showed up. He repeated the sentences that I had just heard, and said in summary, "It doesn't look too good. There is a possibility of skiing with the right leg, but I would not at all recommend the kind of stress that is required during a race. Not even during training." Finally, a decision had been reached. At last, I could forget about the two super-G races in Garmisch at the end of January and hence the Olympic Games in February. Hans Pum was the first to speak. "What would be best for Hermann at this point?"

"I would send him on vacation," Artur said dryly. "Far, far away, to a warm climate. He'll be able to gain some distance there."

What to tell the ladies and gentlemen from the press who were waiting outside? In such situations, Peter Schröcksnadel usually takes over. "Is it completely out of the question that Hermann will take part in the Olympics, or is there still a theoretical chance?" Artur sounded a note of warning: "I would not risk it. If Hermann falls and the tibia with the stabilization spike breaks again, then there would be dire consequences. In that case, we would have to straighten out the lower leg with the nail inside and implant a new one." I imagined this procedure in my mind's eye and was gladly willing to go without it after all I had gone through in recent months. Heini added, "I'm even more worried about the nerve problems in his left leg." The pinched nerve still did not allow for my muscle tissue to be fully stimulated; my left thigh refused to strengthen despite the most sophisticated training methods. My situation was not very encouraging; the right lower leg, which had undergone the surgical procedure, had not yet sufficiently mended. The supposedly healthy left thigh had in the meantime become much, much weaker than the right one; beyond a certain degree of bending it displayed dramatic lapses in function. In other words, the Olympic downhill and super-G were impossible simply because of the high speeds. Nonetheless, Heini, the eternal optimist, dug out his Olympics calendar and said, "And what if we just shoot for the giant slalom?" This race would not occur until February 21, toward the end of the second week of the Olympics. I had a theoretical chance of qualifying for it on February 3 in St. Moritz. Until then, I would still have a scarce six weeks. I knew that this was unrealistic, but I wanted to cling to this last straw. Even if it was only for a few days.

Schröcksi spoke a word of authority: "Then you have to make up your mind within the next week." Because we simply did not want to make the press wait any longer than the Hahnenkamm weekend in Kitzbühel.

Okay, then. I wanted to make the best of the tiny chance I still had, and so I continued my grueling comeback training. The meeting had lasted until long after ten o'clock, and Gudrun, who was now living with me, was waiting impatiently with dinner. Of course, my girlfriend wanted to know what was up. But I didn't feel like talking at the time. Instead, I shoveled down my dinner in moody silence. I don't like to dump my problems on others, no matter how close.

The evening news came on the television, and naturally my checkup was mentioned. "Maier's fight for the Olympics continues," the announcer intoned. "More quickly than expected" I had gotten a green light for race training. I took my painkillers and went to bed. As usual, the night was torture and I tried to delay waking up as long as possible.

I got up exhausted as usual, had breakfast, got into my car, and drove up to Obertauern. I could see Heini's eyes light up when I arrived at his central command post. He hadn't been so sure that I would show up after yesterday's summit. The *Kronen Zeitung* had been placed on the reading rack of my ergometer. "Hermann's mini-chance for the Olympics is ten to one," I read, and then, "Maier only has three weeks left for the big miracle."

The training that day began with twenty-five minutes of warm-up biking. Then weights: one hundred repetitions for the muscle-deficient left thigh on the weighed-down bench press that had been developed especially for me. Then bending and stretching exercises with ninety-five repetitions each, including one-legged knee bends with a big weight on my shoulders. And to end the strength-training session, special exercises for both quads. The quadriceps is an extremely important muscle for skiing because it constantly has to act in its function as a shock absorber. I still had to bike for half an hour to promote active muscle regeneration. Finally, I performed my daily stretching and loosening-up routine, lay down on the magnetic field pad, and still had to endure the painful physical therapy.

You don't have to know much about training routines in order to see that this was by no means a pretext workout. During those days I was continually annoyed by idiotic newspaper articles, with stories claiming that I had long ago abandoned any thought of a comeback and was working out only for show. Or that I was simply pretending to be working out to pacify my sponsors. While I was working on this book, I went into Heini's private archives and grabbed the blue folder labeled "Maier Hermann 2001/2002" to check how I had really trained during that time. Today, I am surprised at how much I must have believed in my own comeback. Otherwise, I would never have gone through all that. Do you want to know what I am talking about? I showed up at the Olympic Training Center even during the Christmas holidays. On New Year's Eve, I put in two training sessions: in the weight room in the morning with 170 leg bends as well as knee bends and quad repetitions, and in the late afternoon, when the first fireworks were lighting up the dark sky above Obertauern, I sweated on my ergometer for over two hours.

The New Year began with the usual sessions on the bicycle. On January 3, another strength session was part of the program. One day later, I took off on a special ergometer. On that "yellow monster," developed by an engineer from Slovakia, the force exerted on each pedal is measured separately and transferred to a computer display. In addition, you can program the thing to give you up to 3,000 watts' resistance. Of course, no mortal can overcome that much resistance. For my sort of workout, 500 watts is plenty. I was able to use this special ergometer to help reawaken the upset nerve fibers on my left side by utilizing an extremely high frequency of revolution. It was also helpful in diagnosing muscular imbalance. At any rate, Heini was thrilled that my legs were completely synchronized only a few short months after the accident.

January 11, 2002. I had to appear at a sponsor event in Obertauern. My training took so long that I barely had time to shower and then dash into the main hall in my jogging suit. Coca-Cola had booked me to motivate 250 retailers. While Werner Grissmann, the "interim world champion" of the 1970s, introduced me, impressive images from my Olympic and world championships victories flashed across the big multimedia wall, accompanied by a soundtrack, Queen's hymn "We Are the Champions" in Dolby "surround sound." I was getting goose bumps. At the moment I was jumping onto the stage, I wanted nothing more than to be part of the Olympics. But by the following weekend I was in such terrible pain that I finally surrendered. After a long discussion with Heini and Andy, I called President Schröcksnadel and informed him of my decision.

You are always smarter in retrospect. I know now that after the accident, I continually let myself be rushed into situations that I just wasn't ready for. Skiing brought me nothing but pain at that point. I was shocked at how few people could manage to see the person behind the "Herminator" mask. I started to question seriously whether my comeback ambitions made any sense at all. On the other hand, it was the magic word "Olympics" that had been driving us to seemingly superhuman efforts. I felt the same as my coaching team. We had been driven by the thought of somehow making the impossible possible. At some point during this period, I lost control over my body, which is a top athlete's biggest asset. Suddenly, I had lost all connection to reality, and everything became worse and worse. I would say that all of us hyped ourselves into something that just wasn't realistic.

The topic "Olympics" was finally off the table, and now it was a matter of pulling together a press conference in a matter of two days. The press director in Kitzbühel wanted to schedule us for the small interview room. But when he found himself receiving more requests for information about the "Maier appearance" by the minute, he finally agreed to let the event take place in the big press room. And even that turned out to be too small.

January 16, 2002. "The line from Kitzbühel has been interrupted. We are asking for your patience." This text announcement was displayed for several minutes to the 469,000 viewers who wanted to find out live on this Wednesday afternoon at 1:15 P.M. what decision I had reached. The media hype on that day was not to be compared with any of my previous Kitzbühel victories. For the first time, the press center of the biggest World Cup event was not sufficient for the media storm that ensued after the Hahnenkamm story. Seventeen cameras, 203 print journalists, and dozens of photographers had knocked the Gamsstadt press center out of commission. I had shown up very much on time and had sat down at the podium along with Peter Schröcksnadel and Heini. Then, suddenly, the lights went out. It took about fifteen minutes for power to be restored. That morning, Austrian National Radio (ORF) had taken an opinion poll among the ski journalists. Only Charly Pointer, the old fox from the *Kronen Zeitung,* was absolutely certain that I would throw in the towel for the Olympics. The others had guessed that I would at least leave a back door open for myself. When I explained without reservation that I would not be participating in any of the Olympic events, most of the journalists sat there with their mouths open.

". . . I HAVE DECIDED NOT TO COMPETE IN THE OLYMPICS."

Verbatim transcript of the press conference, Kitzbühel, January 16, 2002.

PETER SCHRÖCKSNADEL: You all know that Dr. Trost conducted a routine medical checkup one week ago. In the course of this exam it was found that the leg has grown back together well, and that the callus formation around the fracture region is progressing better than expected. We have not been taking it easy. Time and again we have been accused of putting on a show. What we really wanted to do is to seize every possible opportunity in order to give Hermann the chance to start at the Olympics. From a purely medical point of view, that should be possible. How far Hermann is personally ready to take that step, how much his level of conditioning would allow for such a step, and how much he feels in a position to compete during ski races, to win races—all that he is about to tell you himself.

HERMANN MAIER: Hello, everybody. I am glad to see this many journalists once again, since I have been out of the loop for a considerable period of time. August 24, the day on which my accident happened, was a very difficult day for me. My first thoughts were, "Will I ever be able to ski again?" The doctors—supervising physician Trost, senior physician Papp, and senior physician Karlbauer—all helped me a great deal. I offer them my undying gratitude for my being able once again to stand on two feet. That also makes things look very, very bright for the future. We started working out with a hand ergometer as early as September. Since then, I have been working out continually, all the way up to last Saturday. It has been extremely exhausting, but considerable progress has been made. Thank God. We certainly haven't forgotten about skiing in the meantime. I already skied once before Christmas, before the official press engagement, and it looked very good. I also skied on January 4 and got the go-ahead from Dr. Trost, who let me know that the bone had grown back together to the point where I could ski once again. I never thought too much about the bone itself, since I was certain it would hold up because I received such outstanding medical care in that regard. But actual skiing closer to racing parameters didn't work the way I was used to. I was unable to turn properly, and it just wasn't any fun. It felt like the slope was more or less being imposed on me. That's why I have decided not to compete in the Olympics. This is certainly not an easy decision, but there simply remain too many

(continues)

(*continued*)

unresolved problems, especially in my left leg, where the nerve still does not work properly. The muscles are not yet being innervated in the right way. The foot is still rather numb. On the right side I am still struggling with problems as well. I am not able to apply more than a small amount of pressure. Thus I have tried to come to a wise decision, which was very difficult for me. I thought, "Really, it doesn't make much sense. There just isn't enough time." I am very sorry because of my fans and for the people who have stuck by me through all this, who maybe were still keeping up their hopes. But my main focus is simply on the coming season. I will invest everything into being able to ski once again halfway decently, in being able to enjoy the activity once again. That is the most important thing to me. All I can say at this point is that I want to wish all the Olympic participants the best of luck. I hope they will represent Austria in a worthy manner, and that they will return home bearing lots of medals.

HEINRICH BERGMÜLLER: Hermann worked very hard on himself for the fifteen weeks just before the training camp in Chile. He had reached his peak physical performance level ever. After the accident, he kept working out; he has been working out for almost fourteen weeks up until now. As it turns out, the biggest problems ended up being the problems on the left side, which are rooted in nervous function. No doctor was able to tell us, "It's going to take three months, it's going to take half a year." Nevertheless, we kept working and steadfastly hoped for improvement. For instance, there was a 100 percent gap in the back of the thigh two weeks ago. We hoped that the nerve channel would open up further. But that is happening at an exceedingly slow pace. Hermann is to be admired for having worked so single-mindedly, and having put himself under such pressure. But it surely is a reasonable decision on his part not to tempt fate by taking such a risk, but rather to let everything heal completely and go to the starting line in top form.

OLIVER POLZER, ORF: Has this decision really only been taken during the past few days, or has there been an attempt to keep the topic alive in order possibly to benefit the sponsors?

MAIER: No, I don't think I am in a position where I have to advertise on behalf of my name. I have accomplished too much during the past few years to have a need to do that. To be honest, it is more important to me right now to achieve a measure of repose. I didn't start working out immediately after my accident in vain. Otherwise, I could have leaned back and said, "Yes, I'm going to take a bit of a break for once. It'll heal up; it'll all happen by itself." But even in September, when I looked at the calendar, it was my big plan to come back in Garmisch. I thought, "If I am healthy enough to be able to train and ski through the gates in January, then I'll come back for the two super-Gs." Unfortunately, that's not working out timewise, hence the decision. I did not work out until this past Saturday in order to put on a big show for everyone. I simply do not need to go to such lengths. Otherwise, I'd rather be in Australia with the aborigines and play on my didgeridoo. I really tried everything, up to the last moment.

SCHRÖCKSNADEL: It was not we, but the media, who hyped this matter up. We have tried to keep down expectations rather than encourage them.

ORF: A relatively short time after the accident, Artur Trost said that it would not be prudent to ski with such a stabilization nail in one's leg. That metal component is still inside. Is it possible after all to race with such a thing?

MAIER: That should actually not be a big problem. There are several metal parts inside. That really doesn't make a difference as long as I am not in pain. A nail in your foot doesn't detract. As long as the bone is fully formed and stable, nothing much can happen, except if the leg is once again broken. But that really should not happen.

ORF: When are you planning on competing in a race again? Is there even a theoretical chance that we will see Hermann Maier at the next Olympics in 2006?

MAIER: That really is a long, long time away from now. I am going to try to gain some distance for the time being so that I can train properly for the next season. I want to be able to enjoy skiing once again. I will prepare with great diligence and hope that I will get back to where I once was on a physical level, maybe even to a stronger level, although I don't necessarily need to prove anything within the sport of skiing. Anything I can achieve at this point would be an encore.

ARD RADIO: What concrete problems does your left, in fact uninjured, leg cause you?

MAIER: After the injury my pelvis was so big that I barely could have fit into Ottfried Fischer's underwear, which are rather sizable. There was tremendous swelling, and considering the massive contusions, I am amazed that my pelvis didn't shatter in the process. Maybe that would have been better, because then there would have been more space for the nerve pathways to conduct more efficiently, and I would have had more sensation in my leg. Unfortunately, all this is taking a very long time. Even though I can exercise the left leg, there is a big difference compared to the right

(continues)

(continued)

one. The left leg just simply doesn't work up to a certain level when weights are being lifted. If I get below a certain angle, I simply can't get up again. If I compete in a race and I can't stay on course, the gate referees as well as the spectators are in danger. I do not want to put anyone in such a position!

ULLI NETT, ZDF: Have you come to this decision all by yourself?

MAIER: I did not want to disappoint all those who have labored on behalf of my Olympic comeback: the team at the Olympic Training Center, my doctors, my family. I did not want to hurt anyone. Thus, the decision was extremely difficult for me. The fact that I won two gold medals during the last Olympic Games is surely an advantage in this regard.

ZDF: Will you be part of the games in Salt Lake City in some capacity, or will you be watching the Olympics from home?

MAIER: I believe I will fly to a place where there is no television. Maybe somewhere in the bush. I will do things that I enjoy doing.

I drove back to Obertauern with Heini and Knut with a great sense of relief. In the car, we chatted about trivialities. Since I had made my decision a few days earlier, the press conference had been only a formality for me. Somehow, I was glad to have left the media hype of Kitzbühel behind me. That sort of thing is bearable only when you have won.

Heini talked me into coming to Obertauern one more time for strength training on the "day after." Since I had nothing better to do, I agreed. In my head, though, I was only thinking about my upcoming vacation. I used the time until my departure to get things done that I usually have no time for. I went shopping like a normal person, and I picked up some vacation pamphlets. Because I had finally accepted the fact that I needed to forget my sport for the time being, it was important that I get away from it all and spend time among ordinary people.

January 29, 2002. I was sitting next to Andy Evers in the Austrian Airlines Airbus 330 on my way to Miami. We were both glad to have escaped the media frenzy. In the meantime, new speculations about whether I would ever return to the slopes had begun. In addition, strange, nebulous insurance stories such as "ten million if he doesn't race" (*Sport-Bild*) were floating through the media. Because my attempt at a comeback in time for the Olympics had floundered, the reporters also needed to get their "secret plan" stories out of their heads. Thus, they were looking for new topics in order to get on my nerves.

Should I have behaved differently toward the media and gone completely underground? Would I have had a choice? Hardly. For every time we did not take a firm stance with respect to a rumor or a story, it immediately was interpreted in a certain light, according to someone's agenda. To me, it seemed to be most prudent to tell everyone what the deal really was at certain appointed occasions. Sometimes, I used my homepage (www.hm1.com) as my mouthpiece.

It was in that spirit that I conducted the information release during my vacation. Because I did not feel like having the paparazzi hanging around, I kept somewhat of a "vacation diary" with nice pictures and vague geographical references on the Internet, but I announced the exact location of my vacation only after I returned home. Thus, the press played their merry game of speculation, and by guessing "Caribbean," some of them were not far off.

I will always remember that vacation! Key West was the perfect hideaway, and we didn't even have a fixed address. A friend had made his houseboat and crew available to us. We savored the "pirate's life" to the fullest. We floated along Florida's Everglades, did some diving or fishing, and slept in until it got so hot belowdecks that we couldn't stand it any longer. We left the boat only to take in nourishment. Since I was still very much underweight, I did not have any problems enjoying the fare. I was not very picky: burger with fries and a Coke, fresh fish, steak. The captain brought the finest wines out of his quarters. Finally, I had my appetite back! We didn't get bored for a moment. Every once in a while, a private diving instructor came on board and let us in on the secrets of the undersea world. While the sun was burning down on our heads, we were studying the English-language manual for our underwater diving certification.

The more distance I gained from what had transpired back home, the crazier my attempts at a skiing comeback seemed to me. While I attempted to haul the oxygen tank across the deck of the boat, I looked down onto my stork's legs and just shook my head. "Really, it's unbelievable. What were we thinking? How is someone who can't even carry an oxygen tank supposed to compete in ski races?" I was relieved not to be part of the hubbub surrounding the Olympic Games.

I was also truly glad to be in a place where people didn't recognize me. I didn't have to try to walk properly all the time. No one was asking why or how much I was limping. And no one judged or commented on what I was doing. I enjoyed the feeling of anonymity. That was the biggest luxury I could have asked for.

However, my pain was unbearable at times. I could feel the bone fragments of my fibula, which had been allowed to grow back together without surgical intervention, grind against one another, which hurt enormously.

February 9, 2002. Change of scenery. Andy had to go to the Olympics in Salt Lake City in his function as a coach, and I was allowed to fly on to the Bahamas. I had arranged to meet at Miami International Airport with my press spokesman Knut and my friends from the film team who were still working on the documentary "The Journey Back." The meeting in the huge terminal went well, but it took an eternity to get through security. Once again, my titanium spike presented the airport safety workers with a great mystery, especially since the recent attacks of September 11. Thus, my implant caused me more than physical pain. We talked so long that we missed our flight to Nassau, and we finally took off on the last flight of the day, after midnight. There, we were met by the personable Austrian consul, accompanied by his Russian girlfriend in a bright pink suit. He offered us a bungalow in the sleepy little resort on Paradise Island as our headquarters.

It was a bit too quiet for us there, and after two days we moved to Club Med. Kevin, the Franco-Canadian manager of the resort, hadn't a clue who we were at first; but a fax from an Austrian colleague and TV spots from way back in Nagano, which were being aired as part of the Olympics coverage, quickly opened his eyes. Suddenly, we were given the run of the club's entire range of activities. Kevin even lent us the club's fitness trainer, Nancy, as well as Michelle, the pretty waitress from the oceanfront bar, as extras for the beach shots in our documentary. He also furnished us with a pickup truck and an assistant to help us during the filming. So we took the stationary bicycle out of the fitness studio and hauled it from one breathtaking spot to the next. Toné, the cameraman, had the idée fixe that I had to ride on the ergometer in every conceivable location and situation. The bike was placed in front of an antique swimming pool, on the white sandy beach, under palm trees, or on a whitewashed veranda, while Michelle stood in the background with an orange rescue buoy à la *Baywatch*.

To top things off, Toné got the idea that it was permissible to trespass onto private property. "This backdrop with the ocean and the palm trees simply can't be beat," he enthused. "The estate belongs to a wealthy country singer," our assistant explained. "He's not home." Following Toné's urging, we heaved the ergometer across the fence, pushed the porch furniture aside, and voilà, I was pedaling on someone else's veranda. That was quite a kick. Right then, a Jeep Cherokee pulled into the driveway, and I envisioned myself in handcuffs for the second time in my life. The singer, an athletic-looking man in his mid-30s, appeared completely relaxed once he saw the lights and the camera. Knut explained to him what we were doing there, and offered him a bag of Milka chocolate as a bribe. "Don't let me interrupt you," said the owner and disappeared into his garage. I couldn't believe it. "Incredible that we're getting off so easy," I marveled and waited in vain for the flashing blue lights.

It was on that day that the Olympic super-G took place in Salt Lake City. But that didn't faze me any more than our break-in fazed the country singer. I advise anyone who succumbs to seasonal depression to escape to the Bahamas. You are in a different world, and not a soul is interested in the sport of skiing. Not even during the Olympics. Because of the many Canadian tourists, a few ice hockey games were being broadcast live, and of course there were many reports about the bribery scandal surrounding the Russian figure-skating gold medal.

On the day my brother was competing for a medal I discovered that CBC Canada was showing the snowboard competitions live. Curiously, the only event that I really had personal interest in was the only one I was able to see live. I was glad to see Alex make the second-best time during the qualification run. I was truly thrilled that for once, he was able to play the major role in our family. My parents had traveled to Salt Lake City to root for him. On the day of the snowboarding finals, I, too, was biting my nails in front of the television. Unfortunately, Alex was unlucky during the drawing in the main event, was eliminated against the Olympic champion, and ended up in tenth place. I called him at the first opportunity and consoled him. "You just wait another four years. Keep in mind, you're younger than I am." After all, Alex had already won three World Cup races and one world championships bronze medal. I was sure that with his kind of ambition, there was more to come.

At the time of the men's downhill I was lying on the beach, and the results came to me in the form of a short text message on my cell phone, compliments of the "results service" from my homepage. That was it, though, for race results because my cell phone was stolen on the fourth day and my contact with the rest of the world was severed. With the end of the speed events, Andy was allowed to leave Salt Lake, so he took over from Knut and accompanied me on my shark-diving expeditions. It was quite impressive to approach so close to those sea bandits. We checked out an underwater James Bond set, the sunken ship and airplane wrecks that had served as a backdrop in *Thunderball*.

During the second week, we spent most of our time out of the water. I had discovered a love for kayaking. Along the horizon, about two hundred yards out, the surfers were in pursuit of the perfect wave, and I was drawn to them in my kayak. Wouldn't you know it! One of the wave riders addressed me in German and with an Austrian salutation: "*Servus.*

Aren't you Hermann Maier?" As it turned out, he was a relative of Austria's BMW chief, Felix Clary. He was out with two pretty ladies and a friend, and he envied me because I was able to glide along the waves smoothly, while they were being thrown about by the waves. I lent him my kayak for a spin, and then I returned to my paddling.

I DON'T WANT TO DIE IN THE OCEAN!

It turned out to be a dangerous adventure. First, the kayak was thrust against my left shin with such force that blood came squirting out. I could only count myself lucky that it didn't get the right shin. I don't even want to think about what could have happened to my transplant. At any rate, I did not let this deter me and kept paddling through the white spray with a weak feeling in the pit of my stomach: "What if the sharks smell my blood?" On the other hand, salt water is beneficial to healing. The waves got bigger and bigger. Huge waves, six to nine feet high. I had to laugh when I saw Andy being grabbed by a wave and lifted right out of his green kayak. At that moment, I, too, was lifted up and thrown into the water. I bobbed up to the surface. "My kayak!" It was floating off at least sixty feet away. I swam over to it, and just as I was about to grab hold of it, the next wave came along. The kayak was gone for good. I would now have to swim back to shore. Andy was fighting in his kayak, but the riptide was carrying both of us off sideways. I held on to his kayak until a gigantic wave grabbed us both. I let go and watched as my friend was hurled into the wave as though he were being rammed into the side of a hill. A few moments later, I was pulled down into the depths. I struggled back to the surface, and found myself in the open ocean. Everything started spinning around me. I was reminded of motorcycling, when the wake of a big truck yanks you back and forth. And it kept getting worse. As soon as I was at the surface, the next breaker pulled me back down again. I felt like I was inside a washing machine during the spin cycle. Damn it, where's the beach? My only point of reference was a huge luxury cruise liner that was anchored in the harbor about three hundred yards away. I fought like this for about a quarter of an hour. I was starting to be gripped by fear, and I thought, "You should pump your feet so that you can use your hands once your feet are too tired. Don't let yourself become weak in all four extremities!" I thought about Christl Haas, who had drowned in Turkey a short while ago. "What a coincidence, here goes the next skier!" I did not want to believe what was happening: "Now that I've survived the accident, I'm supposed to drown in the ocean?" I had had many adventures in the water, had plunged off sixty-foot cliffs without being harmed. But all that was nothing compared to what I was going through now. Drowning? No, I did not even want to think about it. I am a good swimmer, and I was wearing a life jacket. Without that it would have been over for sure. We had completely underestimated the situation. Suddenly, Andy showed up again in the midst of the watery tempest. He had lost his kayak, but had gotten hold of mine. I clung to the kayak and yelled, "We've got to get in. It's a matter of life or death!" Somehow, we escaped the chaos of the waves, paddled to the beach, and dropped onto the sand, exhausted. Now we could see that we had drifted a good five hundred yards. Our struggle had lasted more than two hours. The boat rental place was already closed. Not a soul would have noticed if we had drowned out there. Then, we saw the remnants of the green kayak. It had been smashed to bits against a rock jetty!

February 23, 2002. Back in Austria. I was again in the grip of reality. I had not yet been home for twenty-four hours and was still fighting jet lag and sleep deprivation. I was yearning for rest. But that was not to be. It was my privilege to spend a day with the lucky winners of a game show. "A day with Hermann Maier," it said on my schedule. Such events were not always a piece of cake in my current physical and mental state. Arriving in the town of Haus in the Enns valley, we were welcomed by a brass band. How happy I had been only a few hours ago. I should never have come back. We rode up in the gondola to the Hauser Kaibling ski area.

There, we made our way among tipsy ski tourists tanning themselves in the sun. When they saw me in the snow without my skis on, some of them offered some sarcastic remarks. I had to give many autographs with personal comments and pose for pictures. I kept saying to myself, "You've just got to get through this, and this, too, shall pass."

But one television interview really was the last straw during my "successful" return from paradise. The reporter knew just what to ask me in order to hit me with a sledgehammer. I had gone off as far away as possible in order not to have anything to do with the Olympics, but the reporter kept harping on that very topic. I told him that I had not registered anything from the Games and hoped to be left alone on that sensitive topic. But the man kept stomping around my weary nerves and continued to dig and dig. When he asked me, "What did you think about the super-G?" I answered, "Who won that one?" The reporter was so perplexed that he looked at his assistant for help until he remembered: "Aamodt." The interview was being aired during prime time, right between the first and second slalom rounds, and all of Austria seemed to be talking about it. The refrain was, "Doesn't Hermann Maier rejoice with his colleagues over their medals?" Once again, I had to clarify things on my homepage: "I am proud of our sixteen medals," I let it be known, and, "I congratulate Eberharter Steff for bringing the entire set of medals back to Austria!" Thus, peace had returned to the homeland, and I was allowed to be myself again, at least for a few days.

FLASHBACK

WHEN THE HANDCUFFS WENT "CLICK"

Aspen, Colorado: That sounds fashionable and exciting. Unfortunately, the truth looks a bit more sobering. The existence of a professional ski racer has a lot to do with routine. Even though I don't have regular office hours, I can still tell you exactly where I will be during what week. Would you like to know, for in-stance, what I am planning to do during the middle of July in 2006? If no red Mercedes or similar mishap interferes, I will be approaching Zermatt on Saturday, July 15, in the passenger seat of my coach's car for the purpose of high-altitude training on the famous glacier.

Every year, about ten days after the start of the World Cup in Sölden, we travel to Colorado at the beginning of November. That's where we make all the preparations for the races in North America. Because most slopes aren't fully prepped at that point, we start with our training at Beaver Creek, above ten thousand feet. In 1998, one year after my phenomenal climb in the world of ski racing, we ended up in Breckenridge once again. Breckenridge is one of those fake western resorts that doesn't offer much besides miles and miles of slopes en-hanced with artificial snow and bone-dry air. Oh, yes, they do have their own microbrewery. One day is more monotonous than the next. In the morning it's skiing, then lunch, then the mandatory rest period, then nothing for a long time, and then a jaunt on your stationary bicycle. Because of the risk of overex-ertion at the high altitude, Heini prescribed only a few perfunctory minutes on the home trainer. That sort of regimen didn't nearly exhaust my physical re-sources, however.

What else is there left to do? Luckily, at the time I shared a room with Andi Schifferer, a like-minded companion who came up with exactly the same sort of nonsense that was going around in my own head. We hardly missed a prank, and we completely agreed in regard to the proper use of our free time. We frequently ambled over to the Breckenridge Brewery & Pub and had one or two pitchers, the type of thin beer that is brought to you by the quart, *after* you've shown them your driver's license, mind you. Those excursions to the pub were our only diver-sion, and our teammates noticed them with chagrin. "The two of them are going out quite a bit," they mumbled, and waited to see whether our downtime diver-sion would have a negative effect on our performance on the slopes. At the time I felt so strong and confident that I didn't even begin to worry. However, the con-stant ski workouts started getting on my nerves to such a degree that after a few days I really started yearning for the first race, the giant slalom in Park City, Utah. The more we trained, the more I decreased my radii, the more I used my edges. Little did I know that this technique was exactly the wrong one to use on the American artificial snow. I judged the conditions more and more aggressively, and developed into a total power racer. In the meantime, I lost more and more of that sixth sense, that delicate balance between truly knowing the slope and still having a feel for the race. Even though I still continued to dish up record training times, I had lost the magic edge that is required of the true champion.

Then it was time for the long drive from Colorado to Park City, a drive that I still remembered fondly from the year before. This time, however, everything was difficult. You see, during the year of my sensational Olympic season (1997/1998), I was so much in demand that all lights were focused on me. We had to drive a BMW, my sponsors' logos had to be displayed prominently, I couldn't go without my signature hat, and I had constant requests from reporters. "Hermann, show us the title page of that newspaper." "Can you juggle three snowballs?" "Put on that cowboy hat!" "Let's see what you can do with that cattle rope." I constantly had to pose for the camera, even while I was eating. The press had their camcorders running while I was loading the trunk of my car, and I had the feeling that they would have followed us the whole six-hour drive through the Rockies, filming from the next lane, if they had had their way. Everything was on my nerves big-time.

In Park City I completely withdrew, but in the end I was able to muster the right attitude for the race. Finally, I was hungry again to perform to my utmost limit. I had won the initial race in Sölden 1.6 seconds ahead of Stephan Eberharter, and I hadn't even gone to my limit then. Now I wanted to come in at least two seconds ahead of my competitors. I liked the course. It was the same slope where I had won my first World Cup giant slalom a year before. Besides, I went to the starting line with a healthy portion of anger in my gut. For the first time ever, my name was mentioned in conjunction with doping rumors. "Hermann Maier or Hormone Maier?" blared the headlines of the Swiss tabloid *Blick*. Needless to say, it was a story devoid of any facts or foundation. Such outrageous insolence! Especially since even back then I was probably the most tested ski racer in the world.

During the first round, in which the start was set somewhat back down the hill (to my chagrin), I was able to get in a test run and still had a comfortable lead of

0.35 second over Eberharter. During the second round, I wanted to make a really big showing. It went like clockwork; even at the first split time, where the slope runs from the shallow to the steep portion, I was able to increase my lead. Then I went into a curve in top form and thought, "Now I'll really show them!" Exactly then I touched the deep snow with my boot at the steepest part and slipped into the next gate. That was my first slipup in 677 days. Is it any wonder that I was incredibly disappointed over my own stupid mistake? I should have won that race in any case. Our own video measurements showed that I was 1.1 seconds in the lead at the time of my slip.

Thoroughly disappointed, I slid down on the side of the slope and disappeared through the barricade in the direction of the hotel taxi. What on earth would I have done down at the finish line? I hadn't been chosen for a doping test, only the top three contestants had to show up at the press conference, and the victory ceremony was a nonissue. I rode back to the hotel and threw myself on my bed. I was completely indifferent to how the race ended up. A little later, Schiffi showed up in our room. He was moping over his fifteenth place. We stuffed our equipment into our bags, checked out of the hotel, and went to Adolph's, where to my delight they had Stiegl beer from Salzburg. I ordered a bottle right away, to the tune of six bucks. I just didn't care that day. So the two of us sat there, like real heroes, and pretty soon we were having a jolly old time. Actually, I should have been attending an autograph session I had been "sentenced" to earlier, but I just wasn't up to it. That's when the Atomic chief of competition, Toni Schutti, showed up and convinced me to go anyway. Once there, I ran into Stephan Eberharter and congratulated him on his victory. Only later did the press try to make a huge story out of the fact that I hadn't extended my best wishes to him right at the finish line. To this day I do not understand the big deal they made over this incident. At any rate, I'm sure we had more fun at Adolph's than the others had at the victory platform. Then we were on our way back to Colorado. In Aspen, we had a super-G on the program. The superexclusive ski locale conjured up visions of high-society gatherings and was reputed to be a secret party mecca. And that is exactly how I would come to remember the town.

Once again, a dumb mistake cost me the victory, and that in my favorite race, the super-G. But I tried to force myself to victory, skied one of the worst races of my life, and came in second. Afterward, I wanted to put Aspen's famous nightlife to the test. I felt that I had earned it after three weeks of overseas monotony, and besides, we had a day off before our flight up to Canada.

For me this meant specifically two days to completely shut down. Here, too, Schiffi was my faithful companion. Maier and Schifferer, the famous duo, now made their entrance at the Caribou Club, a hipster bar for wannabe actors, movie starlets, models, and pseudo-VIPs, for a warm-up session. We couldn't get in, so we went on to the next joint. There, we ran into two Viennese newspaper correspondents who have been writing about ski racing longer than I have years to my name: Wolfgang Winheim, from the *Kurier*, and Charly Pointer, from the *Kronen Zeitung*. As usual, they unearthed memories from the "good old times" when Klammer, Stock, and Schranz were the names to conjure with. "Compared to those guys, you two are as upright as altar boys," teased Winheim. I took his putdown more as a dare. We continued our tour of Aspen in the hopes of finding a place where there was really some action. But the true crème de la crème of Aspen, residents such as Don Johnson, Martina Navratilova, and former president Gerald Ford, and the extremely wealthy folks who live there prefer to hold private parties, which are in great demand starting around one o'clock, when most of the bars close. We finally ended up at exactly such a private bash. A wealthy ski fan took us—Schiffi, Kjus serviceman Hans-Peter Habersatter, and me—up to the mountains into one of those five-million-dollar chalets. The owner of the house immediately made friends with the merry Austrians. As we related our exciting exploits and regaled our hosts with back-to-back Ostbahn-Kurti songs, the night passed away in a flash. I somehow didn't even notice that most of the guests had long since left. It was high time to call a taxi. We still had to get back to the hotel, pack our stuff, and get down to Denver to the airport, a good 180 miles of challenging driving. I turned to the butler and said in my best English, "Please, man, call us a taxi." We waited and waited, but no taxi came. Time was getting really tight for us. The situation called for someone to take the initiative. I turned to Schiffi. "If no taxi shows up, we'll just have to try to take a car instead." Wouldn't you know it. I found an old, decrepit rust bucket that in true American fashion had the key stuck in the ignition. We got in and took off, though with some hesitation. We *had* to get back to the hotel, after all. I didn't feel totally comfortable with our course of action, though. I thought, "Who knows, maybe this dude is going to look for his car tomorrow. The next thing I know, they'll call it theft." I didn't want to take the risk, especially in the United States, so we returned the car. Thus we had only one option left: a long, long hike.

It was freezing cold when we started walking. Slowly, it began to grow light. Out of the gloom arose the hulk of a forklift at a construction site. Since I have a background in construction, I've always felt a magical sort of attraction to forklifts. Then I discovered a whole lot of other construction vehicles. There was no holding me back now. I climbed into the forklift and looked for the key. I figured that in America they use the same hiding spots as back home, either behind the visor or underneath the floor mat. Before we knew it, the key had turned over in the ignition and we heard the engine sound—*roooaar*. It was music to our ears. Schiffi climbed up onto the fork, and I lifted him up and down. That's when I discovered my favorite toy, the dream of every child: a heavy-duty Caterpillar without a roof with the leather seat out in the open and operational levers on both sides, the convertible among construction vehicles, so to speak. I recalled instantly how as a little boy in Reitdorf, I would sneak up onto the property of the adjacent earthmoving company. There they were, the yellow objects of my desire, the ones I would have loved to operate just once. Finally, life had presented me with such a chance. I knew right away that I could start the thing without a key. It didn't take long: *brrrrrrrrrrrrrrrrm, brrrrrrrrrrm, brrrrrrrrrm!* roared the engine. We were enveloped in a dark cloud of diesel exhaust, and the Caterpillar was in motion. I let Schiffi have a hand at the controls and went back to my forklift, and both of us stepped on the gas with gusto. It would have been just the thing for us to ride into Aspen like that. But all over town there were posters for the super-G race with my picture on them. So much for the Herminator. I concluded that this feat would be too much for me after all. Just a bit later, another boyhood dream was about to come true: We would be allowed to ride in a real sheriff's patrol car *with* the lights on.

For now, we had to make do with a two-wheeled vehicle. We discovered an old Steyr military bicycle on the wall of a house, where it had been hung as a decoration. I remember thinking, "Such a shame about that old bicycle! Doesn't do much good in its current function, but it would sure help us out a whole lot right now." It didn't take long for the bike to come off the wall, and off we went, Schiffi up front on the handlebars; Hans-Peter, who was still with us, on the bike rack in the back; and me, presumably the only one in a condition to drive, pumping the pedals. Remarkably, that old Steyr bike could easily handle its load of about six hundred pounds. Even without air in the tires. Thus we rattled down the street, accompanied by the muffled staccato of the air valve, which was hitting the compressed snow at rhythmic intervals. Then, the back tire came off. I tried to compensate by backpedaling and weight redistribution, but because of the jerky motion the passenger behind me was bucked off. It was really good going now, and we were out of time at any rate. "Just keep on going," said Schiffi, who was still precariously balanced on the handlebar. That was Habersatter's good luck, because we had barely made it into town when we encountered a police car. "I sure hope they aren't looking for us!" I thought. Just then, the lights and siren came on. Blast it! Someone must have called the police because of the construction vehicle noise.

Suddenly, we had feature roles in a chase scene worthy of a Hollywood production. I threw the bike aside, and Schiffi yelled, "Run, run!" With the police car in front of us, Schiffi turned right into a vacant lot. I was planning to go off to the left, but I slipped, and was now lying in the street directly in front of the cops. Like a heavy-duty criminal I had to get up and put my hands on the roof of the car. I was frisked for weapons and I felt like I had just robbed a bank. Now the fun was over for sure. I tried to placate the officer: "What's the big deal? We didn't do anything; we were just riding a bicycle." He countered in true American style: "You are criminals!" I had to put my hands behind my back, and I thought, "Oh no, now you've really done it." I thought of a trick that I knew from the movies: If you make a fist with both hands, your wrists will have more free space once you're cuffed. "Click," went the handcuffs. Then I climbed into the sheriff's Jeep, and we went on our way. "Where is your friend?" the cop wanted to know. "No idea. How am I supposed to know that?" It didn't take long for the message to come in over the radio: "We got him!" Now they also had my buddy. He had tried in vain to outwit them. When the patrol car that had been called in for reinforcement turned up next to him, he stopped inconspicuously to tie his shoelaces, as though he had nothing to do with all this. The trick didn't work, though, and we came up on them just as Schiffi was being interrogated in the street. My policeman got out of his car to speak to his colleague. Even though I had handcuffs on, I somehow managed to twist around in such a way that I could open the door and climb out. It seems they had never seen anything like this. I stood up behind the policeman and asked, "What are you making such a big fuss over?" That's when the officers lost it completely. I was pushed back into the car and driven off. During the ensuing drive they seem to have recognized me, since they became increasingly relaxed and quite friendly.

On our way to the Pitkin County jail we passed the hotel where the Austrians were staying. A very embarrassing situation. Our teammates were waiting to check out in the lobby, while we were in the patrol car in handcuffs. The policemen told the trainers at the check-in to follow us to the police station.

At the station, I had a real change of heart. "That's really the end," I thought. "Now they'll throw me in prison." I tried to explain to the officials why we were here and that it had been our last evening in Colorado. In a few hours we would have been gone anyway. Finally, our coach, Toni Giger, and our PR spokesman, Manfred Kimmel, showed up. The PR man just laughed, while Giger sported a serious countenance and scolded, "What have you two done now?" Finally, we issued an official apology and returned the bicycle to its rightful owner, whom I enlightened with, "Did you know that this bicycle was made in Austria?" The whole family was amazed when the young man whose face was smiling from all the posters around Aspen suddenly showed up at their door with a "borrowed" bicycle. Giger donated a superior bottle of red wine from his private collection, and off we went. On the way back to the hotel we had to endure a serious lecture. The mood was very tense indeed. Luckily, we were able to get out of Aspen after all. I will remember it as a most unhappy place. The town is good only for partying.

We were hoping that the whole affair would soon be forgotten, but the opposite was the case: The sheriff's office had released a press statement, and I was able to read a report about my arrest in the *Denver Post*. As luck would have it, it was the reporters from Austria (who flew to Canada a day later) who had brought the paper with them for our perusal. Needless to say, we were the main topic of conversation in Austria. Even my mother was interviewed about the incident. But she took the whole thing with humor and seemed to empathize with my youthful antics. Soon, we were all able to laugh about the incident wholeheartedly. But as we would discover, that was not to be the end of the story.

Two months later, I flew back to Colorado with great expectations. I was about to embark on my first skiing world championships. No one would be winning the super-difficult "Birds of Prey" downhill course just by chance. This much I knew after my super-G victory and my second place in the downhill during the "dress rehearsal" of 1997. If there was such a thing as justice, then I would glean the downhill gold medal that I had exchanged in Nagano for the most famous crash in skiing history. Even though I could hardly wait to finally let loose, my joy in anticipation of the race came to an abrupt halt. After we landed in Denver, I drove the 130 miles up into the ski country along with my teammates. Beaver Creek is the exclusive resort close to Vail. Before we checked into the hotel, we stopped by the grocery store to do some shopping. That's where I happened to glance at the newspaper stand displaying the *Vail Daily Trail*. I was used to seeing my mug on the cover of this paper by now, but the accompanying headline made me slightly uneasy: "Maier May Be Marked Man in Vail." That didn't sound so good. I carefully read the article and was amazed at what was written there. It was the story of our visit at the party back in November, with a few details quite distorted. The owner of a snowboard shop claimed that I had ruined the transmission of his car, a 1986 Honda Acura, and had subsequently taken flight. I couldn't believe it. I'm sure I didn't sit in that old bucket for more than two minutes, and I am certain that I didn't break anything. Okay, maybe we did a few little doughnuts on the ice, and stepped on the gas just a wee bit. But surely it wasn't as bad as had been portrayed. If I could trust the newspaper story, I was in danger of being arrested immediately for automobile theft, facing a fine of up to $500,000 or even a jail sentence of two to six years. I reflected quickly on my situation. What to do next? Fly back home immediately? On the other hand, I didn't have any problems passing customs on my arrival in the United States, and that is where you usually get hung up if there are any warrants out for you. So it couldn't be so bad after all. When I got to the Hyatt Regency Hotel, I saw the Austrian journalists in a huddle, whispering among themselves. I couldn't hear what they were saying, but somehow I was certain that I was the principal topic of conversation. I crept up to my room along a back passage. Barely five minutes later, the phone was ringing. It was Schiffi, who was still back in Austria. "What's up over there, Hermann? They haven't locked you up yet, have they? Should I even bother flying over there?" I calmed him down. "Everything is under control so far. I'll figure out what's going on, and tell you whether you should come." It was time to find out exactly what was going on. My support personnel had gathered all the facts, and I could hardly believe it. It was on account of this thirteen-year-old pile of junk that the owner was making such a big noise? Several dubious witnesses were now claiming that we had ruined the transmission during wild car chases across the ice. How could I now prove the opposite? It was my word against his. I wanted to move beyond this story, so I met with the man who was trying to bleed me at a lonely airport in the mountains. It was just like in the movies. I pulled out a wad of banknotes and personally took care of the matter. With the money he got, he probably was able to buy a Honda Acura a decade younger than his original model.

My legal troubles seem to have set the tone for the rest of the World Cup preparations, which were fraught with interruptions. The season that had begun so promisingly with the record head start in Sölden was accompanied by bad luck and numerous glitches. The poor event planning of the International Skiing Federation (FIS) did the rest to make this season a challenge. They had scheduled the famous Hahnenkamm weekend in Kitzbühel exactly one week before the World Cup opening in Vail. You have to put yourself into the shoes of a ski-racing competitor: downhill training from Tuesday to Thursday, sprint downhill on Friday, classic Hahnenkamm race on Saturday, slalom on Sunday. Overseas flight and all the jetlag that comes with the eight-hour time difference.

May 1973. I'm only six months old and curious about what this world has to offer.

I could already walk at ten months old. In the snow, the mini-Herminator was truly in his element.

Hiking in the countryside around Salzburg, Austria. Alex, my little brother, points the way: straight to the top!

■ March 25, 1995. My first appearance at the Austrian championships in Spittal/Semmering. My racing suit was a gift from the former Olympic champion Anita Wachter (I patched the holes in the knees with stickers). The orange boots I bought at a sporting-goods shop. With a starting number of 130, I end up in eighteenth place. Next to me is Alex Reiner, president of Salzburg's ski federation, who is taking notice of me for the first time.

■ Fall 1996. I'm taking part in a bricklaying contest, and I have no chance against the reigning world champion.

A series of photos of my downhill start at the 2000 World Cup final in Bormio, Italy, the steepest start of all the downhill races. You can see the determination on my face. Now go for it! That was the old Maier, before the accident. The new Maier does not attack quite so aggressively.

Aare, Switzerland, 2001. My most emotional World Cup final. I catch my eternal rival Michael von Grünigen with a convincing win in the grand slalom.

(next page) February 13, 1998. The crash of the century, captured on film, flew onto the pages of sports journals around the world.

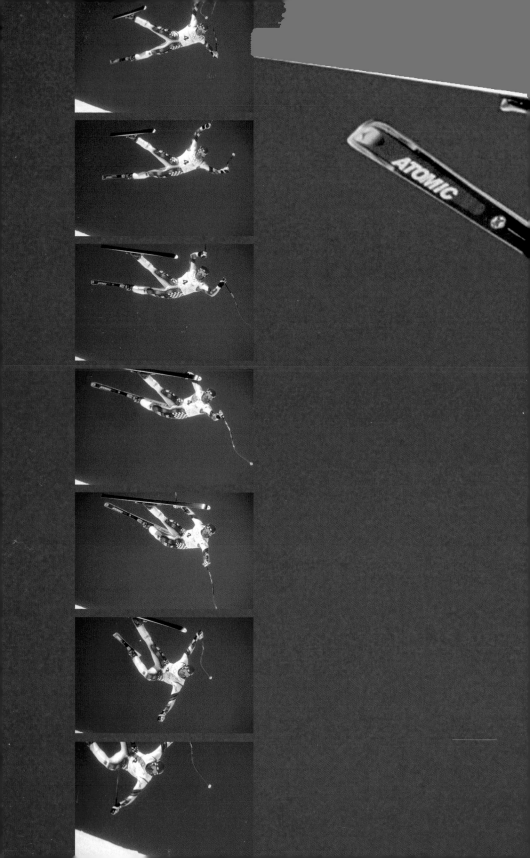

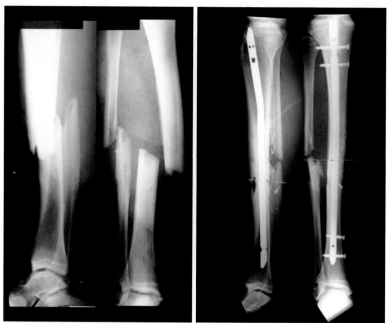

■ August 24, 2001. Before and after: the X-ray shows where my broken tibia was fixed with a fifteen-inch titanium rod fastened with four bolts. My surgeon, Artur Trost, decided to let the fibula mend on its own.

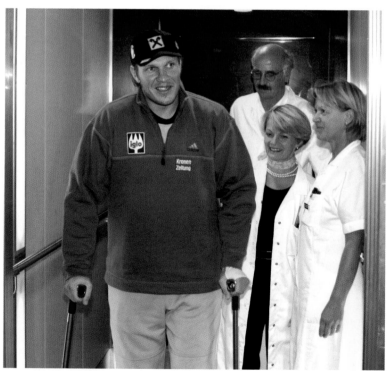

■ September 14, 2001. Released from the hospital, I walk out on crutches, accompanied by my surgeon, the head nurse, and the hospital's physical therapist.

During my recovery, I begin biking on oxygen. It takes time for my body to adjust to the high altitude in Obertauern.

Today I am able to smirk about Atomic's X-ray advertisement, but during rehab I was astonished to see the ad.

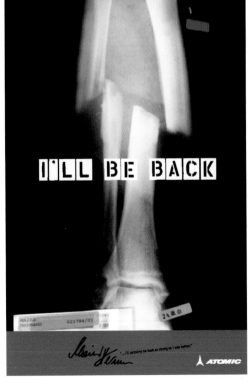

I'LL BE BACK

(next page) Skier in trouble at the downhill in Sestriere, Italy (2003). I feel like I'm skiing on two Coke bottles.

■ July 5, 2003, 3:47 P.M. I'm the first nonprofessional cyclist to enter the prologue of the Tour de France! I'm glad the fragile time trial bike can hold my 200 pounds. I even have a personal service car with "Hermann Maier— Austria" signage.

■ January 8, 2003.
Training on the Reiteralm,
near Schladming, Austria.
Only a few people realize
that my comeback is
days away.

■ 2003 World
Championships,
St. Moritz, Switzerland.
I gave away gold, but at
least I took silver. The
longer I think about it,
the more brightly that
medal seems to shine.

■ November 27, 2004, Lake Louise, Canada. Joking around with Bode Miller.

■ I face the camera for hours during an advertising campaign for Carrera in 2004.

■ With ice-skating queen Katerina Witt.

■ March 11, 2004, Sestriere, Italy. Crystal globes number 13 and 14. That's how it's done! In the super-G, I take revenge for the previous year's downhill disaster.

■ Good skis! This time I can't complain about my equipment.

2005 World Championships in Bormio, Italy

This page

■ *(top left)* The downhill at Bormio is on one of my favorite slopes, but in 2005 it was not meant to be. ■ *(top right)* Total concentration. My grand slalom gold-run. ■ *(bottom)* The speed disciplines were bumpy.

Opposite page

■ *(top)* On my way to gold. ■ *(bottom left)* Arriving in the finish area. ■ *(middle right)* Grand slalom world champion 2005. I can't believe this dream came true! ■ *(bottom)* Victory ceremony. Few can imagine how much this gold medal means to me.

■ Nagano Olympic gold medal ceremony, 1998. I've long dreamed of returning to Olympic competition, and the 2006 Olympic Games in Torino, Italy, will make my comeback complete.

World Cup opening ceremonies on Saturday. World Cup super-G on one of the world's most dangerous runs on Tuesday. Really unbelievable, what they expect from a professional skier. I should have just left out the two races in Kitzbühel and taken my time traveling to the States as I had done the year before. But somehow, I didn't dare do that this time.

So, I planned a softened-down "safety version" of the race that was doomed to failure from the beginning. Maier is either 100 percent or not at all. Sure enough, I crashed during the second heat of the downhill sprint and had to get out of the race. During my first "real" Hahnenkamm race I had to acknowledge, as our head coach at the time, Werner Margreiter, put it, that "even Maier has to submit to Newton's laws," and content myself with eighth place. By the time I skied the combination slalom I was so cranky that my elimination was almost preordained.

I had exactly one day left in Obertauern before my departure for the United States to recharge physically and mentally with Heini's help. I finally took off with mixed feelings and went from bad to worse, finding myself distracted with the whole Aspen incident. After the unfortunate "car theft" story was finally over, I was able to concentrate on the reason for my trip: "Operation World Cup Gold" had absolute priority this season. Then luck was on my side. Before the super-G, I was totally tense, but I still won gold, together with Lasse Kjus. That was symptomatic of our head-to-head season. After that, the big pressure was gone and I delivered one of the best downhill races of my life. My technique? I didn't show my style during practice, and gave it my all during the race. I raced to my very limits; there wasn't much left to give. I was as aggressive and sharp as my red racing skis. I practically devoured the gates and tore down one marker after the other. Indeed, this was one of my attack-happy races. I skied with the knife between my teeth. Now I could enjoy ski racing once again. That was truly a success to be savored.

Although the giant slalom was still on the program for that week, I felt I had earned a few beers after this accomplishment. Still, I was responsible enough to leave the big celebration at the Austria House before midnight and get a ride back to the hotel. There, Arnie's friend Franz Weber, a former speed-skiing world champion, was waiting for me and said, "Arnold would like it if you came up to his suite for a glass of wine." It was an invitation that I could hardly turn down. I had visited Arnold in 1998 at his estate in Santa Monica before our joint appearance on Jay Leno's *Tonight Show*. Arnold's mother, Aurelia, who was still alive at the time, had made Wiener schnitzel and apple strudel, and we had a lot of fun. It would turn out to be even more fun at the Hyatt in Vail. At the suite, Franz Klammer and head coach Werner Margreiter were waiting. I was in a euphoric mood after the two World Cup victories, so I dared Arnie to a match of arm-wrestling. "Wow! Your arms are bigger than my thighs," I marveled as Arnie propped his elbow on the table. While I gathered all my strength and tried to push the Terminator's hand toward the table surface, Arnie kept chatting along. He was really starting to get to me! "Pay attention!" I demanded, but he just left his arm right there.

I have no idea how long the party lasted. But of one thing I am sure: Arnie left first. As he retreated to his bedroom, he wished me luck for the giant slalom. "You show those boys!" Unfortunately, I was out of power by then. I was eliminated during the second heat and thus gave away one more medal. But with two gold medals, I really couldn't complain. On the airplane home I summed up my exploits contentedly: I had reached my goal for the season, had purchased a rusty 1986 Acura, and had eliminated any fear of being put on a watch list.

Chapter | 8

AM I ALL
WASHED UP?

During this time, my relationship with Gudrun came to an end. Officially, we were still a couple, but unfortunately, there were more and more disagreements. Small, insignificant things, which in sum became a big burden for both of us.

Perhaps there was simply too much going on. My accident, the pain, the worries concerning my future in the world of sports, the involved rehabilitation on top of my training, which in itself was very taxing. Gudrun had graduated from law school and for the first time was completely steeped in her work as a jurist. I, on the other hand, felt hemmed in. I realized this fully only after my return from the Caribbean. Before the accident, I had my competitions, training camps, travels from one exciting staging ground to the next. That was my world, my job. I felt like this freedom had been taken from me and suddenly everything around me had become too narrow.

I was going through a severe depression, something that was attested to me even in writing. During an electromyography exam in Salzburg's Christian Doppler clinic, the speed of nerve-impulse conduction in my legs was being measured. The neurologists found that I had a deficit in my ability to lift up my leg, as well as sensation impairment in the regions of my right outer calf and my left inner thigh. I also was given a psychological evaluation, which put it in black and white: *During conversation, a certain lack of motivation and increased tendency to worry can be detected, whereby the patient's spontaneity also seems somewhat impaired.*

I did not know where I stood. Can I continue to ski? Will I ever be able to ski properly again? What will the future bring? Should I continue to invest all my energy in sports, or should I start something new right away? All those thoughts were playing into my relationship with Gudrun. Of course, I was not an easy person to be around at the time. I was always moping about, grumpy, unhappy, and unable to let off steam. The world of sports had been my escape valve.

Because I didn't know for months at a time how things would progress, certain crises were almost programmed. Somehow, it all became too much for me. I started to second-guess my relationship: "Aren't the problems in connection with my job enough for the time being?" I tried to analyze my psychological state: "If on top of everything else there are constant crises between me and my girlfriend, I won't be able to get any peace at all. I won't have a clear head for anything." I had a choice: either abandon my career, or again concentrate 100 percent on my comeback. Thus, my decision was made: "I'm going to end the affair and see to it that I achieve something in sports." Even though I let our relationship hobble along on a lukewarm autopilot for a while, the trajectory was clear to me: "I am going to call an end to this affair."

March 10, 2002. I was still struggling with the pain stemming from my injuries when the World Cup circus pitched its tent at my door in Flachau. In addition to the physical pain, there was the mental agony, because in truth I would have loved to compete on my home turf. Some of my fans seemed to be able to sense my pain, since they had fashioned a thick bandage around the leg of the Hermann Maier statue in the parking lot at the base of the Achterjet gondola. According to the script, I was supposed to make a grand entrance along with a snow princess at the victory ceremony and bear the big crystal trophy for the overall World Cup victory. It was obvious to me that I had to play along. Anyhow, the whole thing wasn't that uncomfortable. After all, this was my hometown and I was glad to see several familiar faces for the first time after a long hiatus. I was yearning to show my face in public once again. I did not want to give the impression that I did not rejoice in anyone else's success. I also did not have to justify anything, since I wasn't able to participate actively in the race. Even before the start of the race, I was limping from one press engagement to the next. That was just fine. I had to play my part, since I was the poster boy of our ski federation. Moreover, there was a PR event in my own interest: I was launching the "Herminator Power Bar." And I had even missed the journalists, who normally just get on my nerves.

And so I showed up at the giant slalom, the last race of the season. I climbed up onto the podium for the TV interviews and watched as the skiers came down the World Cup slope. It was an odd feeling. I felt like an outsider, one of the spectators, and suddenly I saw everything from a new perspective. I just thought, "In a few months' time, I'm supposed to go back to the starting line. I am curious to see what that will be like." A thousand thoughts were whirling around in my head. How fast will I ski? What path will I choose? Where will I be standing? Am I still in a condition to deliver a strong performance such as during my last World Cup race, the 2001 finals in Aare? Back then, I had skied all of them into the ground during the giant slalom, pried the "small" crystal trophy for the giant slalom away from my Swiss rival Michael von Grünigen at the last second, and won with a lead of 1.14 seconds. When I realized how close all the times were in Flachau, I thought, "Incredible, they are all skiing well, and so close to each other. How on earth did I manage to win all those races with such a big lead back then?" For me it was the most normal thing in the world to be well out in front during such a race. But here, everyone was fighting for a margin of a few hundredths of a second.

I cared little about the results during the finals. I was thinking seriously about my future. I knew that the season was over, and with it my time of rest. From now on, it would be all business for me. That was exactly the impetus I needed. "Now it's time to get going, to gain some momentum. I don't want to miss the boat!"

With my thoughts already at the World Cup preseason, I jumped up onto the big podium at the finish line and congratulated Stephan Eberharter for his overall World Cup victory. I was not allowed to hand over the trophy in person to my successor, because the petty FIS protocol did not permit such a gesture. Steff probably couldn't have cared less. I would like to say in this regard that my hat is off to him for his accomplishment. It was not easy to take over my scepter so seamlessly. After all, the Austrian nation, already spoiled with skiing success, had exerted enormous pressure on my team colleague with their high expectations.

The race "Eberharter versus Maier," which had been styled a "duel of the giants" by the media, affected me only tangentially. My fiercest duel was with the Swiss skier Michael von Grünigen, even though this competition took place only in the giant slalom. Thus, the domestic media had to artificially inflate the supposed struggle of the giants Maier and Eberharter. That struggle was rather one-sided, if we take a look at the cold numbers. Eberharter had achieved six World Cup victories and two world championships titles during his ten World Cup seasons thus far (granted, he did not fully participate in all those seasons). Compared to that, during my four and a half seasons, I had managed forty-one World Cup victories (actually forty-two if you count the 1997 disqualification in Val d'Isère due to the "red-line affair"), two Olympic gold medals, and two world championships titles. In terms of crystal trophies, the outcome was twelve to nothing in my favor. During his first season without me, Eberharter made ten appearances in the World Cup and won Olympic gold in the giant slalom. In my second injury season, 2002/2003, during which I was able to compete in only five World Cup races (and won the super-G in Kitzbühel), Eberharter scored nine victories. This means that Eberharter celebrated nineteen victories over the two years during which I was injured. During my comeback season, 2003/2004, when I celebrated my fourth overall World Cup victory with five separate successes, Eberharter won four races. You can refer to the statistical details in the supplement "My Personal Racing Diary" (beginning on page 271).

March 11, 2002. Relieved that the World Cup train had departed from my hometown and the spectacle was finally over, I checked into Salzburg's Pierer Sanatorium. There, the remaining three lateral bolts that had affixed the foot-long titanium rod to my right lower leg were removed. We chose this specialized clinic because only there were we able to have my leg treated with painful shock wave therapy. This type of treatment had to be conducted under full anesthesia, and was used to speed up the mending of the fracture, which still was not complete. Even before the surgery it was obvious that the titanium rod would remain inside my leg for at least one more season. Artur assured me without reservation that a comeback was possible even with the stabilization rod in place. When I awoke from the anesthesia, Artur was standing at my bedside. "Everything is okay," he said. "When full force is exerted on the site of the fracture, your leg will be able to sustain the pressure within a few weeks." I had to smile. I replied, "When I no longer have so much metal in my body, I will once again dare go outside during a lightning storm." I took the three bolts home as trophies.

March 18, 2002. For two full months I had largely done whatever I pleased. If I felt like it, I took out my cross-country skis and stepped onto the slope right below my house. Or I took off on my mountain bike. I just wanted to stay halfway fit. Without a timetable that dictated the course of my day, without lactate checks, without painful physical therapy, without sweat-inducing strength training, and, most of all, without the stultifying hours on the ergometer. While the time-out was good for my state of mind, my body missed the targeted training goals. The checkup following the shock wave therapy showed that the mending of my bone fracture had reached a plateau and stopped. No one wanted to talk me into anything at that point, but for me that was a wakeup call. I was eager to start a disciplined workout regimen once again.

As usual, once I have gotten something into my head, I formulate a plan, and this was a plan that I did not share with anyone. While my competitors were recovering from the racing season and taking it easy, I wanted to get going with some serious hard work. Only thus could I make up for the gap that had been opened on account of my accident.

This was my plan: Use the last snow in Obertauern to get back into the swing of things, then glacier training in Zermatt in the middle of

July. During the month of August, I wanted to make a big effort once again in Chile so that I could surprise everyone with my comeback during the World Cup preseason in Sölden. In order to pull this off, I would have to engage in some tough basic training. The time to start was *now*.

Because of the light endurance training during my time-out, I had kept my body in shape. Therefore, the most important task at this point was to undo the physical deficits that had arisen since my injury. I still had problems with my equilibrium. I had a hard time keeping myself balanced on my right leg, something I tried in the shower every day. On top of that there was the constant pain, that horrific bone-on-bone feeling. So I checked in with Heini shortly after my release from the Pierer clinic and started in on my strength training a few days later. As usual, Heini threw himself into this assignment and came up with a workout program together with me. It is this kind of dedication that I so appreciate in my trainer. As a former athlete himself, he knows exactly what is going on inside of me. Because he realized that I needed some distance, he had left me alone for weeks at a time. Then, when I got serious, he fully dedicated himself to the task and was once again there for me around the clock.

I showed up at the Olympic Training Center for strength training only every couple of days. The rest of the time I worked out by myself, mostly on the cross-country course. That seemed like an ideal workout for me at the time. It provided me with the necessary contact with the snow, let me focus on skiing, helped me with my sense of balance, and simultaneously was a valuable endurance builder. I knew that the lifts in Obertauern would be open until Ascension Day, May 9, so I could still dawdle for a while until I got my real equipment out of the ski shed.

May 2, 2002. Andy seems to have been waiting for my call. "Let's roll!" When it's a matter of skiing, the two of us don't need many words. We drove up to Obertauern in the morning and sat in the first gondola, which took us up to the Zehnerkar. The slope was deserted and frozen in several spots. I put on my skis and pushed off. I dug the edges of the skis into the snow and waited to see what would happen. I could do it!

Granted, the pain was still there, but it was being held in check. The most important part was that in contrast to the unhappy attempts from last winter, my feeling for the snow had returned. I carved across the frozen patches. Yes indeed, skiing was starting to be fun again. That was one of those key days that I circled in red on my calendar. "Just you wait! This could work out once again," I thought. I still had a sense of numbness in my right foot, but my left thigh seemed to be working again. The complete lapses of function had disappeared, and I could once again bend my knees and exert pressure, at least to a degree.

Of course, there was still fear. What if my right ski gets caught? What if my lower leg is twisted? One dumb crossover move and it'll be broken again. Considering the kind of condition I was in, I once again went to the very limit of my capabilities. My confidence rose with each turn. "Yes, I think it's doable." Andy gave me the feedback that I needed. We could both tell that skiing on the difficult slopes of the Zehnerkar was possible. I even carefully approached the speeds I had been used to, and I was glad. "My courage hasn't left me after all."

What none of my coaches could have guessed is that if I had experienced trouble on the slope that day, I would have broken off my comeback training immediately. The situation would have become critical. Most likely, I would have lost my sense of focus because I would not have seen any sense in the continuing drudgery. After all, I was rehabilitated for the normal activities of daily life, so why endure the grind day after day? Who knows, my career could have been over right then.

May 6, 2002. I took up systematic conditioning once again. It was just like every year at the outset of the season. At the beginning, biking was still fun. Even if I was sitting on the same ergometer for the umpteenthousandth time, there was a new aspect to it. Time and again I felt like a schoolboy who is thrilled to be breaking in a new notebook at the start of the school year. As nice as it is to get going, as quickly do the daily training blues catch up with you. My biggest problem was the fact that I could still not run properly. At least on the ergometer, I was making great strides. I improved my performance in the moderate compensation region by eighty watts in only one month.

May 26, 2002.   Finally, a change of pace. An outdoor setting, and what a setting at that! For the purpose of bike training I journeyed to Tuscany with Heini and Andy. We biked extensively through the breathtakingly beautiful hill region surrounding Grosseto. All in all, we biked 335 miles. Andy was in my wind shadow, and Heini was driving the companion vehicle. He had his hands full with the wrong road maps, the crotchety local population, and his nonexistent Italian. With all this, he was sometimes pushing the limits of my patience. For example, he once stopped completely without warning and for no apparent reason. I wasn't able to get out of my pedal clips on time and crashed onto the asphalt. Luckily, I got off with only a few minor abrasions.

In the afternoon, we usually held a running session on the beach. I didn't want to rush into it and started out at a leisurely pace. I tried every day to up the ante and was able to increase my performance markedly by the end of the week. Both training and climate were beneficial to my injured legs. I noticed that they were beginning to function better and better. At the end of our little Italian stint, we made a stopover at the motorcycle world championships race in Mugello, where I was able to observe Valentino Rossi and company on their fat tires. While I was strolling through the competitors' quarters, I felt a certain kinship with these athletes. Motorcycle racing and ski racing have a lot in common: high speeds and enormous amounts of centrifugal force in the curves, which require a keen sense of balance. Back home, I started up my BMW right away and biked along the curving mountain roads near home.

June 3, 2002.   After the training camp in Tuscany, I felt almost like a cycling pro. I had proof of my endurance conditioning at the time when I received the results from my lactate test at the Olympic Training Center. "Hermann, you're back to your old self again!" said Heini with great excitement. He was so taken with my values that he wanted to know where

I ranked in direct comparison with the world's top bicycling professionals. He thought I could sign up to compete in the prologue to the bicycle tour around Austria. "Why not the Tour de France?" I asked boldly. So Heini sent a fax to the Tour de France director, Jean-Marie Leblanc. He did not take us very seriously at the time and instead sent me an invitation to the VIP booth. One year later, Heini's dream would become a reality.

July 12, 2002. When I checked into the federal sports center at Faak am See with Heini and Andy, I felt like a student athlete at summer camp. Faak held positive reminiscences for me. Once before, in 1997, I had been to the Carinthia region with the ski team and had enormously enjoyed the conditioning training there. Back then, as now, the few days in that relaxed atmosphere had caused a remarkable improvement in my performance. During the following season, I would embark on my World Cup debut. These are milestones that you remember for your entire career.

The training course eleven months after my accident may well have been the most important in my career. Track and field was exactly what my training had been lacking. The idea for this type of conditioning had been my own. I had begged my trainer: "Heini, you have no idea how much I could use a change of pace! Couldn't we integrate some new elements into my training?" Heini, a former decathlete, couldn't have agreed more. He stuffed a discus, balls, special running shoes, a weightlifting belt, and other equipment into his trunk and planned a state-of-the-art track-and-field program. In the meantime, he was able to empathize with me even more. In order to stay in shape, he had himself resumed a workout regimen of several hours every day. He has already lost fifty pounds and is seriously starting to think about running a marathon.

Before we got going in Faak, I sat on a little dock at a nearby lake at sunset, looked at my thighs, and almost felt like crying. Especially the left one was so skinny that I felt like a stork. I did see that I was making progress on a daily basis, though. I felt like I was starting to live again. Yes, I was turning into an athlete once again! I got rid of my excess energy right then and there. I climbed up to the three-meter diving board and dived into the cool lake. Back flip, one-and-a-half-turn front flip, double front flip: not a problem! I did some awesome dives. I threw the discus, juggled the shot-put balls, and struggled across the hurdles. Every day I was conscious of how my body was reacting to the exertions. Because of the endurance training, my body-fat percentage had been reduced to a bare minimum. Every muscle fiber was well defined.

I was experiencing the same phenomenon as Lance Armstrong did after his struggle with cancer. It is not at all surprising to me that Lance weighs less now than he did before his illness. If I had exclusively concentrated on endurance and not combined it with strength training from that time forward, I would be as lean today as a bicycling professional. Somehow, I felt like my body was being created anew. After all, I had started over from scratch, and had a completely new development phase behind me. I was surprised at how capable of learning my new self had become.

Despite this progress I was still far from being able to function normally. I was restricted in almost every one of my movements. But I was able to start normal running again. Granted, with a higher pulse rate than before, but I was grateful that I finally had an endurance alternative to my customary bicycling. The time in Faak had turned me into an athlete once again, an athlete who was able to put on his skis two weeks later in Zermatt and make a big stir.

July 20, 2002.   I can think of more enjoyable activities than skiing in the summertime. And more comfortable ones, too. The glacier training in Zermatt is a rather exhausting activity. Even the journey up to the Matterhorn in your car, on steep mountain roads across narrow passes and across the train relay station, takes an entire day. There is a general parking prohibition In Zermatt. Your luggage is carefully loaded into electric shuttles, which take you to your hotel.

Everyone else was long asleep, but until late into the night I had to try on my ski boots. I had had these new boots specially fitted, and I was now trying to get used to them. Before, my ski boots could never be tight enough for me. Now the most important thing was that they be comfortable.

In the morning, I had to get out by six, sometimes even five o'clock. Then came the big haul up to an elevation of almost thirteen thousand feet. I had to transport everything I needed for the day in the gondola: a full backpack, two pairs of skis, ski boots. But when I saw the Matterhorn reaching up into the cloudless sky, when I breathed the marvelous glacier air, I once again experienced that wonderful feeling of total joy that I had been missing for the longest time. The documentary film team was along for the ride, and I started singing the classic folk tune "Rosamunde." I sang so loudly that the tourists in the gondola had to smile.

I perceived it as a true luxury that I was able to step into my boot at the top of the ski slope without feeling any pain. Everything was still very sensitive in my right leg. I stepped into my bindings and skied off with a good feeling. Sure enough, my skiing was fully operational from the very first turn. I had the encouraging realization that I was aware of my injured leg only from time to time.

Since I had been so excited about skiing again, I had come here with Andy and ski serviceman Edi Unterberger three days earlier than planned, and so I already had three days of training behind me when my team colleagues saw me on the slope for the first time since the accident. They were watching me like hawks. Somehow, they couldn't help but notice how well I was feeling inside my skin. I had long become accustomed again to the high speed and was even skiing into the first gates. I slalomed down powder slopes and was in my element once again. Because skiing reporters from all over Europe had announced themselves in order to witness my skiing comeback, the ski federation had organized a media day on the glacier. Thus, more than thirty reporters came to the foot of the Matterhorn. The Austrian journalists either put up with a six-hundred-mile drive or they flew into Geneva or Milan. The Swiss reporters approached the glacier from Zermatt. Maria Rosa Quario, the former world-class skier, came to the mountain from Cervinia together with her Italian colleagues. A Japanese photographer stepped up to me with all of her four-foot-seven and gesticulated, "Be as strong as a bear."

"I'm not there yet," I answered. "Maybe that'll come later!" The *Kronen Zeitung* had a headline the next day: "Pure Ambition in His Eyes," quoting ski federation men's head coach Toni Giger, who had come up to the glacier like the rest in order to get a look at how I stood on two skis. For the Austrian daily *Die Presse*, "the Herminator" was "back to his old self," and the *Bild-Zeitung* celebrated me on page one as the "Winner of the Day." Only the Swiss *Blick* ("Maier is back to skiing, but how?") remained skeptical as usual: "It seems unlikely that this man could ever win again after the injuries he has sustained."

To top it all off, Andy had the Telemark skis brought out, and I demonstrated my newly won skiing sensitivity even in this difficult discipline. I was happy to have once again found my rhythm. Hans Knauss patted me on the back and said with approval, "Well, things seem to be coming along just fine!" I was so thrilled that I rewarded myself with a proper farewell party. While Andy took care of the beer keg, I attended to the music. In addition to the fact that it had gotten a bit late, I must have been paying scant attention to the volume. At any rate, the coach of an American college team stormed in and threw an enormous fit. I can't say exactly what time we did finally make it to bed. I know only that we missed one gondola after another in the morning. When we finally made it up onto the glacier, the slope was already too soft. I called it a day, packed up, and returned home. The glacier course had far exceeded my expectations as it was.

August 14, 2002. Super-G time trials in Portillo, Chile. My racing instinct had been reawakened. I was hypermotivated and was almost back to feeling superior, like the year before, when it happened: After a wide turn I was pushed into an extreme backward position while skiing through a depression in the snow. I lost control of the outside ski, and *wham!* I felt a stab in my right leg underneath the transplant, and I knew instantly,

"Ouch! Now I'm in trouble!" I halted my descent and touched my lower leg. I was mad and I cursed, "I wanted too much, like a real moron!" I tried again, but nothing was working. I couldn't even walk normally.

Back at the hotel, I wondered what had really happened. Had a healed spot underneath the transplant opened up again? For the time being, I treated the injury with ice. Gitti Auer, the ski federation doctor who had come along, wanted to make sure that the bone hadn't been damaged, so she insisted on having an X-ray taken right then and there. The procedure turned out to be a true adventure with the stone-age equipment at the medical ward, which was part of the hotel. Gitti tried to calm me down. "Everything is okay, nothing snapped, nothing broken." Even if the bone's integrity had not been compromised, she warned me during my laser treatment, "Something like this can take a while." Nonetheless, I wanted to ski again the next day. However, since I couldn't get into my ski boot, I dismissed the idea at once.

The summer training during Chile's winter had begun so well. After the success in Zermatt, I had started out a few days before the others with lofty ambitions. I was looking forward to winter snow, to off-slope powder skiing, and to the first gate training in simulated racing conditions. I truly savored the wonderful conditions at the foot of Aconcagua, which rises to a height of 22,800 feet. The marvelous landscape in the Andes was covered with a deep blanket of powder-dry virgin snow. When I plunged onto the steep slopes and the snow was whipped up on both sides of me, I felt like shouting for joy. I was finally certain: Skiing, that's my life! When the others arrived and immediately started working the gates, I was still plowing through the terrain. I could only think, "Unbelievable! The others just can't see the marvel of nature." I ran wild in the deep powder all day long and experienced one of the most beautiful skiing days of my life.

Then it was time for me, too, to start training with the gates, though without great expectations. My body was still a bit clumsy, and the new boots felt stiff. Last year, I had plunged into the gates with much more pressure, and effortlessly skied from one top time to the next. This time around, everything was hard fought, and at each turn I focused on process, especially when the slope became rough and hard. My path, the turns—I had to plan every detail carefully. I was unable to achieve the tight radii that used to be my hallmark.

Yet I was not altogether dissatisfied. After all, I had made the connection once again with my timed runs and was in the general ballpark. But soon, that would no longer be enough for me. I wanted to be clearly up front again. I was not satisfied with the few hundredths of a second by which I had improved during some of the runs.

As beautiful as skiing was, after one week at that elevation I had had enough. On the one hand, you can't underestimate the physical stress your body experiences at an altitude of ten thousand feet. On the other hand, I was starting to go stir crazy at the lonely hotel complex, the only building along the mountain pass.

Thus I got it into my head to undertake a little bus journey over the weekend with Andy. We wanted to catch a ride to the Pacific coast, to Viña del Mar. This was the type of adventure I had seen only in the movies. We squeezed in among the locals on the packed public bus with all their baggage, roosters, and other live animals in cages. What can you expect for 2,400 pesos, or just under five dollars? The shaky bus rattled along Los Libertadores, the bumpy national highway, down to sea level. However, there was little seaside charm in the South American vacation mecca. Wild dogs were roaming everywhere. Some of them were scary; others we felt sorry for. We ended up being chased by whole packs of them. The dog with three legs and the dog with one eye were always among them. I felt like Pinocchio, who was chased by the sly fox and the mangy cat. Late at night and completely starving, we made it to a fast-food restaurant. Outside, an especially aggressive dog was waiting for us, and I said to Andy, "Let's buy him a burger before he bites us." While the dog attacked the burger, we were able to sneak past him unharmed.

Because the ocean temperature was only 54 degrees Fahrenheit, we were unable to go swimming, as we had originally hoped. On the other hand, the cool temperature of the air was perfect for running. Along the way, I met a local jogger, who accompanied me on my lonely circles around a racetrack. I would have liked to go for a bike ride as well, but the guy at the bike rental shop wanted to palm off a bike with flat tires.

Unfortunately, the pleasant outing to the ocean turned out to be a mistake, because once I got back to the high elevation, I wasn't exactly ready to roll. On the very next day, we continued with super-G and downhill races. I felt right away, "This isn't going to pan out." I wasn't concentrating fully and I was tired, yet I skied to my limit. And so I was practically begging to be injured.

Deeply disappointed and depressed, I left. During the flight home, I racked my brain. Was it necessary? Why do I always have to overdo it? I could have just skied with normal effort. But that's what I'm like. There's only black or white, all or nothing. There was never a middle ground.

Heini picked me up from the airport and took me straight to Artur at the trauma center. I got a thorough checkup right away. Artur enlarged the digital X-ray on the monitor and didn't seem concerned in the slightest. Yes, he even could see a silver lining to the mishap in Chile. "The bone withstood this extreme test of force without damage. Now we have proof that the site of the fracture has mended well."

"What is hurting so much, then?" I wanted to know.

Artur had a suspicion. There must have been some tissue that was either damaged or torn in the region of the transplant bulge. He couldn't tell me how long that would handicap me. Just to be safe, he pronounced a skiing prohibition of several weeks. Which wasn't a big problem, since snow training was planned only toward the end of September.

I spent the one-year anniversary of my motorcycle accident with Heini in his car. We were on our way to Austria's Burgenland province for some bike riding. Andy followed in the "support vehicle." Before we set off for the domestic glaciers to prepare for the World Cup, we wanted to work some more on my endurance, which is the foundation of my physical achievement. Unfortunately, the bicycle week at Lake Neusiedel turned out to be a colossal failure. I suffered from the first kilometer. On every little bump, every sewer lid, I could feel a stabbing pain in my right calf. I was unable to take my weight off the saddle. The pain was constant, yet I pressed on and circled the lake on the seventy-mile bike path three times altogether. Andy was usually in my wind shadow. As usual, Heini was driving the support vehicle. At previously arranged checkpoints, he measured my lactate and waved our passports at the border guards as we crossed from Austria into Hungary.

I tried running, but I had to break off the attempt after half a circle around the soccer field. Again and again the pain! No wonder that I slowly started to despair.

The clock was ticking and time was against me. It was already September. It wasn't even eight weeks until the World Cup preseason in Sölden. I began to worry seriously. Because I could tell that this wasn't something I should force, I cut back on my training.

I would never have guessed that the injury that I had sustained in Chile would take such a long time to heal. But the medical problem, which no doctor could explain to me, would stick with me for four whole months. To this day, I don't know with certainty what was going on in my lower leg back then. It seems that some scar tissue in the area of the transplant and around the fracture site may have ruptured.

The pain in my calf accompanied me every step of the way. I was a physical and emotional wreck. But no one wanted to recognize this. My team kept clinging to my blood values, which were okay. In the end, it is completely beside the point whether I have lactate 1.5 or 0.9. The decisive factor is how I am feeling. You can tell when you're in good shape. That feeling is what sets the top athletes apart. We have a special awareness of what goes on in our bodies. Scientists, sports medical experts, and self-proclaimed gurus too often rely on measurable numbers and parameters. If value X is thus, then achievement Y is to be expected. Luckily, that sort of simplistic equation works only in the rarest of cases. Otherwise, professional athletics would be a bit too predictable.

I listened to my body. I could sense clearly that I was in no position to ski at the World Cup preseason in Sölden. If I competed, I'd end up among the top thirty, or if things went really well, among the top twenty.

But what good would that do? I wanted to make my comeback at the very top. And for that sort of reappearance I just wasn't ready yet, even if the media often portrayed things differently. Because of the accident, I had learned to be patient. I was able to wait for things to unfold.

September 12, 2002.   I was seated in the helicopter approaching Vienna. Raiffeisen marketing chief Leo Pruschak was waiting at the foot of Vienna's famous Ferris wheel with my new two-year contract. For my main sponsor this contract renewal seemed to go without saying. Likewise, all my other advertising partners remained faithful to me. Since the Hermann Maier fan in the ranks of Vienna's municipal government was on vacation, I was not allowed (as had been originally planned) to land on Jesuits' Meadow in the Prater amusement park. Thus, I had to be picked up from a military base in the suburbs that had a helipad and shuttled in a private car through Vienna's dense traffic to the Prater. I arrived a few minutes late, but still dutifully went around and around the giant wheel a few times with the journalists. Raiffeisen had published an opinion poll conducted by the OGM institute: My name recognition level had reached 97 percent; when asked to name the most popular Austrian athlete, 74 percent of respondents gave my name. Thus, the sponsors did not stand by me exclusively on the basis of friendship.

Moreover, I was a popular guest at festive occasions. One of the few invitations that I accepted was to Munich's famed Oktoberfest. I decided to humor the biggest Atomic customer in all of Germany, and after an autograph session, took my seat next to him in his private booth at the big beer tent dressed in lederhosen and Bavarian shirt. It didn't take long for the first few guests to recognize me, and shortly thereafter I was up on stage, conducting the Niederalmer Musikanten. When they played "We Will Rock You," the crowds clapped along, and during "Sweet Home Alabama," the first few benches were tipped over. The crowd was exhilarated and demanded one encore after another. But I thanked them and made my exit with an athlete's justification: "You should always quit while you're on top." I had such a good time in Bavaria that I ended up staying an extra two days. Back home, Andy and ski serviceman Edi Unterberger were waiting for me. They had gotten everything ready for the much-needed snow training.

October 1, 2002. I knew that if I wanted to put my skis on for the World Cup giant slalom on October 27, I had to start with racing preparations on the Rettenbach Ferner up above Sölden. But secretly I already knew on my way to the Ötztal that this was not going to happen. The terrain there forces one to be very selective. Except for my one day of giant slalom training in Chile on a slope that wasn't nearly steep enough, I did not have any specific preparation under my legs. In terms of my overall physical shape, I had definitely seen better days. I could not in my wildest dreams imagine how this was all supposed to work out.

It would have turned into a "hop-or-drop" race: Either it works or it doesn't. I had already put my main focus on the North American races. But I had at least to make an attempt. Thus I told Andy on the phone, "Okay, I'll come up to Sölden and give it a try." While my team colleagues were presenting themselves to the press in Pitztal, I started off one valley farther, in Sölden. The glacier slope presented itself soft in the upper portion, and hard and bumpy down below. As usual, I started off simply, which was working out halfway decently. Slowly, I was trying to approach my customary tight turning radius. I listened to my leg, closed the curves, increased the pressure, and waited for the pain, which came upon me promptly. It was déjà vu all over again. Once again I slid on a lump of ice with my inner ski, got into an off-balance position with my weight too far toward the rear, and *wham!* Here came the well-known jab in my leg. I halted my momentum. As soon as Andy gave me a questioning look, he already knew the whole story. "Not a problem on the soft slope, but not a chance on the hard part!" I shook my head and tore the goggles off my helmet. My trainer was in denial, so we stood there in the snow for half an hour and discussed it. The Sölden project had failed. Thus, I no longer had to make that decision.

Without a word, we slowly curved down the switchbacks into Sölden. I was deep in thought. When will I be able to ski again? Will I ever ski a race again? And what should I tell the media? I called my press agent, and a few minutes later, the ski federation fax concerning my Sölden cancellation arrived in the newsrooms. It was important to me to give the whole scoop to my fans: *I want to return only when I am truly fit and able to enjoy skiing once again.* The passage concerning my comeback read as follows: *It is going to happen this season; when exactly, I'm not yet able to tell.*

Back at the hotel, I had doubts about a return this season. Only now did I fully realize that my career was seriously in jeopardy. Like a movie, the past thirteen months during which I had fought for a comeback reeled through my head. At first, we had thought that the Olympics would be possible. Then, I wanted to resume normal training in the spring: another dud. The snow training in Chile was interrupted, and now, in Sölden, it was the pits. I was back at square one. On the drive home to Flachau my situation became clearer and clearer. Is this ever going to work again? What if I have to miss yet another season? Surrender? No! I'll make a new start in the springtime. But that will be my absolutely last chance.

Andy interrupted the silence to try to cheer me up. "It's going to work out. It will just take a little longer." That was small consolation to me. "I trained like a fool, prepared myself like a madman, and what's going to come of it? Another injury!" I was done with skiing for the time being: "I'm going to do something totally different." I was looking for a new challenge, something that would really be a dare. I also felt a keen desire for some intellectual stimulus.

I could tell how my body was fighting the forced attempts at skiing and I was ready to accept that. Together we made plans and contemplated how I could best spend my downtime. Maybe a helicopter flew across the cloudless sky at that very moment; I don't remember. At any rate, I said spontaneously, "I'll get my helicopter pilot's license!" We called Heini, whose advice I very much value, and he was taken with the idea. Yes, he even allowed my endurance training schedule for the next few weeks, which was already sitting on his desk ready to go, to disappear into a drawer, and he said in a fatherly tone, "You should really do what you feel like doing at this point. If you feel like working out again, you can let me know."

He couldn't have given me better advice at that point in my life. I signed up for the first available helicopter class. Starting immediately, I was sitting in a classroom at the Union Air Sport Center in Niederöblarn, in the Enns valley. What no one knew is that in the evenings, I secretly sneaked into the adjacent fitness studio and spun rounds on the home trainer. It wasn't only the workout equipment that interested me. I found myself continually glancing over at the attractive fitness coach. "A nice change of pace," I thought, and pedaled away.

To divert myself, I drove often to the heliport in Graz. Flying completely fulfilled me. I wanted to finish the training in record time and was willing to invest a lot of time and energy. I grappled with the concepts of navigation, crosswinds, the dangers during climbing and descending, air density, and lift coefficients. In very short order I learned to control the machine. The combination of the required technical know-how and a special sensitivity for the characteristics of flight was fascinating to me and completely captured my attention. For the first time ever, I couldn't have cared less about skiing.

October 17, 2002. After umpteen requests from the Vera studios, I was talked into an appearance on Austria's most popular television talk show. I had been snagged with the prospect of receiving the award "Newsmaker of the Decade," which I would receive during the show. During the conversation, I uttered a sentence that would shortly thereafter, ripped out of context, flash across the telex machines of the big international news agencies: ". . . otherwise, it will be the end of skiing for me." Austria was shocked. Even though I had not planned on it, I had given the public material for speculation on a possible end to my career. I was angry because in the TV studio they had talked and talked until my head was spinning.

The sentence slipped out spontaneously, and I had to admit that there was something to this sentiment. Yes, I had even partially come to terms with it: If I can't cut it anymore, then that's the end of that. For the first time I considered possibly entering a different line of work.

The crazy weather seemed to justify my abstinence from skiing. The wonderfully warm föhn winds blew any thoughts of the slopes out of my mind. The winter began without snow, and I was lacking all motivation. I repressed any thoughts about ski training: "Why on earth should I put myself through this? So that I can get myself injured once again? So that I can sink into a deep depression? I don't think so!" On the other hand, I was floating on an emotional high. I was already flying across the sky in a helicopter and was delighted at how quickly I was comfortable piloting the thing. After all the setbacks of the past months, I once again had a real sense of achievement!

THE MADDENING INTERVIEW
October 17, 2002

VERA: And now with us: ski superstar Hermann Maier, the Herminator. [Applause] Congratulations on your award as Newsmaker of the Decade. One more award in your huge, huge collection of trophies. Do you even have any room left with all the medals, awards, and trophies at your house?

HERMANN MAIER: That's mainly my parents' domain at their house. I think we have about seven or eight hundred trophies at the moment. My parents used to compete in ski races, and my brother is a snowboard racer. But this recognition as the "Sportsman of the Decade" is something special. Especially in Austria, where Thomas Muster has been very, very strong in past years. I am truly honored.

VERA: When did you first feel within you that enormous will to win, that special drive that gave you wings?

MAIER: It actually started during my childhood. I always wanted to be the best in all things having to do with sports. I was the fastest runner in school; I jumped the farthest in the long jump and the highest in

(continues)

(continued)

the high jump. Somehow I just get totally involved. In soccer, I had technical problems at the beginning, which I was able to work out. Most of what I was able to do I attribute to my speed. You somehow just get into the whole thing. It is often hard to admit mistakes, to lose when you're used to winning. I learned how to deal with this when my body didn't function right, when I had growth problems at age sixteen. That's when I realized, "Okay, now I have to leave it alone." The whole thing subsided after a while and at age 18 or 19, when I started growing again and gained weight, that's when my will to win returned.

VERA: Is it true that you were told at age 16 that you would never become a top competitor, that you were simply too short, and would remain that way?

MAIER: Yes, but then I said to myself, "Now it's over for sure." Thank God I learned a trade and got to learn about other things. It was very, very important to me that I could work in my job, that I finished my training. I enjoyed it, and I believe that it helped me out a great deal in the realm of sports.

VERA: Well, as we can tell, you didn't remain short; on the contrary, you became very, very, very big. Until that fateful twenty-fourth of August 2001, when you were stopped by that terrible accident. In the meantime, there is an official statement that attests in detail that you were not at all at fault in the accident. Did you ever feel anything like hatred toward the 73-year-old German driver?

MAIER: No, not really. I didn't have time for anything like that. I tried to get over the accident as quickly as possible. There is no benefit in harboring any kind of vengeful feelings. To think, "Why did he make the mistake? Why couldn't he have acted otherwise?" You just have to try to look ahead. That's what I ended up doing. I was lying there in the hospital, and my next goal was to learn to walk again.

VERA: You were twice world champion, twice Olympic champion. Did you never consider giving up?

MAIER: That was all very nice, and I am very content with what I was able to achieve. Only, the time frame within which I was able to get there, it was simply too short. I had four fantastic seasons; others have ten, twelve seasons. For the short amount of time, for the energy that I mustered, for the great life, the physical activity out in nature, it was simply too short. I want to come back. Only as one can see, it is very difficult. Something inside me is fighting it. I hope that I can overcome that and that I can once again make a splash, because it really is about time I got going.

VERA: It was looking good at the beginning of summer. But then, in Chile, there was the first big setback, when you got the contusion where the top of your boot meets your leg. Now once again you have to take a training break because of excessive pain.

MAIER: In the beginning, everything was going wrong. Then, at the beginning of May, when I skied once again, I was still in pain. But then, in the middle of July, it just sort of worked out again, and I thought, "Yes, there is definitely a prospect here." Then the next thing happened in August, in Chile. I was very, very motivated. I skied time trials and for the first time after a whole year's break I was very content.

VERA: They were all amazed, isn't that right?

MAIER: You can't take that too seriously. But it is an approximation, especially when you've had such a serious injury. You ski your first race and see that you're part of the whole thing once again. That was really good, of course. And I could tell, yes, there are still a lot of reserves. I wanted to ski a bit better yet, not necessarily because of the time, but rather, because of my technique, so that I could further fine-tune it. Then I unfortunately made a mistake, of which I have to say, if I had been altogether healthy, my foot wouldn't have suffered any harm, and I would have continued to ski the very next day. But my leg is in such poor shape, so battered up at the moment, that the smallest mistake was enough to leave me injured once again. I have got to get a handle on that, so that it will improve. Otherwise, it will be the end of skiing for me.

VERA: So the World Cup preseason in Sölden is definitely canceled?

MAIER: Yes, definitely.

VERA: The *Kronen Zeitung* wrote that even the world championships is in question. How are you gauging your chances at this point?

MAIER: Well, it's good to see that others are thinking about such things. I myself don't think too much about sports and skiing. I just try to think about other stuff and hope that my leg will get better. I have a goal, and that is to be able to ski again as soon as possible. But really strong exertion does not yet work for my leg. Thus, it is best to be quiet about it, in order to return on a strong footing later on. I hope that such will be the case soon. The most difficult aspect will be coping with the high

(continues)

(continued)

speeds. You usually descend a downhill racecourse at eighty or ninety miles per hour, and you can't really see much. It becomes a matter of feeling the slope, which is hard to get used to again.

VERA: Hermann, you've also made headlines with your private life during the past few years. You broke up with your girlfriend Gudrun last summer. Do you miss her, especially during the times when things aren't going well? Do you regret having taken this step?

MAIER: Relationships come, relationships go. I don't think that she would be able to help me much at this point. I have to get out of difficult situations by myself. She has a lot on her plate as well. I think one shouldn't burden each other in this regard.

VERA: If we look back ten years, what was your life like back then?

MAIER: I was hard at work back then, I was in construction, and I was very, very ambitious. I already had my own construction crew, I had a company vehicle, which was something special then, and I just had a lot of fun doing what I was doing. It was nice, when you're building a house, and you see that you're making progress. There are jobs where you do stuff and you don't see your progress. It was a difficult time, and in the winter, it was very cold. At age 20, I started working as a ski instructor, thank goodness. Then I had two jobs, and there was some variety.

VERA: Is there something you liked more about the time back then compared to now?

MAIER: Yes, we always had a mandated coffee break at nine o'clock; I kind of miss that now.

VERA: In December, you'll be 30. Do you sometimes feel like time is running out for you in competitive sports?

MAIER: Not at all. In that sense I am not really used up, except for my foot down there. Other than that, I haven't had any major injuries. I went into competitive sports pretty late, at age 24, 25. Considering that, there surely is time left for me, as long as that thing down there gets better.

PART II

(previous page) October 23, 2005, Sölden, Austria.
A dream come true! My first grand slalom World Cup
victory in almost four years. I never expected to win
a season opener again!

Chapter 9

THE VICTORY
OF MY LIFE

K eep all requests away from me," I told my press spokesman on the phone. "No interviews, no photo shoots, no TV appearances. I don't want to see a soul, not even the documentary team." I had made my point.

I was sick and tired of the idiotic stories and rumors that were constantly making their way through the media. "Maier is only appeasing his sponsors," they were saying. "He'll never come back!" And in whisper tones, "Maier's management is bluffing the whole world." Obviously, no one seriously believed in my comeback at that point. My sponsors, however, were really standing behind me, in addition to my family, my coaching team, and my true fans. Not one of my faithful advertising partners even hinted at possibly letting go of me.

On the other side were the tabloids. Regardless of what I was doing, they wrote about "PR strategies," "insurance speculation," and my "advertising value," which I was supposedly trying to keep alive artificially. I could no longer listen to all this. It wasn't my fault that more journalists showed up at my press conferences than at those of my active skiing colleagues. I couldn't have cared less about how many of them were present. My comeback work was no public relations ploy. It was strictly the will to come back that drove me, surely not the money. I probably would have cashed in more from my insurance policy had I stopped skiing. But there was nothing I was yearning for more than being able to stand there once again at the starting line in the freezing cold. To compete in ski races, that's my life. What good would it do me to sit at home and count banknotes?

What should I have done? Say nothing? Then, they would say, "What sort of a pointless game of hide-and-seek is this?" Or should I tell the public at an opportune moment what was going on? I chose the latter course. Nevertheless, my entire comeback work was belittled as "PR strategy." I trained for months on end while I was in considerable pain, tried everything humanly possible. An army of coaches and professionals were giving their very best under conditions of great personal sacrifice. Then you read, see, and hear base remarks that you can't help but take personally. That really hurt me, and put me into a deep depression.

The Maier intermission during November was good for all of us. I took my helicopter lessons, spent time with old friends, and made some new friends. I started feeling well again and was at peace with my life. My leg functioned adequately for daily activities, and I didn't really miss the athletics. There were more important things in life.

My only "appearance" was for Heini's fiftieth birthday. My trainer had invited us all to a medieval feast at the castle in Werfen, where we dug in with our bare hands, just like the beloved comic characters Asterix and Obelix during the brave Gauls' traditional farewell banquet. A photographer friend of Heinrich's sent some photos of the event to the newspapers.

Because the media were slowly running out of Herminator stories toward the beginning of December, a speeding ticket on the autobahn served as an impetus for a tabloid scandal. The facts: I was traveling on the Salzburg autobahn on my way to the airport because I had to get to Cape Town for a commercial shooting. I had left my company BMW at home in the garage, since a very good friend of mine wanted to drive me to the airport in her VW Golf. Because everything was once again planned out to the last second, I insisted on taking the wheel of the seventy-horsepower car myself. We were gaily chatting and I failed to check the speedometer. I must have been going a few miles over the sixty-mile-per-hour speed limit. At any rate, a policeman in civilian attire pulled me over and seemed quite annoyed. Since I wanted to continue on my way to the airport as quickly as possible, I did not engage in lengthy negotiations, but instead accepted the citation. I had barely arrived in South Africa when my traffic trespass caught up with me. The first few agency reports arrived at my hotel via fax. Apparently, the officer had informed the domestic media. Most of them did not deem the facts worthy of even a short mention, except for one small daily, which went way overboard. They came up with this huge scandalous story that took up an entire double page, with wild speculations and a tasteless insert in which they listed fatalities that those on the ski circuit had caused by speeding.

Actually, I was glad to be in South Africa at the time and to find out about the latest scoop only via fax or short message service. The Raiffeisen crew had picked Cape Town as the location for an advertising shoot because they required a sun-drenched hotel swimming pool with the requisite bathing beauties. After two exhausting days of shooting, I lay down by the pool and let the sun beam down onto my pale skin. "Longing for home," complete with an ad-agency artificial tear, wasn't altogether fake, though. In the meantime, without my noticing it, my leg had stopped hurting. A few days before my departure, Heini had suggested treatment with a novel ion magnetic induction therapy system called PAP IMI developed by the Athenian professor Panos Pappas.

The PAP IMI box looked like a two-hundred-pound combination of a washing machine and the *Star Wars* robot R2-D2. The high electromagnetic energy output, which introduces negative ions into your body, removes dead cells from your system and stimulates the formation of new nerve and muscle tissue. I agreed to this experiment with much skepticism. But lo and behold! After each treatment, I could feel a tingling sensation. That was a good sign, since my nerves and muscles were considerably damaged, and the leg that had undergone surgery was practically without sensation as a result. From now on, the magic box would always accompany me along my journey back.

There I was, sitting in the sunshine, fingering my transplant, when suddenly I had a positive feeling. Was the combination of time-out from training and treatment with the PAP IMI device starting to work? If so, then the only thing that was missing was a real winter!

December 6, 2002. I climbed out of the airplane in Salzburg carrying a gigantic wooden giraffe that Raika manager Leo Pruschak had given me as an early birthday present. I was met by a camera team and a handful of journalists. Heini arrived bearing a cake, and I blew out the candles for the camera. There were two parties planned for my thirtieth birthday. The official one took place at a Flachau estate, then I celebrated with my friends in Obertauern in a more intimate setting. There I received a nostalgic pair of wooden skis, which I tried out next to the Lürzer Alm at a late hour by sliding down the mountain to the ski bar, where I came to an elegant halt. I know that this may sound ridiculous, but when I felt the new snow underneath my skis, I suddenly had that itch again.

Starting immediately, I showed up at the Olympic Training Center regularly between helicopter lessons to resume conditioning. While the snowflakes were dancing around outside my window, Heini looked at me and said, "Don't you want to start skiing again?" He must have been reading my mind. My secret wish from South Africa had really come true. Winter had come at last, and I could sense my yearning to ski grow with each passing day.

Before I could really get moving, I had to go to Vienna for a sponsor presentation and an ORF sports Christmas party. There, an altercation was narrowly avoided. Since Stephan Eberharter had injured himself that very day in Val d'Isère, it was not beneath the reporter to ask the following idiotic question in front of running cameras: "Is it motivating to you that you might possibly lose a very, very strong competitor? After all, he was king of everything at this point . . ." I gathered all my poise in order not to lose it right then and there, and answered, "I believe that this is a very, very unfair question, one that did not even occur to me." Then I added, "If Steff starts, then he starts, and if not, then so be it. None of this will make my leg any better."

Is a competitor's injury convenient to me at this time? What a venomous sentiment! From a human point of view, I was terribly disappointed at such a vicious train of thought. A sports rivalry must never escalate into hateful feelings. My mood had toppled within just a few seconds, and I couldn't wait to get out of there. Vienna had disappeared beneath a deep blanket of snow, and the traffic was snarled chaotically. I almost missed my plane to Salzburg, which would have been of little consequence. When I looked up flight OS 917 on the departure monitor, I read "Canceled." Thus, I could forget about my conditioning training in Obertauern for that day. I reacted quickly and rented a car. A stewardess, who was also on her way to Salzburg, asked if she could hitch a ride. I was still tired from the day before and seized the opportunity, saying, "Yes, but only if you drive!" What a nice change of pace. While we were struggling through the snowdrifts on the west autobahn, I thought almost exclusively about skiing, despite the attractive distraction in the driver's seat. I knew now that the plan that had been spinning around in my head could finally be realized. I would collect my strength in record time and charge up to my top level of performance. That sort of thing is precisely where my strength lies. I felt that the time was ripe to stage an attack. Thus I started my comeback blitz.

I had nothing to prove to anyone. This was a matter neither of titles nor of medals, but was strictly for the sake of one objective: I wanted to make the comeback. Only then would the matter be closed for me. Let it be said that he came out of nowhere, achieved everything in four years, was taken down by a car, and came back in the end. Then the circle would be complete. I was completely obsessed by this narrative. If I had not had it in the back of my mind during this entire difficult time, my plan would never have worked out.

"OPERATION COMEBACK":
NO ONE HAD A CLUE

December 17, 2002. There were perfect conditions on the slopes, so I made my decision shortly before going to sleep. "Tomorrow, I'll do it! All by myself!" No convoluted explanations, no justifications in case it didn't work out after all. I did not want to have anyone watching me. So I didn't tell a soul. Not even my family. Especially not my trainers. I had already assembled my ski equipment. The next morning, I stopped by the Atomic ski shed and grabbed the first two pairs of giant slalom skis I saw. Not even Edi, who normally keeps skis on the ready for me for any kind of training, knew anything about my solo stint. In Obertauern I simply went up to the lift and asked meekly, "Will you please let me go up once?" I didn't put any pressure on myself. "If it works, it works," I thought. "And if not, then I get out of my ski boots and drive home!" On the chairlift I let my skis dangle and once again probed deep inside myself. In such situations, I always think back one year. What was going on at exactly this time one year ago? If I compared the pain from back then with the present, I was content indeed.

I took off expectantly. Very carefully. Thoughts about my painful skiing trials thus far arose within me. My expectations weren't too big at any rate. "If it works better this time than when I quit in Sölden back in October, then I come out ahead." I skied hesitantly. Since I was very careful not to get into an extreme backward position, I constantly relieved pressure from the sensitive area on my lower leg. It was more than a mere slide down the mountain, though. Things were really happening, though in carefully measured doses. Fear still accompanied me. "What if I slip on my inside ski as in Chile or Sölden? Will I once again get that pain in my calf?" Nevertheless, I quickly started approaching my limits once again. Watch out, you're about to slip! But it was only a scare. Fabulous! I felt no pain! The first day was a complete success. I grabbed the telephone: "Andy, it's time!"

There was only one thing for me to do. "Tomorrow, I'm going to step on the gas." During such phases, nights are very important. How will your body react to the new exertion? Will there be problems? But everything stayed within the green zone. At this point I realized that my dream of a comeback this season could still become a reality. My next thought was, "Now I have to get going with the right kind of training. Now I have to do gates!" Which is exactly what I did. I struggled through the first gates in Obertauern, and I was fully back in my element. Suddenly, the fear of a new injury became secondary. After two cautious runs I again went to the limit, until I almost slipped again. But even this situation could not dampen my enthusiasm. The leg was holding up! After I zipped across the finish line, there was an end to the secrecy. Yes, I wanted to race again!

December 23, 2002.   Shortly thereafter, my cell phone rang. It was men's head coach Toni Giger, who had been traveling with the team since the beginning of November. He was keeping up with the news via telephone. "We hear only good news about you," he said. Now that my comeback was taking concrete shape, it was time for a thoroughgoing discussion. How many more days do I need for free skiing? Which trainers should be there? When and where do I start with time trials? For these types of logistical matters, Giger is my most important adviser next to Andy Evers. A few hours later, we were sitting at Salzburg's Tennis Point. "Let's get going," the head coach suggested while he was getting out his laptop. We reviewed the World Cup dates. One of the lines caught my attention: "January 14, Adelboden, Giant Slalom."

"Yes," I thought. "I would like that!"

On Christmas Day I was in water up to my waist. With hip boots and a fishing rod, I was wading through the icy cold Inn River alongside the ski federation president. Peter Schröcksnadel had invited me, and we were standing next to each other silently. It was sort of a strange atmosphere. I let nature and the tranquil setting have their effect on me. I could tell that this was the calm before the storm, the beginning of a new chapter altogether. Before, it had been Hermann Maier I. Now it was time for Hermann Maier II. As usual, Peter supported my plan. He had a word of warning, though: "The most important thing is your health. Please be careful that you don't overdo it." Back then, he didn't suspect that we would meet again only three weeks later to announce my racing comeback.

From then on, things began happening lightning fast. Andy was already in Bormio, where two downhills were planned within two weeks. After he got the okay from Giger, he left Italy even before the races in order to support me as best he could. Next, I called my serviceman, Edi Unterberger. "Edi, there's work to be done again."

December 29, 2002. For the last few days of the year, we relocated to Carinthia, to the Turracher Heights. On this occasion, I let myself be seen for the first time by my slalom and giant slalom colleagues. They had to work out under extreme conditions. The slope was icy and rippled like a washboard; it had sudden drops and in the lower part was incredibly steep. "Good heavens," I thought while taking a close look at the run. Nevertheless, I tried my no-holds-barred daredevil style, which at times had made me unbeatable before my injury. But I had to abandon that technique. I quickly realized that during my absence, things had changed. The giant slalom skis had gotten a bit shorter. I had problems with the fast back-and-forth motion required for a successful run. Was it a matter of strength that I was now missing? Or was my technique outdated? Soon I realized, "Lad, you're skiing a bit too straight." Of course, the final measure of confidence was lacking, and I was still afraid of the sudden drops. But I bravely finished the run despite the brutal slope. Andy encouraged me as much as possible. "You couldn't have worse conditions during a race." I was concentrating on the next two runs. Each time, I inched closer to the racing times of my colleagues. I continued to increase the pressure on my boot, since I wanted to know "Will my leg withstand this?" It held up, and I went to the Olympic Training Center with an upbeat feeling. "Heini, should I still risk it this season? If I don't do any more races, I might regret it later." My trainer took away my last remaining doubts. "Why not? You're in good enough shape, that's for sure!" Thus, it was a done deal for me. We could plan my return to the World Cup circus!

"I'll be back!" I promised my fans on my homepage for the new year. But no one seemed to take that seriously.

January 1, 2003.　Word of my ski outing to the Turracher Heights had gotten around in journalistic circles. In strict secrecy the Herminator was skiing again, I could read from the bold letters in the *Kronen Zeitung* after two days with my ski federation team colleagues. Then lo and behold! Slowly, they were starting to believe my announcement: "If there's any chance whatsoever, I'll be back." According to the papers, the training runs on the Turracher Heights proved at the very least that my words weren't just meant to reassure the sponsors.

January 4, 2003.　Since I was in no mood to be hounded by reporters during each training session, I accepted an invitation to Sterzing. Markus "Spartacus" Sparber, a South Tyrolean sports scientist with the Austrian Ski Federation team, had organized everything perfectly, right in his own front yard. He had found a perfect slope (the Rosskopf), which has a similar layout to the one in Adelboden. I was floored when I arrived to find a slope that had been expertly groomed just for me. Spartacus had obviously mobilized half the village. Twenty volunteers had skied down the slope, and the little snow that remained had been pressed down to a compact ribbon by a specially ordered snowcat. In addition, two Ski-Doos were waiting, which made the lift unnecessary, and Spartacus took his assignment so seriously that he had even obtained the weather forecast from the Italian air force. He assured us that he had enlightened only his own mother (in whose house we were invited to stay), the snowcat operator, and the operator's boss for whom such ostentatious preparations had been made. I was not sure whether I should really believe him.

At any rate, the "secret training" became a public spectacle in short order. Soon, I could hear calls of "Hermann, Hermann!" Hundreds of spectators had accumulated along the barrier net, and after I was done with my training, I ended up giving autographs for over half an hour. I didn't really mind, though. I was so happy that I was once again allowed to do what I do best. The training was a lot of fun. With every run, I regained more of my old self-confidence. For the first time, I was training again in front of an audience. After each training session, we were well cared for at the Sparbers' home. I filled up my carbohydrate stores (truthfully, I must have overfilled them) with the homemade noodles, which were served in huge vats. We started out with salad and prosciutto, followed by the noodles, which I assumed to be the main course, so I took a second helping. But I hadn't counted on the veal schnitzel with potatoes, as well as the plate full of cakes for dessert. There were also plates heaped with Christmas cookies everywhere. "I've never seen a person who can eat so much," said Frau Sparber while she cleared off the table. "And I have never been given so much to eat," I replied with gratitude.

In the meantime, our hosts' telephone was ringing every ten minutes: ORF South Tyrol, *Tiroler Tageszeitung*, Radio Tyrol, RAI, *Dolomiten*, and others wanted the details of my "secret training." Frau Sparber wasn't only an expert cook; she also did a great job of shielding me from the media. All in all, the whole stay was a worthwhile digression. Despite the bad weather during the third day, we were still able to conduct a perfect super-G training. When we left Sterzing, I knew that I had taken a big step toward my return to the World Cup!

A CRASH TOOK AWAY MY
LAST REMAINING DOUBTS

January 8, 2003. Only a few people seem to have realized how close my racing comeback really was. During the second week of January, time trials on the Reiteralm near Schladming were planned for a majority of the giant slalom and super-G group. I felt strong enough once again to face my team colleagues, who would soon become my competitors. So I called Edi and asked him to get the very best equipment out of the ski shed. Unfortunately, my serviceman was back in Bormio at the time, where training had resumed for the next downhill race. He jumped in his car the very same night and drove the entire 285 miles of mountain roads back to the Atomic plant in Altenmarkt, where he prepared my skis until the wee hours of the morning.

At 6:45 the next morning, Edi had already boarded the first gondola up to the Reiteralm, loaded down with six pairs of giant slalom skis. Next to me, Hans Knauss, Christoph Gruber, Christian Mayer, and the up-and-coming Thomas Graggaber were doing their warm-up. The ski federation trainers were staking out a giant slalom course and installing the electronic timing system. It was a perfectly gorgeous, icy cold winter morning, with the thermometer at −4 degrees Fahrenheit. The rippled, hard slope appeared to be in sensational condition, lacking nothing compared with a World Cup slope. In the meantime, the ski federation bosses had arrived along with alpine skiing director Hans Pum and men's head coach Toni Giger. They were glancing across the shoulders of Andreas Evers and Walter Hubmann, who was the trainer of the super-G/RTL group (WC3) at the time. There was tension in the air, as though this were a real race. All those present seemed to realize that if I could keep up with the country's best giant slalom racers at the time, then there was nothing in the way of a speedy comeback.

After almost two years without a race, I was yearning for a sense of accomplishment in terms of directly measuring my skills against those of my competitors. I went to the limit and really gave it my all. I was the fastest one that morning! I could hardly believe it. With so little training! Trainers and service people were standing around in the finish area, studying the computer printouts with the interval times and shaking their heads. "Hermann is fit. Otherwise, he never would have made it down this slope," Hans Knauss informed the reporters who had traveled there. Everyone was sure. "He will race again, all right!" I put my head down onto my ski poles and closed my eyes. Images from the past months were passing in front of my mind's eye in time-lapse fashion. An adrenaline rush was coursing through my body. It really looked as though I would be able to fulfill my dream of a comeback in Adelboden. The classic race in the Berner Oberland was to take place in exactly one week. I associated the place with wonderful memories. After all, I had won all three of the races that I had skied there, and in 1998 it was with a record lead of 1.24 seconds ahead of local champion Michael von Grünigen.

Now a cool head was in order. My comeback would be announced only at the end of the week. Because it was not entirely certain, after all. I had three training days ahead of me on the Reiteralm. I was so obsessed with my work that I barely paid attention to the peripheral activity. Thus once, as I left the ski change area, I pushed off at full throttle. In the process, I crashed into a teenaged girl, who curiously enough was overjoyed by the assault. While I was helping the young lady up, she proudly announced to her girlfriends, "I was run over by Hermann Maier!" More and more ski vacationers discovered me and asked for autographs and souvenir photographs. Somehow, it felt good to experience such rituals again on the ski slope. My self-confidence grew daily. As strange as it may sound, the incident that really prepared me psychologically to race again was a wild takeoff during my second day on the Reiteralm.

Once again I was trying to maintain my tight line. While doing so, I underestimated my strength deficit, as well as the developments in equipment that had taken place during my absence. Because of the more tapered fit of the skis, stronger forces were released, and these additional forces are what tripped me up. It was one of those incidents that I remember to this day in minutest detail. I am pulling through the curve. Relocating my weight to make the left turn. My leg gives out, and I pull off a real "highsider." The ski tips point upward all by themselves, as though I were a real ski jumper. I can no longer withstand the pressure and begin to climb. In the air, all the alarm sirens go off in my head. "I am such a moron! Why do I have to risk so much only to get hurt again?" But miracle of miracles, I touch down and glide to the edge of the slope.

Carefully, I shake off the snow and listen inside myself. But the jolt to my leg that I have so much expected to feel at this point doesn't come. I am uninjured. I am indescribably relieved. "If my leg can withstand this, then there's nothing that can prevent my start in Adelboden!" One thing was certain: Bone and rod are holding fast. Considered from this point of view, I was truly grateful for this fateful mishap. In the meantime, people around Austria were pricking up their ears. As is often the case, the *Kronen Zeitung* charged ahead: "Everything is ready for Hermann's dream comeback."

January 12, 2003. Hundreds of fans went to my homepage to convey their congratulations and encouragement. Hundreds of press requests had been made to my press spokesman within the past few days. But I did not allow myself to be talked into a statement; I wanted to concentrate exclusively on my comeback work. The media seemed to understand that. What I couldn't prevent were more and more spectators arriving on the Reiteralm. They all realized that after this week of training, there would be a decision about the exact timing of my comeback. No one really was prepared to believe that the giant slalom in Adelboden in two days would be a serious consideration. It was still dark outside. I was sitting in the car next to Andy on the way up to the Reiteralm. On the radio, there was a report in which ski expert Adi Niederkorn was speculating about my comeback in Adelboden, which ended with the words "realistic comeback, PR gag, or sponsor appeasement?" and in conclusion, the misleading final sentence: "No hotel room has yet been booked for Hermann in Adelboden." Was I ever glad to be putting an end to all this tiresome speculation.

There was a giant slalom course staked out on the Reiteralm, and I knew that if I could make it down halfway decently three times, then I would be at the starting line two days later. At this point, such things were no longer an issue for me. I finished by snatching the best time from local champion Hans Knauss, coming to a stop, giving my racing skis to Edi, and driving down into the valley with Andy. Ski federation president (as well as fishing companion) Peter Schröcksnadel was waiting for me at the Hotel Pichlmayergut, where he extended his congratulations. After conferring with Hans Pum, who was at the downhill in Bormio, we gave our blessing to the press statement before it was faxed out into the whole world in German and English via the ski federation distributors.

I had to concentrate 100 percent on my start in Adelboden. And so it was important to me that everything I had to say on the subject of my comeback should appear in the press statement. And I wanted to prevent any speculation and possible disappointment. Therefore, Schröcksnadel specified my initial goal as "a finish in the top thirty."

MAIER RETURNS TO
COMPETITIVE SKIING IN ADELBODEN

Schladming, January 12, 2003

A year and a half after his serious motorcycle accident on August 24, 2001, Hermann Maier will surprisingly return to the racing slopes for the giant slalom in Adelboden at this early point in time. After the renewed injury sustained during summer training, which was graver than suspected, it was not foreseeable when Maier would make his comeback into the World Cup. The 30-year-old Flachau native has recovered from this renewed setback much faster than expected. He began light ski training at the beginning of this year and has made enormous progress in recent days.

The final decision regarding the comeback was made Sunday morning with Austrian Ski Federation trainer Andy Evers during the giant slalom training after second opinions were received from men's head coach Toni Giger and alpine skiing director Hans Pum on the Reiteralm. Ski federation president Peter Schröcksnadel, who was present on Sunday, gave his blessing to the comeback and said, "Hermann once again enjoys skiing, and I thus can see no reason why he should not go to the starting line at this point." The federation president reined in expectations, however. "It is now important that he feels his way back into things. A position among the top thirty would be a first goal."

Ski federation men's head coach Toni Giger emphasized the solid preparation of the three-time World Cup overall winner: "Whoever knows Hermann knows that he leaves nothing up to chance. He gave an excellent impression on the first day of training on the Reiteralm." Alpine director Hans Pum, who was announcing Maier's comeback together with Giger from the sidelines of the slalom in Bormio, said, "I am glad that Hermann is able to return to the starting line in a fit condition and ski for Austria. I am fascinated by the fact that he took the stress and strain of a comeback upon himself after such a grave injury despite his great successes in the past." Schröcksnadel added, "Hermann is disproving all the naysayers who claimed that he would never again ski in a race and belittled his comeback attempts as a PR charade. Neither Hermann nor his sponsors have any need for such nonsense."

"Skiing is simply a lot of fun again, and for me, the greatest fun is competing in races," Hermann added in support of his decision in favor of a comeback.

TOP THIRTY? I WANTED TO WIN!

Secretly, of course, I wanted more. I knew my training times from the Reiteralm, and normally I was able to improve my times during a race. So I took off with a different resolution altogether. I wanted to win! I thought, "If everything is just right, if the conditions are perfect, I can end up way toward the front, maybe even more." Yes, I wanted to win! Of course that was an illusion, but such a thought has to be inside every ski racer's head.

Without much time to brace myself, World Cup madness descended on me. Eternally long drives. Eating at highway rest stops. Number drawings, press conferences, slope inspections, equipment checks, and team meetings. TV cameras were lying in wait everywhere. Photographers and reporters were watching every move I made. I was once again the transparent sports celebrity, and if they had their way, they would shine a light right through me around the clock.

Between sending off the press statement and departing Flachau, I had a scant hour and a half left to myself. Ninety minutes to drive from Schladming to Flachau, shower, eat, and store my equipment. I had to postpone eating until we were en route, because Andy was already at the door, and a few minutes later we were on our way. It was shortly before midnight when we arrived in Adelboden. We had barely unpacked properly when the reporters were crowding around my door. They took pictures of everything: Maier with his luggage, Maier with his ergometer, Maier as he checks into the hotel. No one dared ask a question at such a late hour, though. Really, no one seemed really to believe me anyway. I had gotten the same corner room as during my last victory in 2001, and I was extremely glad finally to be in bed.

The Swiss tabloid *Blick* was sitting in the breakfast room. "Maier is back!" I could read in big red letters. "The best thing that can happen to the sport of skiing." "Nice welcome," I thought, not suspecting that the same paper would be putting me down even before the race.

Nothing would ever again be as it was. Before my accident, barely a journalist had deemed it worth the effort to show up for a slope familiarization. The day before a giant slalom, the racers are given a chance to study the terrain. That is usually of interest only to the active racers, the trainers, and the service people. But this time around, the photographers were stepping on each other's skis on the side of the slope. In the finish area, a cluster of reporters was waiting.

But I had concerns of a different kind. The famous Kuonisbergli, which includes the most difficult giant slalom run in the world, was baring its teeth. It was smooth as a mirror. I started out hesitantly. "Madness! I have to go down this?" But there was no turning back. I tried to think positively: "I've won every time I've skied here thus far." I really liked the slope layout, and long runs are to my advantage to begin with. The first run put me in an optimistic mood. "This isn't going so badly." After all, we had trained in icy conditions on the Reiteralm. I went down another two times, got into the groove of things, and thought, "Really, it's working out just fine!" I gave a few brief statements to the television people while I was still out in the snow and then marched, crowded by more and more people, straight into the press center, where a crowd of journalists was waiting for me. Two hundred seven reporters altogether, more than ever before in Adelboden, had received accreditation for the occasion of my comeback race. I tried to convey all the major points in a few sentences. They all picked out one sentence in particular: "With me, everything is extreme, even my comeback."

When for the drawing I rappeled down from the second story of the Hotel Bär on a steel cable and zoomed over the heads of 4,500 screaming fans onto the stage, I was back in my element. I drew the number thirteen and offered special thanks over the loudspeakers to those of my fans who had not written me off.

January 14, 2003. My coaching team was hiding the *Blick* from me with good reason. Sure, my comeback was topic number one. However, the time for friendly gestures had passed. The tabloid wanted to keep all possible scenarios open and had done an informal survey among the Swiss ski team. Each quotation was a punch below the belt. The crowning comment came from the Austrian serviceman of my opponent Michael von Grünigen: "Maier will ski a few gates, come to a halt and say, sorry folks, nothing doing. Then his insurance has to pay up, because Hermann can no longer perform his job." Aside from the fact that his idea of the way insurance compensation works is completely off base, I was annoyed that anyone capable of standing upright on two skis felt inspired to comment on this situation, and in the process give it a slant that simply wasn't true. What on earth is going on in the heads of those people? Obviously, they assume that their own malicious train of thought must also apply to others.

I couldn't escape my own comeback. Every TV channel and every radio station were awash in talk about it. That certainly added to my stage fright.

Early in the morning, when I was riding in the car on my way to the slope familiarization, I was silent and unapproachable. Without a word, I took my skis out of the trunk and stood in line at the T-bar. While I studied gate after gate and tried to remember key passages, I realized that overnight, everything had become even more difficult, more brutal. I could feel the sheer ice. The long slope had been prepped with water from top to bottom.

Over seventeen thousand fans provided a record backdrop on this Tuesday, a normal working day. Maria, the physical therapist who had been instrumental in the meticulous effort of teaching me how to walk without a limp at the Olympic Training Center, had been working for the German women's ski team. On this January 14 she got into her car early in the morning in order to witness my comeback live. When she became stuck in traffic and realized that she would arrive too late, she knocked on a stranger's door and asked, "Do you have a television? If so, then please turn it on right away. I have to see Hermann Maier!"

THE POINT OF NO RETURN

The "Herminator" banner with the good-luck pig was hanging in the finish area. Right below it stood my parents, who are always there during important moments. The official racing clock was showing 10:22. Almost a million viewers were witnessing my comeback live in front of their televisions. I was more nervous than at any other time in my career. Jan, the masseur, was handing me my goggles. "I'm on now," I thought, "and there's no going back!" I had finally returned to the starting gate, 508 days after my accident. How hard I had worked for this moment! I had invested 294 training sessions and over a thousand hours of training, I had biked almost six thousand miles, had lifted over eight hundred tons of weight to strengthen my compromised legs, and had been pricked in my ear over two thousand times for a lactate check. Then came the extremely brief fine-tuning on skis, which I had conducted with more scientific precision than ever before. Now the moment had come in which I had to recall and put to use all of this within a minimal time frame. How often had I dreamed of this moment, how many times had I played it out in my mind! Now I had only a few seconds until it was time to put all that into practice. It was a strange feeling, one I was barely familiar with. It was almost as though I were having an out-of-body experience. Suddenly, I felt like I was actually standing next to myself. I started thinking, "If that happens to you on this steep hill, then you've already lost."

Beep-beep-beep-beep. Beep! The electronic countdown ticked off the last five seconds. I felt I was in over my head, and suddenly I was in a panic, asking myself questions: "What on earth am I doing here? What kind of attitude should I have? Should I attack? Take it easy? Should I ski for a victory, or just try to make it down the slope halfway decently?" I started out with ambition enough, but after four, five gates I made my first mistake. I simply wasn't skiing as aggressively, or with the same agility, as I was used to on this hill. Then I made one dumb mistake after another. I was not willing to take the full risk, and time and again I gave in. Especially during the uneven sections, I was losing time. Then the biggest problem. My strength totally left me. This had happened to me on a few occasions, but this time around, I was completely unable to recover. I gave up mentally and bumbled across the finish line in an upright position.

When I saw the slow-motion playback of my finish, I thought with alarm, "Who on earth is this coming down the hill?" That skier looked anything but good. The display showed my lag against the winner, Didier Cuche: 3.34 seconds. I thought, "Well, my friend, that's nothing to brag about!"

I was done with this race, and not for a moment did I assume that I would qualify for the second round among the thirty best times. While I was standing in the finish area, giving eternal interviews, a member of my coaching team kept nudging me and saying, "You can still make it." After fifty racers had descended, I was in exactly thirtieth place. But then Kalle Palander, with starting number fifty-six, took away any remaining illusions. When I realized that as number thirty-one I had missed the qualification for the second round by only five hundredths of a second, I was somewhat assuaged, and indeed, a joyous feeling welled up inside me. "I am in the ballpark!" I had lost only six tenths of a second to the completely healthy Lasse Kjus. I realized that I was far from being back to my old form. Even though it would have been great to ski a second round, my disappointment quickly dissolved, and I started to enjoy the interviews in the finish area. Following that race, I had a frightening experience with the cheering crowds. I had witnessed nothing like it either during my Olympic or world championships victories or during my triumphs in Kitzbühel. When I left the cordoned-off finish area, a horde of screaming fans rushed toward me, and I was almost crushed in the ensuing melee. My press spokesman bravely tried to shield me from the human wave, and a British cameraman who happened to be filming the scene kept yelling, "Keep moving, keep moving!" Had I stopped, I would have gotten stuck and the situation could have become extremely threatening. As it was, we were pushing with all our strength to get to the car, which had stopped at the closest possible spot. I was incredibly relieved once I was able to close the car door behind me.

On the drive to the hotel, I mentally took stock of the situation. My mental balance did not come out so badly. My leg had held up. I crossed the finish line, and I almost qualified for the second round. I encountered a few journalists in the hotel lobby, and no one quite knew whether they should be content or disappointed. For me the prevailing sensation was definitely one of contentment.

Luckily, I had planned ahead and brought along my downhill boots. Edi, who always counts on all eventualities as a matter of course, had the long skis in his luggage. Thus, there was nothing to keep me from trying the downhill after my first accomplishment. On the very same day, we moved to Lauterbrunnen, barely an hour away, where all the equipment was moved into the Wegeralp alpine train, which transported us directly up into the Jungfrau range.

January 15, 2003. Wengen fit into my comeback concept not only from a geographical point of view. The longest of all downhill classics with its lengthy gliding sections was ideal for the purpose of getting me used to the high speeds required for this race. My first time again on a downhill course was a strange feeling. I asked myself, "How will my leg react during the jumps? If I cross the Hundschopf passage incorrectly, I will crash down in the flat section." That was the last thing that my mended lower leg needed right now. I started out nice and easy and began to reacquaint myself with the speed and the jumps from the very first training run. During the second run I even had the fastest interval time for the Hundschopf passage.

I already knew during the run that I was quite fast, and I slowed down at the finish S. Yet I came in tenth, which earned me the bad starting number of twenty-one. This is how it works: In order to make the downhill as suspenseful as possible, the International Skiing Federation (FIS) had instituted a new rule during my absence according to which the top thirty contenders have to start in reverse order based on their times during the last training run. The one who was fastest during training starts with number thirty, the second fastest with number twenty-nine, and so on. Because the low numbers are the better ones during critical weather conditions, we are forced to conduct embarrassing slowdown maneuvers during the final training run so that we don't end up with the higher numbers.

Even though I messed up at my first trial with this new rule and came in too fast during the last training run, I did not let this mishap spoil my enjoyment of the event. I was in a jovial mood during the interviews, even if the questions repeated themselves with monotonous predictability. Thus I tried to bring some variety into the boring question-and-answer session with my answers. When I was asked about the Hundschopf jump, I quipped, "I was worried that my titanium rod was going to stick out of my boot and tear up the slope."

I was looking forward to the first of the two downhills, because I was used to giving it an extra boost during the actual race. But the relaxed feeling I had had during the training runs was completely gone as soon as I crossed the starting line. I tensed up, stopped fighting, and just kind of let myself drift across the finish line. Twenty-second place was a bitter disappointment. On my way out of the finish area, I saw a former colleague of mine sitting in a wheelchair. For the first time since his horrific crash in 2001 at Val d'Isère, Silvano Beltrametti was present in person at a ski race. We immediately hit it off and had a long talk. It was an impressive conversation; I can only admire Silvano for the joy he exudes after this grave turn of events. Our paths would be crossing frequently from then on.

This encounter let me completely forget my surroundings until my PR man reminded me that we had to get back to the hotel. In the meantime, however, all the shuttles had left. I was so annoyed about that, and about my mediocre performance, that I walked the mile and a half back to the hotel. That gave me a chance to think about everything in peace and quiet.

Okay, my gliding motions no longer worked as they had before the accident. Since the surgery, I no longer stand completely straight in the ski boot with my right foot. Instead, it points outward a bit. In addition, there is still a lack of sensation due to the damaged nerve tissue. Both of these handicaps have remained with me to this day. The longer the gliding passages, the more I have to grapple with these problems.

Yet, I was not ready to call it quits. I called Heini and complained, "I'm tired, worn-out. What should I do?" My trainer, who always comes up with something, got on the phone and mobilized all the glucose stores that were stocked at the medical center in Wengen. Our team doctor mixed the small ampoules in the right ratio into the saline solution, and late at night the fluid was dripping into my veins. My empty muscle cells were being replenished.

The next day, I was indeed doing better. I started off with a somewhat easygoing attitude. It was still dark as we slowly made our way up the mountain in the Jungfrau train. I decided with certainty, "Today, I'll ski as though I'm doing a relaxed training run." Edi had prepared yet another type of ski, and off I went. Seventh place during my third race, a dream result! With this feat, I convinced my critics for good. Karl Schranz, the only Austrian overall World Cup champion before me, had to revise his opinion, which he had published in the *Kronen Zeitung* the day before, by 180 degrees: "I was wrong," Karl confessed with sporting fairness in his column. "Hermann was able to reconnect with the racing circuit much faster than we would ever have thought him capable. Until Kitzbühel there aren't many, but still a few, days left in order to improve even more. This is going to be most interesting," he wrote as though predicting the future. ORF was jubilant over their 1.5 million viewers and a market share of 83 percent. That was a record for Wengen. "World Wonder Maier," I read in *Blick*, and I asked myself, "What will they write in case I should really win something this season?"

KITZBÜHEL IN CHAOS

January 20, 2003. The Hahnenkamm press chief had asked my coaching team again and again, "So, will Hermann be starting in Kitzbühel?" For me, this had never been an issue. As soon as I felt fit enough, I wanted to take every opportunity to qualify for the world championships in St. Moritz at the beginning of February. Kitzbühel was my last chance to do so. The schedule, with its training runs from Tuesday through Thursday, super-G on Friday, and the classic downhill race on Saturday, was ideal for my situation. I wanted to inch slowly toward my limit during the training runs and then really make a splash.

Hermann Maier and Kitzbühel: a love affair that was growing slowly but surely. I had canceled in 1998 in order not to jeopardize the Olympics; then 1999 brought a crash during the downhill sprint because I wanted too much: only eighth in the classic downhill, and out in the combination slalom; 2000 brought victory in the super-G, fourth in the downhill, third in the combination; in 2001, triumphant in the super-G and downhill within twenty-four hours. I would not have dreamed of ever topping that performance.

Kitzbühel, 2003. In a way, I was glad once again to be an active part of this mixture of myth, tradition, high-tech performance, fan hysteria, and showcase for the beautiful people of the world. I knew what was awaiting me: overcrowded hotel lobbies, VIP invitations, and PR appointments; closed-down driveways, narrow alleys, and attendants who strictly follow orders and prevent even winners from getting to the awards ceremony without the appropriate sticker on their windshield. So I put the ID tag around my neck, something I can afford to skip in every other World Cup location on earth, because the people there know my face by now. In Kitz, there are three times as many reporters as at any other race. I was fortunate to be able to prepare myself for the grand occasion in Oberndorf, three miles away from all the action. But you have to grant it to Kitzbühel: a perfectly prepped slope in any kind of weather, where the tough get going, and spectacular TV images that mesmerize millions of people around the globe.

In fact, I was in my element on Kitzbühel's downhill course. I did have a weak feeling in the pit of my stomach when I thought about the many left swerves and especially the long, diagonal downhill portion at the Hausbergkante. That would be the first sustained force exerted on my right leg, which still sported the titanium rod. During the first training run, everything was just about perfect. During the steepest portion of the descent, the radar showed that I had the fastest speed at 68.9 mph. At the final drop just before the finish line, we even accelerate up to 95 mph, but in accord with FIS whim, there is no radar there.

I was already looking forward to the second training run, because I wanted to test "my" line. Unfortunately, I did not get a chance. From then on, snow and fog turned the Hahnenkamm week into a weather nightmare. After Wednesday's training was canceled and the prognosis for Thursday did not offer any improvement, I went home to Flachau with Andy and Edi, where I conducted super-G time trials in heavy snowfall. The super-G that had been planned for Friday was canceled in the middle of the course inspection. Luckily, President Schröcksnadel was able to insist on a postponement until Monday after tough negotiations with ORF. Otherwise, I would have missed my last chance at qualifying for my favorite event.

On Saturday, Kitzbühel continued to be barraged by heavy snowfall. But the organizers wanted to hold the most prestigious of all downhill races at any cost. It was snowing and snowing, and the fog had settled down on the Hahnenkamm to stay. The race was pushed around all over the place. After almost three hours of waiting around, we were confronted with a foul compromise: extremely shortened racecourse, start at the "old corridor," so no "mouse trap" and no steep escarpment. What was left of the much-feared "shaft"? You get going up above and *wham*, you're at the finish. That was no real race for me, yet it would be counted as the classic Hahnenkamm downhill. They were allotting full points, full prize money. It reminded me of the eight-minute prologue at the Tour de France. Right away, people were saying, "The shorter course will favor Maier, since he is in poor condition."

"If only they knew," I thought. "Was I not the fastest during the training run? Did I not surprise everyone on the longest downhill a few days ago?" But that didn't help me much at this point. I tried to think in positive terms: "Even if I don't like the shortening of the racecourse, I'll still give it my very best!" So, I really stepped on it for seventy seconds. Once I had crossed the finish line, I felt like I hadn't done anything. Yet, sixth place was an astounding result. I was the third-best racer from Austria, and had made good use of my last chance during the last downhill before the world championships. All that, even though I once again had not taken maximum risk because of the compression right after the Hausbergkante. In fact, I had never dared to do that in Kitzbühel, not even during my downhill victory of 2001. Just as in Wengen, at the Minschkante. There are passages where you're better off not putting it all on the line and thus tempting fate. During the transverse passage I thought of my injured right leg, and during the prep for the final jump, I opened earlier. Even though I was thinking, "Stay down, stay down!" reason was telling me, "No, get up!"

That's why I was faster than Rahlves, the eventual winner, in the upper portion, but gave away more than half a second in the lower portion.

Immediately after the downhill I wanted to flee from the ski capital, which had in the meantime been flooded by a host of fans. No way was I willing to show up at the ORF studio as a "guest of honor" along with the best five competitors. I just wanted to get away. But I wasn't allowed to. I still had to make an appearance during the evening gala in the VIP tent because I had already made a prior commitment to a sponsor. I couldn't get away until 10:30, and I went straight to Flachau with Andy.

While the slalom racers were fighting through the gates in dense snowfall in Kitzbühel, I really had to train for the super-G one more time, which was madness in this kind of weather. After all, I hadn't skied a super-G in twenty-two months. I was still lacking the feeling, that complete confidence at the proper racing speed, which is enormously important especially in this event, where you have to make tighter turns, yet have almost the same speed as in a downhill race. In Flachau, on my home territory's slope, I got the conditions I was looking for. I also encountered the exact same weather conditions that I would have during the race itself a day later: fog as well as dense snowfall. I cruised through the gates almost as though blindfolded, and once again carefully inched toward my limits. Because I often exert myself more during the training runs than in the actual race, I ran the danger of crashing several times. But that was exactly what ended up giving me the cutting edge!

MY GREATEST VICTORY

January 27, 2003. Shortly after six o'clock, the nurse was knocking on my door. I looked out the window. Out of the dark night sky, big white snowflakes were falling. "Couldn't it stop by now?" I complained, while my right ankle was being massaged. Previously, I had always been the last one to crawl out of the sack, but now I had to endure the painful ankle-mobilization procedure before breakfast. After the treatment, I slipped into the breakfast room. On the table, a portable radio was crackling. "Please, not a cancellation!" I thought. Andy was already out on the slope for the jury inspection. He would inform us via radio immediately if the situation changed. But the radio remained silent.

As in days past, Knut was the one driving me past Kitzbühel via Reith up to the Fleckalmbahn. I took my warm-up skis and went to the slope inspection. Despite the poor weather, I was in a good mood. I had one of those "this is going to be your day" feelings.

Despite the critical weather situation, the organizers wanted badly to hold the race. The starting time had been pushed up to 10:30, the start interval between racers was shortened to seventy-five seconds, and the commercial breaks after racers number fifteen and twenty-two had been canceled. Thus, everything happened really fast.

It seemed to me as though the race had only just begun when I was standing at the starting line, number twenty-two. It was 521 days since my motorcycle accident. A strange feeling overcame me. "My first super-G, unbelievable!" Finally, I had the chance to show what I could do in my own event. The super-G is custom-tailored for my abilities. You have to have certain technical skills and experience in addition to a willingness to take risks. There are no trial runs during which you can experiment and try out your line. Only one slope inspection, and then you're on. You drill the transitions, the most important gate combinations into your brain, and come up with a line in your head. There are no boring gliding sections, just one technical passage after another. And lots of tight radii executed at top speed. Yes, this was my race! I had won almost every one of them. The last one I had won, however, was now a while back, on March 4, 2001, in Norway's Kvitfjell.

I catapulted myself out of the starting gate. Not as explosively as before my accident, when everything had functioned with an almost unreal certainty. I had to find my rhythm, which was not easy. Had I tried to transfer my aggressiveness to the skis as I used to, it would probably have slowed me down. My new tactic was starting to pay off, and I hit my stride. Now the fighting spirit had really seized me. "Okay, now is the time to step on it! But don't charge ahead like a battering ram." That sort of approach leads to disaster on the Streif. I had to fight. I tried to gather speed at every one of the gates, and caught the upper passages nice and clean. Only one time I overlooked a small snow mound, and my right ski was lifted up beneath me. I was able to make a correction right away, though. Most of the time, those small interludes, which are such a boon to the spectators, are a good sign. They let you know that you're traveling fast. I took the Hausbergkante with a measured amount of risk. From then on, it was nothing but a struggle, incredibly taxing, little visibility, and the gates awfully close together. It got loud inside my helmet. "This is a descent!" I thought, while I was making my way through the gates in the dense snowfall. Often, you only have a tiny fraction of a second to make the right decision. Since the allotted time for the slope inspection had not been enough for me once again, I almost took a wrong turn in the lower portion. Just as in the downhill, I lost precious fractions of seconds there. When I saw the number "1" light up next to my time of 1:20.48 in the finish area, I stuck out my tongue in my typical victor's pose. Inside of me, everything was screaming with relief. I was jubilant, for I was sure: "Now they *have* to take me along to the world championships!"

I was a long way from winning the race, though. Up above, there were nine racers who could pose a danger to me. I looked up toward the Hausbergkante as though in a trance. There was Christoph Gruber. I counted along during the last seconds of his run and sighed a breath of relief. 1:20.59. Grubi was slower than I by only eleven hundredths of a second. "A close shave," I thought. "If the next skier comes this close, I wonder whether I'll even end up among the top three!" But the remaining racers all had bigger lags. Eberharter made for a suspenseful run, but then "+0.15 seconds" showed up on the display board, and third place.

I realized what had happened. "Unbelievable, I won!" And in such inclement weather to boot. Not in my wildest dreams could I have counted on this! For a few moments, I completely forgot about the world around me. There were a thousand things going through my head. The accident, the first steps, all that hard work. I felt immeasurable gratitude toward all those who had a part in making this possible for me. I realized that I had accomplished something unique! Not only did I feel like crying, I really cried. "My biggest victory!" I stammered into the TV microphone during my first flash interview. Nothing could top this. Not even my Olympic victory after the crash of the century in Nagano 1998. As though in a trance, I stumbled across the finish area, where I could make out my mother standing on the other side of the barricade among the loyal Herminator fans underneath the lucky-pig banner. A thick layer of snow had collected on her wide-brimmed hat. We hugged each other. In such moments I know where I belong. No big words are needed. What had this woman gone through in the past twenty-two months? The worry about her boy, my moodiness, the mean defamations. She had witnessed close up how hard I had worked during this whole time, how I suffered setbacks time and again. She had never doubted my comeback and my ability to win once again. But that it would happen so quickly! If you work hard, are willing to make some sacrifices, and never cease to believe in yourself, then, with luck, everything will end up coming back to you at some point.

I remembered my humble beginnings, when I failed to make the Austrian Ski Federation team. Even back then, the good side prevailed. Even back then I knew, "I will make it, no matter what the others are saying."

Slowly I again became aware of my surroundings. One by one, people were struggling to get through to congratulate me. Andy, who had been there for me in all kinds of weather, at any time of day, during each and every snow training; Edi, who had spent more time with my skis than with his family; Schröcksi, who had always believed in my comeback and had helped me along time and again with his paternal advice; Toni Giger, who had kept open the door for me to the federation team; alpine director Hans Pum: They were all there on that memorable morning.

I was really starting to fall in love with Kitzbühel. Everything was different on that Monday morning. The VIPs and drinkers were gone, and only the true fans remained. The grandstands that usually held the hangers-on were now occupied by rejoicing school kids. I suddenly felt like I was at a real sports event. And I was surprised at how many fans had gone to the trouble of coming to root for us on this normal workday despite the numerous postponements.

In the finish area, I was being shuttled from one television station to the next. I wanted to make time for the newspaper reporters as well. Many of them had accompanied me since the beginning of my career, and I could feel how they were rejoicing along with me. A victory podium was being put up right there. While the national anthem was played, I once again got goose bumps. My eyes became moist again, and I sent a short prayer of thanks heavenward.

I still had to go to the international press conference in the media center. Because most of the journalists were filling their newspapers with the emotional statements I had made in the finish area, they let me go again after just a few minutes. I still had to get back to the hotel, pack, and get back to Flachau. Back home, the mayor had quickly and with minimal notice organized an evening reception along with a brass band, TV coverage, festive speeches, and everything that is part of such an occasion. I just *had* to show up on time.

I sat next to Andy in the car and took a deep breath. During the drive home I finally had some time to myself. No pictures, no autographs. But the five o'clock news on the radio brought me back to reality. "Did I really just hear that?" I shook my head and looked questioningly at Andy. There was the doctor who had left the Olympic Training Center three months after my accident being brought out of nowhere back into the equation. He was said to have had a significant part in my comeback victory. "Unbelievable, the people who have to promote themselves," I remarked with annoyance. Sitting next to me was someone who truly had a big part in this success, and he had not even been mentioned. I wondered how this pronouncement had come about. During such moments I find it difficult to take the ephemeral, superficial media reports seriously. Normally, I don't let these kinds of things get to me. I try to push them far away and not let them bother me. Unfortunately, though, this sort of unsubstantiated coverage has an effect on public opinion in my country. Moreover, it is difficult to counter something once it has been uttered. Corrections usually show up in small print. After all, who likes to admit that they were wrong?

With one stroke, my life had taken a decisive turn. Once again, I was a performance athlete, and as such a guarantee for success. I no longer garnered compassionate looks. On the way home I was able to walk into the highway rest stop with my head held high. I was once again there for something that I work toward, that I live for. I was once again allowed to carry on my profession with complete self-confidence. I had already shown the proper attitude in Adelboden; it just hadn't worked out quite yet. Thank goodness the victory was only thirteen days in the making.

When I got home, all of Flachau was out in the streets. Autographs, interviews, pictures. If I could have, I would have shaken hands with every single person out there. But I had to get to the improvised *Zeit-im-Bild* outdoor TV studio next to the Achertjet valley relay station, where I was being spliced live into the news broadcast along with President Schröcksnadel. Later on, when we were sitting and relaxing at the Reslwirt hotel together, suddenly my cell phone rang. It was Arnold Schwarzenegger:

"My heartiest congratulations!" he said. After a few admiring sentences, Arnie added, "Celebrate unstintingly." He could count on that!

More than a few days of rest was not possible, however. I barely had three days left before my departure for St. Moritz. One was blocked out for the Olympic Training Center, and I was also planning on doing some time trials.

January 31, 2003. During my trip to St. Moritz, we took a break in the South Tyrol to do some giant slalom training. Since more than one hundred requests for interviews had reached my management since my victory in Kitz, the ski federation had organized a press conference, in which my super-G colleagues Stephan Eberharter, Christoph Gruber, and Hannes Reichelt also took part. I still had half an hour. I took advantage of the window of time to make myself comfortable in my hotel room. I always put great emphasis on that. I even dare to claim that I am the most orderly member of the ski team. My room is always the tidiest, and everything has its place, from my ski boots to my helmet and goggles as well as the electrolyte energy drinks. Since I am usually in a big hurry, I hate hunting around for stuff. I even got a chance to lie down on my bed for a few minutes and just breathe before my press spokesman gently knocked on the door. "Let's go to the press conference," he said. "A few folks should be there by now."

We walked past the reporters' cubicles and the area for the print journalists. I was amazed at how quiet everything was. Two days before the beginning of the ski world championships, and everything still seemed abandoned. How wrong I was once again: All the reporters had squeezed into the big press conference hall. I could not believe it. A jumble of voices, a barrage of flashes, camera teams jockeying for position. I had only seen such scenes on television thus far, when American presidents hold their state-of-the-union address. Completely perplexed, I asked myself, "What in the world is this all about? What kind of world championships is this going to be?" Once I had regained my composure, I was glad about the reverberations that my comeback had obviously triggered. Especially since the word on the street had been that the sport of skiing was on the decline.

WITH TEARS IN MY EYES

The first live TV interview at ORF with Rainer Pariasek

RAINER PARIASEK: Hermann Maier, it's outrageous! A further chapter toward immortality in the realm of sports. A trite question, but I will pose it nevertheless: What is going on inside of you right now?

HERMANN MAIER (with tears in his eyes): I don't really know what to say, I am so surprised! I would never have thought that it could work out so quickly, and I am beside myself with happiness.

PARIASEK: Could it be that there were a few tears in your eyes earlier?

MAIER: Yes, indeed. I was deeply touched. After my accident . . . one of my most beautiful triumphs, if not the most beautiful.

PARIASEK: You would really classify it as such, even with your Olympic victories and world championships titles?

MAIER: Yes, completely. After this injury, after it was looking so grave, and all this now after such a short time span. I can only say thank you to everyone, a beautiful feeling!

PARIASEK: How much were you hoping that the race would take place today?

MAIER: I thought, "If it doesn't take place, then we have to come up with something else." This year, only a few super-Gs have taken place. My whole life I've always made the best of every opportunity.

PARIASEK: How did you feel while Stephan Eberharter was racing?

MAIER: I was quite content there in the finish area when I was still in the lead after Steff came in. I had realized that he was in the lead in the upper portion. I thought, "If I end up second, that's a great result too." But a victory is that much sweeter.

PARIASEK: It is almost like a script for a Hollywood story. You already knew that your trajectory was upward. But did you realize that you could already win?

MAIER: I was hoping I could. During the downhill, I knew things are happening. I skied with the utmost concentration and did very well on that short course. That's when I realized that something might work out. I hoped that the super-G would take place. The slope was really good. Visibility could have been better, but I made it through pretty well. The skis also performed very well. Everything has to come together just right.

PARIASEK: Your comeback in Adelboden was only thirteen days ago. How were the past two weeks? Were you aware of time passing, or did it all happen as though in a dream?

MAIER: In Adelboden I was still a bit unsure. I wasn't quite able to get into it fully. I didn't know for sure. I thought, "What exactly am I doing here?" Mentally, I had a really hard time. In Wengen I wanted to tear everything up during the race, but that backfired on me. Then I said to myself, "I'll just ski more relaxed," and seventh place resulted from that, then sixth here at the downhill, and now, suddenly, victory. An unbelievable upward trend, and that after such a long break.

PARIASEK: Who were the most important people on your way back?

MAIER: I don't really want to mention them right now. Otherwise, I'll forget a few, and then they'll be upset. I can only say thank you to everyone, especially those who've stuck by me. There weren't many left who were still giving me a chance.

PARIASEK: You said after the downhill, "The hand brake is still skiing along a bit." Was it completely released today?

MAIER: Yes, I think so. Especially considering the poor visibility, I can't complain. If I said I didn't attack fully, that would surely be an untruth. I gave it my best; you can tell from the results. All the competitors were good racers; I was just a bit luckier.

It certainly didn't look like it on that day. Some of my team colleagues were a bit peeved because all the spotlights were on me, but most of them reacted in a positive manner. "If that wasn't a motivating factor for my young colleagues who are allowed to take part in this championship . . ." I thought as I sat down at the podium. My name tag had long been knocked over in the hubbub. After the photographers had settled down, the press coordinator opened the microphone for the obligatory question-and-answer session, and I must admit that I truly savored all the interest in me four days after my triumph in Kitzbühel.

February 2, 2003. Bright sunshine, −4 degrees Fahrenheit. Marvelous conditions for a super-G. I was fully motivated. Will I be able to crown my comeback with a medal in the world championships? Unlike my opponents, I had never before skied on this mountain, which boasted more transitions than any other course. Yet I resolved, "I am certainly going to up the ante!" And that's exactly how I started out. Above, I skied really perfectly. I kept to my short line. However, our hand was exposed. Even in Kitzbühel I had used an old, carefully tried and tested ski prototype, unlike my colleagues, who were using their various brand-name skis. I was using the old skis because I had won on them even before my accident. I was not yet strong enough for the new type of ski. The old ski worked better in St. Moritz. But in the meantime, Eberharter, too, was skiing on the same model of the older generation of skis. Nevertheless, no one was able to keep up with me in the upper portion. Then, I made a decisive mistake by thinking, "Now I can let up a bit." Such an approach should backfire in the shortened middle portion. I started to drift prior to my turns and paid attention only to maintaining my momentum all the way to the end. But then I managed to take a completely wrong approach in the lower portion. Normally, you orient yourself on the tracks of the skiers who have gone ahead of you. But I wanted to push through my stubborn ways and instead chose a completely new line. At the place where everyone else had kept an inside line, I headed toward the outer gate instead and realized right away, "I shouldn't have done that. Now I've lost my momentum." I had lost the last of my speed and given away the victory for good. At the finish I saw that I had the same time as Bode Miller. I patted him on the back and said, "Bode, we should be happy with silver or bronze, if we even win a medal. The other racers up above can hardly be dumb enough not to take the medals from us." But that is exactly what happened, and I congratulated Stephan Eberharter on his victory. I knew that I had squandered my chance carelessly, and I alone was to blame for this defeat; in the lower portion I had lost sixty-four hundredths of a second compared to the winner. During the last forty-one seconds of the race, "Eberharter ripped the gold medal from the Herminator's neck," as the *Kronen Zeitung* characterized the scenario, and they got it right. In retrospect, I really cannot complain about silver such a short time after my comeback. Who would have thought?

In fact, I could have gone home and had the titanium rod removed from my lower leg. But I still wanted to give it a try in the downhill. Here, too, my lack of experience on this course was not exactly an advantage. On top of that, several unlucky circumstances all came together. The internal ski federation qualification should have happened during the second of three training runs. But the training was canceled due to inclement weather and I was quickly nominated. In addition to Klaus Kröll, the once-victorious ski racer Andi Schifferer had been left out. Schiffi was so vocal in his disgruntlement that he triggered a nationwide discussion about the connection between merit and the right to race. I tried to stay out of this discussion as much as possible. Since this was my first time in such a situation, it was important to me to discuss the matter personally with my former roommate.

During the return from the downhill training runs, there was an incident on the slope. I had to dodge a tourist, landed in a hole, and took a hit. That was close! But my leg held up even during this incident. The next day, I stepped into my boot and noticed that it was broken above the heel. I called Gerhard, the Lange serviceman. "Now things are critical!" Gerhard improvised by stabilizing the severed parts with two screws. Afterward, both of us spent a whole afternoon to get the boot race-ready once again. I know this sounds crazy, but I did not have a single pair of adequate backup boots with me. Because of the injury I had tested only the one pair of special boots. I had to use them in the downhill at any rate. Not the best of conditions for attacking a race with extremely long jumps. And moreover, the cobbled-together footwear had to protect my injured right leg.

I ended up coming in eighth and missed the bronze medal by only twenty-five hundredths of a second. Unfortunately, I had not been prepared to give it my all and take the last ounce of risk. If you're not completely fit on a physical level, that really affects your psyche as well. It was a combination that would take its revenge. I was glad for Michael Walchhofer, my training buddy from Obertauern. Somehow I was relieved that I didn't have to go to any awards ceremonies or press conferences. I enjoyed not being handed around on a silver platter like a trophy at the fair. For the first time I stayed in the finish area, and it was no big deal. Along with my trainers, a handful of fans, and a few cans of beer, we celebrated the end of a short but very eventful season. I was glad that it was over. The extremely long jumps had been so hard on me that I could feel every one of my injured bones. As I was sitting there with my beer, I found myself thinking ahead to the next season. "Just look at how well things went this year. Now the rod will be removed, and I still have a whole summer ahead of me. Who knows what will happen in a year's time?"

10

ALL GOOD THINGS
COME IN FOURS

During the exhausting and involved comeback season, I had had to turn a deaf ear to all female callers. There just wasn't enough time left in the day to invest in one of life's more pleasant aspects. But as soon as we started celebrating in St. Moritz, once all the competition-induced pressure had ceased, I felt free and unburdened. Finally, there was room for private feelings. I savored this for several weeks at least. I took the time to fly south for a few days, and this time, it wasn't Heini who was my companion. I had met a young woman who meant a great deal to me. But that's where I will stop with the private revelations. To be honest, I am surprised at how much personal information I have divulged in this book. I feel like my comeback story and the exciting things I was allowed to experience in the course of my career are interesting enough all by themselves. Thus, unlike some other writers, I do not feel compelled to expose my private affairs or seek scandalous stories. My experiences are much too special for that, and the affected women do not deserve such treatment.

February 15, 2003. I had another checkup, and after consulting Artur, set a date for surgery. Now that the comeback adventure, including the world championships, had worked out so beautifully, it was time to relieve my right lower leg of the titanium rod that was still implanted deep inside. I realized that this procedure would cost me a few weeks of training. But when was there a better time to do it than right now? There was still enough time afterward to prepare for my next big goal, which was a rather modest one: to compete for an entire racing season. During the last few days before my surgery I was goofing around with friends from Flachau and Obertauern when I got the call from Andy: "We could use one more sparring partner for the giant slalom training. Feel up to it?"

Michi Waldhofer, my training buddy from Obertauern and new downhill world champion, was to start at the World Cup finals in Kvitfjell in the giant slalom. He did not want to fly to Norway without knowing where he stood. Thus, I let them talk me into skiing a few training runs on the World Cup course in Flachau. It happened at one of the last gates: I repositioned my weight, leaned into the curve, and slipped. I still wanted to brace myself on the steep slope, when *wham!* I felt a sharp, intense pain. "Damn it!" I yelled as I lay in the snow, "I've thrown out my shoulder." Michi and a friend were helping me up. Walchi took me to the hospital. We were listening to music and I was hunkered down in the passenger seat, pretending to be too tough to feel the pain. There I was again, at the Aufmesser clinic, in the very same room where I had received first aid on my shredded leg twenty-three months earlier. This time around, I somehow had to get out of my racing suit before they could take an X-ray. That was such an overwhelming endeavor that all the nurses had to stand in to peel me out of my one-piece suit. Compared to this, the process of having my shoulder set was an almost pleasant procedure. At any rate, the season was now over for good.

"What are we going to tell the press?" Harald wanted to know. "Not a word!" I grouched. After my lightning comeback and six weeks in the limelight, I did not have the slightest inclination for publicity of this kind. There's too much whining going on in public anyway.

I had to cancel a ZDF Sportstudio appearance in Mainz, Germany, which had been planned for that evening. We asked the German TV station not to reveal the reason for my absence. They graciously acceded to our request. It is hard to imagine that such news would have remained secret here in Austria.

February 26, 2003.   A year and a half after my emergency surgery, I was privileged to revisit the—now new—trauma center in Salzburg as a patient. Compared to my first hospital stay, when construction vehicles and concrete mixers had rattled around in front of my window, I felt like I was on vacation. I inspected the recently completed complex from a bricklayer's point of view, and I was impressed. I sat on my pleasant patio in the afternoon sun and thought, "It feels just like a hotel here!"

Even if I was here "only" to have my stabilization rod removed, my mental state was not exactly one of relaxation. The week before, I had consulted three doctors on account of my displaced shoulder, and the tenor was, "You should have surgery." But I refused. I was convinced that my musculature was strong enough on its own to heal properly. Besides, I was spooked by the thought of being impaired on both top and bottom.

Thus we stuck with just removing the rod, which was no small feat. Artur cut, hammered, and chiseled around on me for almost two hours. It turned out to be a veritable battle, since, as Artur told me later, the bone had grown firmly around the rod. During the operation, the patella tendon, which connects the kneecap with the head of the femur, was split down the middle. The fourteen-inch rod, which was embedded in the bone marrow of my tibia, was pulled out through the resulting hole. Once again I awoke from the anesthesia as though from a drug-induced coma. Completely confused, I dug out my cell phone, dialed random numbers, and stammered senseless mumbo jumbo. I cannot remember a single word I said, but judging from the hints of my friends, it must have been some pretty crazy stuff. Once the painkillers began to lose their effectiveness, my knee began to hurt like mad. The stitches were so tight that I could not even think about bending my knee. Walking was out of the question.

"The pain is completely normal," said Artur. "One or two weeks and it will subside." Instead of a cast, I got a white, superlight synthetic brace with holes in it. "You keep that on for two weeks," Artur told me at my release. "Yeah, sure," I said. I was barely home when I took the thing off. I felt too silly wearing it. I wanted to feel like a halfway healthy athlete.

"I just won a silver medal," I thought. "I don't want to wander about with such a lump on my leg. I've had enough of that." Back home, I produced the six-hundred-dollar titanium rod and showed it to my brother: "Look, I took this home as a trophy!" After all, that rod had accompanied me during a victory in Kitzbühel. Today, the trusty implement can be admired next to my Olympic medals as the main attraction at the Herminator fan shop in Flachau.

I was limping around impatiently on my stiff knee. When my goal is to work toward top racing condition, I can be patient. I have a plan, which I carry out over the course of weeks and months. But with things like this, where it's a matter of healing, it can't happen fast enough for me. If Artur says, "one to two weeks," then I am hoping for four to five days. I felt like the problems with my knee would drag on forever. I did everything feasible to speed up the healing process. Almost daily I showed up in Obertauern for therapy, and at home I treated my knee with the PAP IMI wonder machine.

April 11, 2003. During the traditional World Cup end-of-season gala in Salzburg, I smiled broadly, displaying my brand-new braces to the surprised reporters. Since I had only a few PR appointments at the time, I indulged myself with this luxury to correct the incisors that had been damaged during my motorcycle accident. The pain in my knee was still there. It got so bad sometimes that I treated myself to the occasional Tramal pill.

At any rate, at the beginning of May, I was ready to put in a few end-of-winter ski runs in Obertauern, just as I had done the year before. I had expected to perceive a wonderful sensation of freedom, since I would have more range of motion in my ankle now that the stabilization rod was gone. However, it was once again apparent that I was expecting too much, too soon. In addition, there was pain every time I bent my knees. The patella tendon has to withstand enormous pressure when you ski. Even the smallest sort of irritation causes problems. Even at this point I could guess that these problems would accompany me throughout the following season. Nevertheless, I was yearning to commence with the training buildup toward my comeback season, and I started doing endurance-training sessions in Obertauern. During the morning, I stepped into the pedals, and in the afternoon, I went running around the soccer field in Flachau. The tendon was still hurting. But I had to get through this.

I had problems with biking as well, and never was able to apply more than two hundred watts of resistance. Yet I could tell how my endurance was improving. But I was looking for some variety. Thus, as in the year before, I included a week of bicycling in Tuscany in the buildup to the ski season. It went really well. When I got back, I felt like a cycling pro. So I said, almost in jest, "Heini, why don't you sign me up for the Tour de France again? I'm going to badger them until they finally let me bike!" I gave no more thought to my joke.

June 11, 2003.   I was sitting on my ergometer in Obertauern when Knut handed me the cell phone. I gave my press agent a questioning look. "What now?" Normally, there are no interruptions during my training. On the other end was French journalist Patrick Lang, a friend of the deputy director of the Tour de France. "We did it! You are going to be in the Tour!" A childhood dream had come true for me. I would get to take part in the biggest cycling event in the world. One minute before the racer with starting number one, I was to open the four-mile prologue to the centennial Tour.

All at once, things got a bit hectic in my usually serene training environment. What does the prologue take? Where could we get a time trial bike? Where do I get fitted for my outfit? Who will give me insider tips? Who can I work out with, and most of all, how should I work out? I had a scant three weeks. During that time, I had to drum up support for Salzburg's bid for the 2010 Olympics, and during the week before the prologue, of all weeks, I had to travel to a congress of the International Olympic Committee (IOC) in Prague. All that was not exactly conducive to my Tour de France preparations. There was another problem: The Tour date coincided with the traditional Milka Chocolate festival in

Bludenz, near the Swiss border. I had already been committed there con-
tractually for sack races, wooden ski skidding, and similar merriment. As
usual, ski federation president Schröcksnadel helped me out of my
pickle. He negotiated a compromise. I would show my face via a satellite
connection from Paris; in addition, I would be riding in a specially tai-
lored purple Milka racing suit.

For a while, everything was top secret. The first to be informed about
our plan was Schröcksnadel's friend, former bike racer Wolfgang Stein-
mayr, who was without much ado declared "team captain." The former
"Race around Austria" winner had procured a time trial bike from the
Italian Carrera team. We met in Carinthia, where I took the splendid vehicle into my care. It weighed a mere 16.75 pounds and had a black, full-
carbon frame, tri-spoke front wheel, and a disc wheel in back, with
Campagnolo components. The gear ratio was 55:11, which enabled me to
cover more than ten meters per pedal stroke. Even though it was already
dark, I spun a few trial loops in the parking lot. On my tight schedule, I
had only two days left for "real" training with this exclusive racing machine. Bicycling pro Peter Wrolich, who was convalescing at the time, accompanied me to the Lungau region, where we took off on lightly
traveled level roads. After only a few meters, I became disillusioned. The
bike wasn't at all a good fit for me. No wonder, since my stature can
scarcely be compared to that of a bicycling pro, who on average is lighter
than me by about sixty-five pounds. In my frustration, I got myself a hack-
saw and corrected the time trial handlebars. With this improvisation I
was able to improve my position on the bike considerably. Yet I saw no
chance of really transmitting my strength onto the asphalt.

July 2, 2003. Salzburg had applied to host the 2003 Olympic Winter
Games, and I had been chosen as ambassador. Canadian hockey legend
Wayne Gretzky had been picked to represent our competition, Vancouver, British Columbia. I was hoping that my name would help the appli-
cation. The points on our side were a competitive edge and a presentation
that really appealed to the emotional side. I had to give my speech in

English. This proved to be a more difficult task than I had at first imagined. I was not allowed to speak colloquially, and because of that I had the proverbial blackout during the final rehearsal. After a few sentences I fell as silent as a fish, and finally left the podium without a word. An awkward silence ensued among our delegation, and even the attractive assistant of IOC president Jacques Rogge, who was in charge of the order of events, did not know how to react to this embarrassing situation. Everyone desperately wanted to help me, but I just disappeared into my room to practice. When it came down to the wire, I held my speech in front of the assembled IOC team and an audience of millions of people in front of their televisions that made everyone's ears perk up. It was a speech that was, in contrast to my colleague Gretzky, given without any notes. I guess I am the competitive type.

Unfortunately, all that ended up making precious little difference. Salzburg was eliminated, and Vancouver got the nod ahead of South Korea. This type of political wrangling is hard to understand for an athlete. I have to completely let go of something like that right away. It's the same as when I read a poor newspaper article about myself. "Don't get worked up about it. That only costs you unnecessary energy." Energy I sorely needed for the Tour de France. From Prague, I flew back to Salzburg on a private jet along with "Kaiser" Franz Beckenbauer and leisurely got onto my bike that very same evening. The next day I conducted my final training, and then we were off to Paris.

July 5, 2003, 3:47 P.M.   I am sitting on the yellow start ramp underneath the Eiffel Tower. "Weird, this thing is much smaller than it looks on TV," I am thinking. Then I can hear my name sounding through the speakers: *"Bienvenue champion d'Olympique Hermann Maier!"* The starting-line official, a small white-haired man, is holding on to my bike seat and counting down while indicating the seconds with his fingers: *"Cinq, quatre, trois, deux, un . . ."* Now I am rolling down the ramp, and I start to pedal as though there were no tomorrow. Behind me, there's a coaching vehicle with my name on it. I feel like a real Tour pro! They all warned me about the same thing—Heini; our team captain; the nice professionals from the Gerolsteiner team, whom I was allowed to join for my warm-ups; even Chris Carmichael, Lance Armstrong's trainer—"Don't start out too fast!" Heini's words are still resounding in my ears: "Be especially careful during the first incline. Otherwise, you'll come down with acidosis." Even I know that much. But the adrenaline rush that seizes me at this moment propels me forward without mercy. I am beating into the pedals, my pulse is up around 180 within just a few seconds. After not even two minutes, my hellish initial speed is starting to take its revenge on me. My muscles are starting to burn; I can virtually feel the lactic acid pouring into every fiber. At least it's downhill by now. I am doing a good forty-five miles per hour when I feel my whole body being shaken up by the cobblestone pavement. Panic! These jolts! Will the Pantani bike withstand my weight under that sort of impact? I feel like my thighs are about to explode. Completely beaten, I veer toward the final curve to the right. But the people are screaming and cheering me on. *"Allez, Hermann!"* Let's go! Once more, I give my last and best effort. I am speeding toward the finish and clenching my fists. Because one thing I know for sure: I did not make a fool of myself! There was no official time kept for my run, but Heini was my timekeeper. It took me eight minutes and forty-five seconds to cover the four miles. As I found out later, that was only seventy-nine seconds more than the prologue winner, Bradley McGee; I was sixty-five seconds behind the later Tour winner, Lance Armstrong, while Gerrit Glomser was twenty-nine seconds faster. The slowest bicycling pro was only thirteen seconds ahead of me.

Once I got back to the Gerolsteiner support post, I rolled past the U.S. Postal Team bus. Lance Armstrong, as the winner from last year, still had over an hour before he had to get onto the racecourse as the last competitor to start this year. He had watched my run on the monitor and jumped out of the bus. "Where's the Herminator?" he asked and extended his hand. "How long did you take?" "Eight forty-five, but I could have gone faster."

"That's fantastic! If you keep going at this rate, some of my colleagues will have to fear for their jobs pretty soon." Then, Lance wanted to see my injured leg; once he saw the bulge on my calf, he just shook his head: "Unbelievable that you can win races with this thing!" Then things got serious for the tall Texan, and he started into his warm-up routine. I was somewhat envious of his private sphere. When I was doing my warm-up an hour ago, the photo reporters, camera people, and journalists had crowded across the barrier and were continuously jabbering at me. And that was not all. Former ice queen Katerina Witt had kept me so long with her live appearance as an ARD reporter that I almost didn't make it into the warm-up circle to limber up on my bike.

Sure, I had expected more, since I know that I can do better. With a bit more time to prepare, better-adjusted equipment, a rounder pedal stroke, and especially if I had listened to the experts, I surely could have improved my time by half a minute. Even as it was, I was surprised by the media's response. I must have stepped into the pedals with some persuasion. According to an opinion poll by the Austrian magazine *Sportwoche*, 83 percent of readers believed that "skiing god Hermann Maier would triumph even as a bicycling pro."

In truth, it was not my time that mattered in the prologue, but the fact that I was allowed to be part of it. I had never before taken part in a bike race, let alone ever sat on such a flimsy time trial bike. It was a singular experience, maybe my most satisfying outside of the sport of skiing. I was impressed by the precision with which this gigantic event, called the Tour de France, was conducted. The next morning, when the entire Tour entourage had moved to the outskirts of the city in front of the Stade de France, I was strolling through the athletes' quarters. I marveled at the enormous ring of vehicles, was amazed at the flexible, mobile infrastructure. There is everything you need in this rolling village, from the newspaper stand all the way to amenities such as a barbershop. Sensational! "The International Skiing Federation could take some hints from these guys," I thought, and secretly envied my fellow athletes.

"Maybe I should do more bike races in the summertime," I thought, because that type of exertion was ideal for me at the time. It helped me to feel once again something like a racing instinct. Once the ski season is over, and after the eternally long summer break, you lose that sort of thing quickly. My body was already displaying withdrawal symptoms for such total effort. After all, I had broken off the World Cup season five weeks ahead of my colleagues.

August 3, 2003.   As opposed to years past, when we spent half the summer in the Chilean winter, this time around we were off to New Zealand, more specifically, South Island. After the hectic weeks leading up to our departure, I savored the peace and quiet and the lack of press engagements, which were kept to a minimum. I was concentrating exclusively on what I had come to do here in the first place: ski training. I liked the idyllic and incredibly beautiful landscape, the green hills dotted with herds of sheep. You can't ask for more if you really want to relax. Finally, I had time to get back to myself. At home, I rarely get that chance. In the end, it is this sort of serenity that is so very important when it comes time to gather strength for the upcoming strenuous season.

September 3, 2003.   Back in Austria, each week was packed with press and PR engagements. As usual, everything happened all at once. Thus, I had to invest two days in an advertisement shoot with ski federation partner Iglo at the Stanglwirt in Going. Training had to continue just the same. I was not even able to take a lunch break. While we were sitting outdoors on the patio furniture that had been placed there specifically for the shoot and I was inviting myself to a quick hamburger, a doping control team was suddenly standing in front of me. I had to interrupt my lunch and look for a bathroom. Since there was none nearby, I went to pee into a plastic cup in the driveway. While I was thus taking care of business, the producer called us back to continue the filming. I was grumpy and hungry. Nonetheless, I had to smile for the camera. I was holding freshly prepared Iglo frozen food in my hand, none of which I was allowed to eat.

PR responsibilities take a lot of time, time that is taken away from my training. In order to keep that loss to a minimum, I try to travel by helicopter as often as possible. My sponsors show a lot of understanding in this regard. I make good use of the flight itself to accumulate flying hours. However, time and again complications arise. For example, my helmet sponsor, Raiffeisen, was planning a season's preview press conference in Vienna's Albertina museum, where Albrecht Dürer's famous painting of a rabbit was being exhibited. That day the weather was so crazy that we had to take a huge detour via Salzburg. Time and again it looked as though we would be halted by thick drifts of fog. We were being shaken about until the flight instructor finally insisted on taking over the controls. In the Vienna metro area we finally had to land, since Knut was sitting in the backseat and threatening to throw up unless we touched down right away. Because the fog was right in front of us, we made two spirals, and that was it. My companion quickly dug out his backpack, which contained a time trial helmet signed by Lance Armstrong for a "Light into Darkness" charity auction, removed the helmet, and then threw up into the impromptu air sickness bag. Forty-five seconds later, we had pulled off the emergency landing. I had never before seen such a pale white face. We were standing in a gravel pit and it was raining. Right then, a rickety truck pulled up, which must have been at least as old as I. The driver offered to take us to the next highway rest stop. I climbed up into the cab and sat down among snow chains and a pair of construction gloves, which immediately evoked memories from my former life as a bricklayer. A Raiffeisen driver picked us up from the rest stop and drove us to the press conference. Because Vienna's western highway entrance had been blocked by an accident, the last kilometer to our destination took a full hour to cover. I finally showed up in the Albertina at 12:22 P.M., a full hour and fifty-two minutes after the official beginning, and admired the handsome rabbit. Not even he believed our tale of travel woe. Once again I was late through no fault of my own.

I had a hard time squeezing my conditioning and strength training in among the ski federation gala, photo shoots, charity golf tournament, sponsor evenings, the traditional ski media day in Vienna, and the most important TV and press appointments.

There was only one topic for the press before the World Cup preseason: "The duel: Maier versus Eberharter." No story was too dumb for the reporters, and we played right along. During the "Day of Sports" on Vienna's Heldenplatz, they had us pose in a boxing ring wearing boxing gloves; we sat down together at the TV studio, and if we were unavailable as a matched set, they helped themselves with cut-and-paste splices. During the interviews, I tried to keep expectations low. The previous season, I had come back as a sick man, and compared to then, I was looking markedly better. But at that point I really could not predict how my convalescing leg would react to the ongoing stress of an entire season. Two or three races on one weekend, training runs ahead of that, eternal drives, flights, time changes—these are all exertions that are hard even on a healthy person. Despite the first few race attempts a year ago, I still regarded the coming one as the true "comeback season," in which I would not be able to gauge until November or December whether I was in shape to go all the way to the World Cup finals. I was yearning for the snow and was truly glad once the glacier training was finally under way.

October 22, 2003. I wanted to get that cutting edge on the World Cup slope in Sölden for the preseason start on October 26. I was dominating the giant slalom time trials with my newfound aggression, and like magic I managed to pull one best time after another out of the glacier snow. Benni Raich was amazed. "Outrageous! You're skiing like a young man!"

"That's fine with me," I thought and let myself be pumped up by his praise. I was trying to up the ante some more when it happened: I got onto the inside of a gate with my right hand and the flag did not come loose in the process, which is not that uncommon during training. I got hung up, was lifted out, and slammed down onto some lumps of ice. My arm and ribs hurt terribly. I skied down and joked, "I guess I broke a rib!" I didn't suspect that I had really been rather seriously injured. That same day I was supposed to go to Salzburg to the "Night of Sports" to receive the special Comeback of the Year award that had clearly been created just for me.

The pain was getting worse by the hour and I slowly began to panic. "Sunday I'm off to a start in Sölden. What do I do now?" No one knew of my problem, and I put on a happy face despite the pain. But when I leaned down to my ski boots after the slope inspection on the day before the race and came up against my rib again, the pain once again pulsed through me. From that moment on, nothing worked right. I could not even push off with both poles, so I arrested my momentum and skied up to my trainer. "Andy, I think I broke my rib!" Something like that always happens when you're least equipped to deal with it. First the knee, then the rib. My coaches tried everything known to man the night before the giant slalom: infusions, injections, drugs. I went to the starting line pumped full of painkillers. The analgesics lessened the pain, but that is not to say that they are conducive to better performance.

October 26, 2003. At the same place where I almost ended my career from pain and desperation thirteen months earlier, I started up my first full season since the accident. Despite all the speculations that were whirling about the media world, I realized that I would not be able to perform miracles. I emphasized at every opportunity that it would be a "comeback season," and I meant it. It was my goal to compete in all the races, to improve my performance step by step, and to win at least a few times. I hadn't even thought about the overall World Cup. Besides, FIS once again tossed a log between my skis: Because I had competed in a giant slalom during last year's season (the one during the comeback in Adelboden), I was put into the lineup as though I had skied the entire season, which meant that I fell back by many numbers. I ended up with the unfavorable starting number of twenty-six. In contrast to the downhill event, a high number in the giant slalom is a big disadvantage. The Austrian Ski Federation's protest against this order bounced back as expected.

When I got to the Rettenbach Ferner, the outside temperature was an unbelievable −8 degrees Fahrenheit. Who would have expected such unbelievably cold weather at the end of October? Gitti Auer, our alpine ski team physician, took blood samples from the racers' earlobes in the finish area. At such temperatures, the samples froze in the little plastic tubes. No wonder we were completely off with our equipment choices. I did not have my ski under control and just kept thinking, "If I push too hard, I'll never make it to the finish." The slope was in excellent condition and terribly fast. But I did not dare go to the limit. I put on the brakes in both races and kept my radii too tight.

When I compared the videos of the training with those from the races, I noticed that I had lost my typically low, close-to-the-slope posture during competition. In the end, I placed sixteenth. I knew that I could do better than that. I just hadn't managed to transfer my skills. I was disappointed. On the other hand, this gave me the necessary impulse. "I have to do something in order to do better at the next race, in Park City." In order to do that, I first had to find out what was really wrong with my rib.

So I turned my back on the glacier as soon as I could, packed my bags, and went straight to the clinic in Innsbruck. Ski federation physician Wulf Glötzer thoughtfully studied the X-rays and finally diagnosed a fissure, which can best be likened to a hairline crack in a porcelain plate. Once again I let nothing seep through to the public, because I simply didn't need any excuses. When I went missing during the next few training sessions at the Reiteralm, however, the journalists pricked up their ears and got wind of my injury. I had no choice but to make a statement. Once again, the reporters felt free to interpret the information according to their whims. The fissure became a "broken rib," and suddenly I was even in "mortal danger." I didn't even want to laugh about this, since that made my rib hurt even more.

MY "GURU"

Whenever I am at my wits' end with a medical problem, when the healing process is taking too long, or when time gets tight before a race, I go to Bayrischzell, to the small practice of Volker Müller, an alternative healthcare provider and physical therapist. It seems to me that this man in his fifties, who is in good shape and elicits a great sense of confidence in his patients, has healing hands. Intuitively, he finds the root of the problem in record time. He then helps me out with alternative treatment options, so that I can get through my next race without major problems. I was doing markedly better after my visit to the picturesque little Bavarian village, even though the rib would cause me trouble for another month or so.

November 11, 2003. Saturday night, shortly before nine. I am busy packing for the races in North America. Ski boots, racing suits, functional underwear, running shoes, electrolyte drinking powder, workout clothes—it's all spread out in an orderly fashion. At that moment, the doorbell rings. A lady holds her ID tag up to me. I respond angrily, "Do you have to stop by with your doping test on my last free evening?" She "had" to, even though she had had plenty of opportunity during the past few days to visit me on the Reiteralm during my training runs, or at the Olympic Training Center. This schedule of doping control had seemed to become a tradition with me.

I made a path for the lady through the orderly chaos and asked her to wait in the kitchen. I knew that this unwanted visit would take a while, since I had gone to the toilet only a few minutes earlier. The visit was anything but welcome, since I was not home alone that evening. I had invited a girlfriend over for dinner. She too was peeved, ignored the woman with the plastic cups, and did not even offer her a glass of water. While I downed massive quantities of apple juice, I got more and more annoyed, and I complained accordingly. Even though I had not committed a crime, I felt as though I were being treated like a criminal. But that's the way they handle doping controls. Everything is recorded: time of day, witnesses, medications that are being taken regularly or those that have been prescribed temporarily due to an injury. Even though I have a clear conscience, I still get a strange feeling in the pit of my stomach each time I fill out the form. It is like a routine traffic stop where you know everything is in working order.

November 13, 2003. When I was finally on my flight to Denver, I breathed deeply. Actually, I breathed as deeply as I was able to. My rib hurt so much that I felt somewhat hampered. As he does for every transatlantic flight, Heini had given me a time-zone-adjustment plan, with detailed instructions as to when I needed to put on the blindfold, which blanket I should use, what I had to drink at what time, how active I should be, and when I was finally allowed to take the sleeping pill. There was no way to think about sleep with this kind of pain, though. Yet, I was relieved. Relieved that all the appointments had been able to be squeezed into the brief time frame. Radio spots, photo shoots with the new ski team outfit, another quick Raiffeisen advertisement shoot in Vienna, and in between, equipment selection, medical checkups, physical therapy, and, of course, training despite the pain.

All that was behind me. From now on, it was first and foremost a matter of skiing. "Now the comeback season is getting its true start," I said to Andy. I was looking forward to the preparation in Colorado. Beaver Creek, the upscale ski resort with its dream location above the World Cup town of Vail, had long become something of a second home to me. Each year, we took several weeks to prepare for the overseas races there. We always stayed at the same fancy hotel, the Hyatt Regency, where room prices start at around four hundred dollars. Jim Steinbach, the hotel manager, is a big fan of us Austrians. He tries to anticipate our every wish and charges us a fraction of the official room rate. Even though Hollywood celebrities are among the regulars at the Hyatt, the hotel management always makes us feel like we are the real stars. There's a giant banner in the lobby reading "Home of the Austrian Ski Team," the hotel employees are all wearing "Ski Austria" buttons, and the workout room has been specially outfitted according to my needs.

As usual during a longer stay, I rearranged my room according to my preference. I cleared a space for my workout bike, which is always part of my luggage. Next to the huge oxygen bottle there is a humidifier, which emits a white mist day and night. Up here, the air is dryer than in Chile's Atacama Desert. Next to the cans of electrolyte beverages there is a huge water tank, and in the walk-in closet I've hung the giant slalom outfit next to the downhill suit and the slalom suit, as well as the all-weather outfits, including waterproof pants and jacket. Downhill and giant slalom helmets are sitting on their own rack above the hangers, and next to them, goggles and substitute lenses. On the floor, carefully arranged, five pairs of racing shoes, including the removable insert that was specially fitted to my leg and foot. On the nightstand is my CD player with my favorite CDs. In case I get homesick, I always bring along some Austrian tunes.

Everything is less complicated in Beaver Creek than anywhere else. You get to the lift right behind your hotel, and on the slope you find dry powder snow; there are more sunny days here than in any other ski town. This all works together to help you get in the right mood. Despite my rib problems, I made good progress in my training. I got into the car and drove for six hours through breathtaking scenery clear across the Rockies to Utah, where the World Cup was being continued.

"If things don't work out now, what then?" I asked myself once I was standing at the start of the giant slalom in Park City. Things no longer gelled the way they used to. Before my accident, I had dominated the training runs according to my whim and then taken a risk or two to get to the finish in record time. That's exactly what I wanted to do now. But my youthful exuberance and the ease with which things used to work out were a thing of the past. I kept gathering too much speed, and compared to the training runs, I still did not put in the necessary effort and the correspondingly low, transverse position on the slope. At least I was starting to approach this goal halfway during the first run. It worked out very nicely, and with starting number twenty-two, I came in fourth. "I'm going to win this one," I said to myself and resolved to attack outright during the second round. This may sound like an excuse, but just as Benni Raich, who was set to go ahead of me, entered the race, the weather began to change. A wind came up, the fog rolled in, and it grew quite dark, and that slowed things down. Benni fell back to fourteenth place, while I came in seventh, but I knew, "Now, I'm back in the giant slalom as well." I had overcome my Adelboden trauma for good. Back at the hotel I scribbled my giant slalom results since my accident onto the notepad that was sitting on my night-stand: 31–16–7. A definite upward trend, with which I had to be content. "I will win a giant slalom yet this season," I knew. Unfortunately, I was wrong.

November 26, 2003. Lake Louise, Canada. Welcome to the most beautiful World Cup location in the world! We stayed at the picturesque Chateau Lake Louise, a remodeled castle. Behind it sits the frozen mountain lake that is tucked in among dark pine forests, and then there's the glacier tongue. Truly a feast for the eyes. I suppose that this unbelievable scenery, the untouched natural surroundings, must be even more exciting in the summertime. I advise anyone who has the opportunity to take a trip to Lake Louise. Such surroundings bring out my romantic side. Unfortunately, the only girlfriends that came along with me are long, red, and have a slim figure and two sharp edges. After all, I'm here to do my job, and the slope is my office. There was enough work to be done for sure: downhill training Wednesday through Friday, downhill on Saturday, super-G on Sunday.

You are aware of the spectacular natural surroundings even on the World Cup slope, which runs right through the national forest. Ten minutes after the second downhill training run, an alarm went out over the portable radio channels: "A bear, I can see a bear!" Whether our sports scientist was simply hungover from the night before or whether he had really seen something from his observation post up in a tree, the mountain rangers would be preoccupied with this hypothetical bear for days. In fact, grizzly bears are supposed to be hibernating at −6 degrees Fahrenheit. It certainly seems unlikely that the three hundred spectators along the slope would have disturbed a bear from its winter slumber.

The extreme cold made life difficult. The equipment became brittle and felt aggressive, and the right choice of materials was made even more difficult. Since I had not skied any gliding curves in a long, long time, I had enough problems even without equipment woes on the monotonous downhill "autobahn." These problems had a negative effect on my run time for sure.

So I should not have been surprised about coming in ninth, more than a second behind the winner. Yet I was thoroughly miffed. "This just isn't any good," I lamented. "Why am I even doing this to myself?" If things aren't going right, I want to fix it at the first opportunity. Am I the problem? My equipment? My training? I asked to be driven back to the chateau at once, which is five miles from the downhill slope, and there I thought about all the variables: "What can I improve for tomorrow's super-G?" While I was taking my shower, I could hear my name through the portable radio: "Where is Hermann?" The coaching team was hunting for me. In the background I could hear the fanfare of the "winner's presentation" in the finish area. I had forgotten about the awards ceremony. A fitting end to this messed-up day.

Each evening before a race, all the team members (from the massage therapist to the competitors) assemble for an internal team meeting. There, everything is discussed: starting numbers, timetable, weather forecast, tactics, trainer positions, shuttle service, meal planning. If either Peter Schröcksnadel or Hans Pum is present, it always takes a bit longer. The president and the alpine director always have an encouraging word in store for the competitors. As opposed to most of my colleagues, I go to dinner only after this meeting. Afterward, I put everything in order for the upcoming racing day, turn on the television for a short while, and then try to fall asleep. That night, though, I couldn't even think about falling asleep. I had to think too much about *my* event, the super-G.

It was almost midnight, and I was trying to get hold of Ed, who was still working in the equipment shed, on his cell phone. But there was no reception out here in the wilderness, so I got into the car myself and drove the three miles along a winding, snow-covered road to Edi Unterberger's ski service container. When I opened the door, the telltale wax fumes were drifting toward me. Ed was standing at his workbench in his "cooking apron," thoughtfully caressing the underside of a racing ski with hands that were all cut up from the sharp edges of the skis. Behind him, carefully stacked against the wall, were fifty-five pairs of skis: the seven-foot downhill skis and the super-G skis, which are shorter by two inches. Each pair was meticulously marked with a number code. The racing skis had been carefully selected from among several hundred pairs of skis before the beginning of the season during twenty days of testing at the Sölden glacier. We had already determined the possible shaping and layering variables during our summer snow training in New Zealand. This was my working equipment for the twelve downhills and seven super-Gs of this season. On top of that, there are twenty pairs of seventy-five-inch "short" skis for the seven giant slaloms. If I have to compete in one or two slaloms because of the combination points, I borrow a pair of short skis for such side trips from one of the specialists. The shaping rules, narrowly defined and spelled out by FIS, play an important role in all this. But the minute, individual differences count as secrets of the trade, even though they are always being found out by "industrial spies." "What are you doing here?" Ed asked with surprise when he saw me. But he knew. If I go to the trouble of searching him out at such a late hour, it must be truly urgent. We talked for a long time about the slope layout, the snow conditions, and the terrain. Of course, I know that Ed is a true professional in his area, but I had prepped my own skis long enough (all the way up to my entrance in the World Cup in 1996). Ed and I (the two of us used to compete in ski races while we were teenagers) understand each other without the need for many words. We quickly decided on a completely new variant in materials, and reassured, I went back to the hotel.

Only a few hours later, I won the super-G. Once again I believed in myself. Suddenly I had found my racing rhythm. That was the turning point. I took the momentum that I had in Lake Louise along into the next few races. I still talked about a comeback season and about my hopes to get through it from a physical point of view. But for the first time, I risked a look at the World Cup standings, and back then I considered Schiffi and Michi Waldhofer, who had won the downhill in Lake Louise and was second behind me in the super-G, as my strongest competitors.

After the tranquil week in the forests of the Canadian Rockies, the travel stress was once again upon us. We had to pack, store all our stuff, drive to Calgary, spend the night at the airport hotel, depart for Denver the next day, rent a car, and head up I-70 toward Beaver Creek, where we once again set up base camp at the Hyatt Regency. That's where the circle of the North American tour closes. I had to have one urgent matter taken care of: A corner of my Raiffeisen logo had come off my helmet when I banged against a gate. This had been noticed back home right away with corporate eagle eyes glued to the television, and we received a critical e-mail about it. John Garnsey, head of the Vail Valley Foundation, personally dealt with the incident. By the first training runs, everything was back in order. In order to supply a sample for the airbrush artist, he had borrowed one of the many yellow "Herminator" helmets that are available for sale (complete with sponsor logo) at the local sports store.

What Wimbledon is to Boris Becker, Beaver Creek is to me. The newspapers call it "Herminator's living room," which is no exaggeration, since I really do feel right at home here. I was at the start ten times before my accident, and won seven out of ten, twice at the 1999 world championships. Olympic champion Bernard Russi had fashioned the "Birds of Prey" course for the 1999 world championships. It has everything that a downhill and super-G course requires. After a short gliding section, it gets down to business, and it's no nonsense all the way to the finish line. There is not a moment's chance to rest, for the run is replete with jumps, extremely steep passages, selective curves, and the enormous altitude with the starting line at 11,427 feet above sea level, which makes this course additionally challenging because of the sheer physical conditioning it requires. I live for such races. The enticement to go to the limit, to challenge oneself: That's the essence of racing. A true racer must always exist in that border region. Otherwise, he gets bored. It becomes an addiction to face the competition, and I am addicted to speed courses like the one at Beaver Creek. Besides, I was sick and tired of the constant discussion in the media suggesting that I might be taking a starting spot from better racers on the ski federation team. I was still a winning racer, and a damned hot one at that.

Luckily, with two downhills and one super-G, I had three chances on my favorite mountain. The first downhill went down the drain. Wrong ski! Why did I have to drag this one out from my training? The slope was much softer than the day before, and I almost got stuck during the upper gliding section and was only in forty-ninth place. "Maier no longer is able to glide since his accident," the media were quick to report. As usual in such cases, my favorite experts were babbling something about "wax problems," when it is simply a matter of equipment choice. Depending on the snow conditions and temperature, a certain model with a certain edge angle is used. Usually, Ed takes two different models up the mountain for the race. He puts the matching warm-up pair into the team car so that it comes along with me right away in the morning when we do our skiing warm-up. The worst thing that can happen to a downhill racer is for the ski to turn slow in the flat passages. Usually, the cause is neither the wax nor the coating, but rather the edge angle, which has been specially adapted to the individual racer, or the shaping of the racing skis. I don't want to divulge more than that at this time.

The next day, I showed all those naysayers a thing or two. Fastest up above in the gliding section, victory with almost a one-second lead. Even if no one wants to believe me, I had skied all the passages the same as the day before. Could there be more vivid proof concerning the importance of the right equipment?

When John Garnsey presented me with the raptor trophy, I had tears in my eyes. I had won another downhill after almost three years, a dream come true. Moreover, there was enormous gratification because of the peculiar interpretation of my injury status and the criticism regarding my guaranteed slot in the downhill. I was sad to see that top contenders such as Pepi Strobl and Peter Rzehak had to watch from the sidelines time and again. On the other hand, I had only "lent" them my slot during my absence. It is not my fault that there is a limit to how many competitors each nation is allowed to bring to the start. President Schröcksnadel once put it like this: "The Real Madrid team has thirty top kickers, but only eleven can play."

December 7, 2003. I dare to claim that during the last day of the North American tour, I experienced more than other competitors go through in an entire season. It was my birthday, of which I was reminded by the congratulatory letters in front of my hotel room door. I was supposed to be sitting in an airplane heading for Frankfurt at five o'clock that afternoon. Between now and then, an action-packed day was awaiting me. During the super-G, I have to sit and watch with starting number twenty-eight as the conditions worsen by the minute. Yet I come in second behind the Norwegian Bjarne Solbakken, who, with number nine, had bright sunny skies. In the finish area, the song "Happy Birthday" is resounding for me from the loudspeakers. Ski federation master of ceremonies Roberto Brunner lets the champagne corks pop and magically produces a whole series of cakes. I am passed around from one TV station to another. While the David Bowie classic "Heroes" is blaring over the speaker system, a victory platform is being put up for the big awards ceremony. I can feel enormous pressure building underneath my racing suit, and I secretly relieve myself underneath one of the grandstands. (Why is there not a single bathroom in any of the finish areas around the world?) I have barely reemerged when someone shoves one of those blue doping control forms in my face. "I can't believe this," I complain vehemently. Again right before my departure, again on an empty bladder. Why did no one think to test me during the quiet weeks here? But this isn't even the worst. In addition, I have to take off my racing suit: fabric control compliments of FIS (air permeability, etc.). But what tops everything is that the doping test is to take place at the height of the midlevel station, at Beanos Cabin. So right after the awards ceremony I'm on my way via Ski-Doo to the uppity yuppie joint where membership supposedly costs fifty thousand dollars. Up there, not even the draft spout is in working order, and we have to drink orange juice along with our spaghetti dinner. Finally, I'm allowed to pee and get back to the hotel. It is already 2 P.M., and the staff there is waiting with the next birthday cake. I stop briefly for a picture, hurry to my room, pack in record time, stuff everything into the car where my reliable press agent is already waiting with his engine

running, and we're off to speed the 105 miles to Denver, with blithe dis-
regard of most U.S. traffic laws. During the drive, my cell phone rings
every few minutes. Friends congratulate me on my birthday and, which is
most exhilarating to me, on my lead in the World Cup!

On the plane to Frankfurt I let myself sink into the spacious business-
class seat, which did not altogether go without saying, even though the
FIS guarantees this perk on every flight to the leading three competitors
in the overall World Cup rankings. Because of the delay caused by the
doping test, I showed up at the ticket desk only forty-five minutes before
departure. My seat was gone, but somehow I was able to get on after all.
Finally, I had a chance to relax and open a can of beer to celebrate my
thirty-first birthday. I leaned back and reflected on the past week. Even I
was surprised that I had a commanding lead in the overall World Cup, because I did not nearly feel the way I had felt before the accident. My right
lower leg was still half numb, and the range of motion in my ankle was
still restricted. My left thigh was still too skinny, since the nerves there
had not yet completely recovered. But, and this gave me reason for being
optimistic, the pinched-off nerves were still continuing to regenerate, despite the doctors' claims that I could expect such healing only for up to
two years after the accident. I always had the same answer when asked the
frequent question, to what degree was I back to my old self, expressed in
percentage points: "70 percent." But I still had hope that at some point,
my recovery would be nearly complete. The American journalists who
were crowding around me at every race always marveled at my bulge and
seemed to have realized the gravity of my injury, which did not go without saying, considering the statements that came from one of my teammates. Thus, I learned from the *Denver Post* during my return flight that
my injury had been played down by many within the world of ski racing
and compared to a routine knee injury: "In the past, many ski racers had
to battle with grave knee injuries or similar matters. Of course, he had a
magnificent comeback. But he only did what many other competitors
would have done as well. The fight for the comeback keeps you alive."
The reporter was right at least with his last statement. This newly won

life was just starting to be enjoyable again. One thing will always remain after the accident: Victories mean a lot more to me than before, when they had something I took for granted.

For years the World Cup schedule has been such that the transition from the North American to the European series of races couldn't possibly be any dumber, or less convenient. Let's say you risk losing your driver's license and make your flight to Frankfurt, and finally get to Salzburg on Monday afternoon. Tuesday, I'm off to Val d'Isère by car, or I fly to Zurich and get picked up there, still with a five-and-a-half-hour drive in store. Thursday, the downhill training gets going. Whoever doesn't manage to halfway recover from his jet lag in this short amount of time is going to stand at the starting line completely exhausted, only to tear down the slope at eighty miles per hour moments later.

I was spared all this during my comeback season. There wasn't enough snow in Val d'Isère at the end of November 2003. Thus, I pedaled away comfortably on my ergometer for three days in Obertauern, joking around with my coaching staff and reading the papers. Then, I leisurely made my way to Alta Badia on Friday, where they had scheduled an additional giant slalom.

December 14, 2003.   I was standing at the start of the steepest giant slalom slope in the world, and I was hungry. Once again I made do with a safety run, and came in fifteenth after the first round. But during the second round I stepped on the accelerator. Up above, I had the best time, seven tenths of a second faster than the eventual winner, Kalle Palander. But then I approached one of the gates too directly, my ski boot made contact with the snow, and I slipped. Done, over! At least I had my giant slalom feel back and I was looking forward to the second round. "Next week, they'll be amazed," I said to Ed on the way home. It was I who ended up being amazed, because after two training runs, one super-G (third place, my worst super-G result since the accident), and one downhill (fifth place) in Gröden, we returned to Alta Badia, and during that race, I completely lost my strength. I felt drained of power and energy.

With twenty-sixth place I collected a measly five World Cup points, and was looking forward to Christmas.

MY HOMETOWN RACE:
ONE BIG NIGHTMARE

January 3, 2004. I know that some were hoping I wouldn't be able to pull it off for once. People are always eager for something sensational, and a poorly performing Maier, well, that's a sensation. They got their kick in my own backyard of all places.

Fiftieth place! My worst out of 136 World Cup races. And that during my giant slalom, on my own slope. But the entire surrounding hubbub became a run through the gauntlet. After all, I knew each slopeside worker, each lift attendant personally, and everyone addressed me, patted me on the back, wanted something from me. I found myself in a constant dilemma. Should I keep walking without saying anything and concentrate on the upcoming race? Then the word is, "Now he's become arrogant, that Maier!" Or do I stop for a friendly chat with everyone? But if you keep that up, at some point, you start losing your focus.

I had been in such good shape during the week before the race. I had felt my giant slalom momentum coming back. But at the starting line, it was all different. I skied in an uptight manner starting at the first gate. No wonder I suddenly found myself sitting on my behind. In any other race, I would have stopped instantly. But I thought of the thousands of spectators that had come to my hometown race. So I got up and skied on; I had to let myself be seen in the finish area at any rate. I did not want to repeat the scene at Park City in 1998, when I sneaked out through the back door. Then they would have interpreted my behavior in all sorts of weird ways right away. But I was sick and tired of those stories. I have learned one thing in the meantime: A true winner must be able to lose and still hold his head up high. But believe me, with my sort of ambition, that is anything but easy. I hate to lose.

I came into the finish area and was there exclusively for the media and for my fans for the next several hours. I patiently covered all the interview stations: first the ORF live position, followed by the important foreign TV stations, then Austrian public radio, and the patient newspaper reporters, who always lean against the fence after a race and wait for the word snippets that are left over after all the television and radio interviews. Since I hadn't made it among the top thirty, and thus didn't qualify for the second round, there was enough time left for the small radio stations and reporters who don't usually get a turn.

Afterward, I gave a bunch of autographs and posed with a fan who is wheelchair-bound, whom I had visited two years earlier on Christmas Eve at a home for the handicapped in Linz. I tried to be there for my fans as much as I could before hiding away behind my own four walls and trying to analyze what had happened.

When I read the papers the next day at breakfast, I could tell how some were really empathizing with me. But there was a good amount of complete garbage being dished up as well. I read, for instance, that I had only thrown out a few empty phrases during my press conference on Friday, that I had not been exposed to any sort of bustle or hype. *No photo shoots, no press, and except for one lightning-fast appearance for the automobile sponsor of the ski federation, no sponsor responsibilities. Supposedly Maier did not give ten autographs in the place he calls home, and where the World Cup holds a race primarily because it is Maier's home.* Okay, it was a terrible race. From a sporting point of view, I accept any kind of criticism. Only when facts are being twisted and, which unfortunately happens quite a bit, things are deliberately misrepresented, and that simply isn't fair.

Believe me, the photo shoot for BMW, where I had to pose with Benni Raich and Stephan Eberharter, was no fun at all, and anything but a lightning-fast appearance! Time and again the word is that I'm always late. This time around, I was on time, and had to wait for Eberharter and Raich. I could understand Benni's tardiness. As the winner of the previous race, he had to jump the usual hurdles. So I had to wait a good half hour in the car of my press spokesman. Fans were constantly coming along and knocking on the windshield. I was already miffed about the results of my last race, but with each passing minute of waiting around, my anger grew. I suddenly remembered the World Cup preseason in France's Tignes, when I showed up for the number drawing at the last second with Andi Schifferer and was hit with a ten-thousand-schilling fine from the Austrian Ski Federation. I just cursed, "I want my money back from way back when!" More and more fans were trudging past our car. Even though I was camouflaging myself as usual with dark glasses and the car's visor, the fans discovered me and started to mill around my vehicle. I always try to approach my fans in an open manner and don't like to be shielded. But this time around, things got decidedly too much for me. The situation was starting to take on a threatening note. A crowd of drunken marauders showed up who were trying to pry open the door. Because they were hitting the window like maniacs, I got out and tried to calm them down with autographs. I had barely made it out when a clearly inebriated lady was standing next to me asking for a photograph to be taken. She shoved a half-empty vodka bottle into my hands. "Well what's up, buddy? Do you still remember us, you know, from way back when? Take a swig." Another woman pressed her cell phone against my ear: "Don't you want to say something? My little girl's on the line. Say something!" A third lady of questionable taste requested that I sign her chest. A nightmare! Finally, my teammates showed up, the picture was taken, and I was out of there. Really, I had imagined my hometown race on the newly christened "Hermann Maier World Cup Slope" a bit differently.

At least a colleague from my own training group (WC4), Benni Raich, had won the race. With no respect for age he had even snagged the World Cup lead from me. Benni Raich had been in top shape ever since the weekend of races in Flachau, while I was still drawing nourishment from my North American success.

January 22, 2004. The World Cup was gathering for the yearly meeting in Kitzbühel. There were five hundred World Cup points to be earned there. I could use a few additional points. Otherwise, I might not even have come. I was plagued by bad back pain. A few days earlier I had slipped while jogging in the snow, and had thrown out my back. It got worse with each passing day. It was so bad, in fact, that I made use of a canceled downhill training run in order to pay a visit to my medical miracle man in Bayrischzell. Volker enabled me to take part in the ensuing four races within four days. The results were as expected considering my mediocre shape: fifth in the downhill that had been substituted for Wengen, second in the super-G, ninth in the second downhill, and fourteenth in the combination. I was most disgruntled by a comment from Daron Rahlves, who had until then always given me the "buddy" vibes. He had heard that I had allegedly made a derogatory comment about his victory from the year before on the shortened downhill course on Kitzbühel's Streif. Which was complete nonsense, of course. At any rate, Daron was getting ready to deliver a counterpunch in front of the journalists: "Hermann Maier shows no respect when others are winning," the American said. "He is a poor loser. He's always looking for excuses for his defeat. Besides, he doesn't look you in the eye when he congratulates you." Apparently, Daron's success has gone to his head and he takes the words that his coach yells at him every time at the starting line ("Ski for the money") too seriously. From a competitive point of view, I was glad that I had held up as well as I did despite my back pain during this demanding program, and had kept up with my World Cup rivals. What no one realized at this point was that Lasse Kjus, who was leading the World Cup after his victory in the first downhill and third place in the combination race, had suffered a meniscus injury during his jump into the "mousetrap."

January 28, 2004. "I'll counterattack in Garmisch," I resolved. And in fact, on the same slope where I had won my first World Cup race on February 23, 1997, a preemptive strike was made in the battle for the overall World Cup lead. Lasse Kjus had to break up his training, his face contorted with pain. He had to undergo surgery in Oslo. Which is too bad, because he would have turned the four-way fight for the big crystal trophy into a fivesome.

After two fifth-place rankings in the downhill, I finally had the starting number that I deserved in the super-G. As the first in the rankings, I entered the race as the last top contender with number thirty. I didn't miss a trick and was assured early of the super-G World Cup victory, my thirteenth crystal ball. Benni Raich had a bad crash and suffered a concussion; luckily, he suffered only a few bruises apart from that. With my victory, I had moved from fourth place to the top of the overall World Cup rankings within twenty-four hours. The Garmisch Kreuzeck has time and again been a fateful mountain for the Austrians. In 1993, I had witnessed its darkest hour live in front of the television. In 1997, when I first passed the location where Ulli Maier had her fatal crash, the horrific memories from back then were going through my head.

February 5, 2004. "Make sure you're holding on to something. In Munich, the results from the court proceedings have been announced." It was my press spokesman on the other end of the line, and he was beside himself. "The driver of the Mercedes has been found guilty." I breathed a sigh of relief. But then came the clincher. "His attorney is trying to present the facts in such a way as to say that you are partially responsible." This sentence hit me like a sledgehammer. I was sitting in the car next to Andy, and we were on our way to the giant slalom in Adelboden. A few minutes later, I heard the report on the radio news. I was furious. The facts were being falsely presented on purpose, never mind that my innocence had been confirmed by a court of law. In the very place where I had celebrated my comeback a year earlier, the accident was catching up to me again. My press spokesman called all the big domestic newspapers and tried to clarify the matter. President Schröcksnadel, along with my attorney, Karl-Heinz Klee, drew up a statement, which was sent out via the ski federation's press distributor. When I saw the national news in the evening at the hotel, I still had reason to be mad about it. Not a word about our statement. I got onto my stationary bicycle and tried to settle down. I had to prepare myself for an important giant slalom. After all the hustle and bustle, I was content with the race. With eighth place, I was able to defend my World Cup lead. Yet I had to wait to go home. As in Garmisch, my name was again drawn for a doping test. I am just as lucky with the doping test "drawings" as my dad was years ago in the lottery. Except that my dad's good fortune actually brought him some money, whereas for me it only usurps my time.

February 14, 2004. St. Anton. I still had the botched world championships from 2001 in the pit of my stomach. I was itching to take revenge. This time around, the conditions were just right. Ed produced a completely new, difficult-to-control, "silver bullet" out of the ski shed for this, the most strength-consuming of all racecourses in the world. I took the risk. In contrast to the world championships, we were finally covering the entire racecourse starting at the very top. I was looking forward to the additional thirty seconds. Since I still remembered exactly where I had lost the championships three years ago, I wanted to do a better job this time around. I had a great attitude and wanted to show what I had given away back then. During the middle portion, with its slow curves, I retained my speed, and down below I gave a great performance. Finally I had that feeling again. "Lad, you again have the power and conditioning that lets you finish a race to the bitter end!" I skied in the borderline region all the way. What wasn't visible on television is that in the Sailerboden section, where there's a speed meter, I skied over a gate and almost sailed out of the race. It was one of my best races since the accident. I had never gone to the limit like that. In the finish area, I was drained and happy all at the same time.

I witnessed the slalom the next day from my bed. I watched in pain as Bode Miller won and came dangerously close to me in the World Cup. Once again, I was badly banged up. Idiot that I am, I had to celebrate my St. Anton victory a bit too exuberantly! In the disco, I must have gotten too close to the bar while dancing, and I once again cracked my rib in the process. I was mad at my own stupidity. On the other hand, when could I celebrate, if not after such a victory? I am just all-around extreme, I guess.

Two days later I paid for my sins. For one of the team sponsors, we had to take part in a "joke Olympics" in Seefeld. As I was sliding down the ski jump slope on my stomach on an inflatable boat, I was bent over with pain. Of course, I didn't want to let on what was really the matter; it was irritating and embarrassing all at the same time.

February 28, 2004.   It was still dark when my cell phone rang. "You can stay in bed," Andy told me from Kranjska Gora. "The slope inspection has been canceled!" This meant that I could travel to the last giant slalom before the World Cup finals in all leisure. It takes me about an hour and a half to get by car to the Slovenian World Cup town from Flachau. "Mr. Maier?" said the customs agent as we prepared to roll across the border on the Wurzen pass. I nodded and thought, "He's probably going to ask for an autograph." But the uniformed officer remained serious: "We have a problem!" I didn't have my passport with me. With a serious face, the agent called his superior in Ljubljana. Nothing doing. I would have counted on anything, but not with the surreal scenario that two months and a day before Slovenia's joining the European Union, there would be no crossing of the border without a travel document. My press agent quickly called around, but neither men's head coach Giger, who had just come out of a team leadership meeting, nor Roberto Brunner, who always keeps a few crates of South Tyrolean red wine handy for just such an occasion, nor the FIS officials could do anything for me. After an hour of tiresome negotiations, we finally turned around, and I considered forgetting about the race altogether. That's when Ed suggested spending the night at the Atomic accommodations, Südrast, in the "three corners" region between Austria, Slovenia, and Italy. A courier had obtained the passport from my mother. I took the document into my possession and fell asleep reassured.

The "passport affair" had somewhat distracted me from my rib, but I still couldn't pull off anything better than twelfth place. Bode Miller, who also had passport-related trouble at the border, took the overall lead away from me with his victory, but during the slalom he and Benni were disqualified. After a side trip to Norway I came to the World Cup finals in Sestriere as the leader.

Now it was all up to me. Whether I was eight points behind or a hundred, Miller was not the problem. I summed it up thus: "If I win the downhill and super-G, then I'm in front no matter what."

March 10, 2004. Everything was somewhat bizarre during the World Cup finals at the Italian ski resort. The downhill was not bad, but I couldn't really warm up to it. As opposed to all the other seasons' races, only one training session for this one had been arranged. That wasn't enough for me. I didn't quite know where I could make up time. Besides, I was irritated by the weather conditions. Spring was around the corner, and we were in the southernmost World Cup location, only two hours by car from the Côte d'Azur. We all agreed: It's going to be warm, slushy, and soft. "A dream," I said to Ed. "Prepare the ski from St. Anton for me. With that I will demolish them!" In the morning, however, it was −13 degrees Fahrenheit. Since the sun was shining brightly, we thought that the slope was going to thaw. Thus we stuck with our choice of ski. It ended up being the coldest race of the season. I even had had a long discussion with Andy and Ed after the training, and we morons had decided on the very worst variable. During the race, I skidded around helplessly starting with the first gate, as though I had strapped soda bottles instead of skis to my feet! "What on earth is going on here?" I dare to claim that not many people would have made it into the finish with this type of ski. On the display board, a lag of over two seconds showed up. "God Almighty!" I thought. "I'll fall behind the top fifteen." Which is exactly what happened. As opposed to normal races, during the World Cup finals only the top fifteen contestants receive points. It was all in vain! One thing was crystal clear to me at that point: "If I end up losing the overall World Cup, I just now gave it away."

Before the super-G, I said to Ed, "No fancy tricks, we'll do everything the normal way." Since after the downhill bust I had complained about the poor choice of material in every single interview, I was under a lot of pressure. Immediately, the word would be, "He's using the ski material as an excuse!"

I knew at the super-G start that it would have to be victory. Eberharter was in the lead, only twenty-two points behind me in the overall World Cup. "If I don't get a move on now, then I'll really be in for it," I thought at the start. Under this kind of pressure, I put down my best super-G since the motorcycle crash: direct, without compromise, without mistakes. At the finish, I yelled so loud that everyone could hear: "That's what it's supposed to look like!"

After the race, we rattled in a military all-wheel-drive vehicle to the doping test. Stephan Eberharter was sitting next to me, staring into space. That was the moment when I asked him the question that had been burning on the tip of my tongue: "Well, how are you going to go about your retirement?" "Yes," he replied, "I'm going to quit, and I'll announce it in the summer together with Uniqa" (his chief sponsor).

There was one more race that we were about to tackle: a giant slalom, on which everything hinged for the World Cup. But it was called off under adverse and dangerous conditions. I escaped to my room and prepared for the start the next morning. That's when one of the coaches called me with the message caught over the radio waves: "Giant slalom canceled!" Canceled, not postponed? When I heard that over the telephone, I could not believe it. I was the World Cup winner. For the fourth time!

I have this theory that life moves in expanding circles. In 1999 I had gambled away the World Cup to Kjus and Aamodt, partly because FIS had stricken a super-G without a replacement.

Benni Raich is six years and three months younger than I. The future, they say, belongs to him. The present belongs to me. We will have a number of gripping duels in the snow, which I am looking forward to.

LISBON, MAY 10, 2004, AND THE AWARD GOES TO . . .

. . . Hermann Maier! As figure-skating grand dame Katharina Witt holds aloft the five-pound, gold-coated "Laureus" award with soccer heartthrob Luis Figo applauding next to me and tennis legend John McEnroe offering commentary, I can feel goose bumps all over. That's when I truly realize what I have accomplished in the past months: I am the world Comeback Athlete of the Year! That is the award I so desperately wished for two and a half years after the accident. A year ago, Ronaldo snatched the trophy right from under my nose, but with the overall World Cup triumph during my comeback season, I had seized my last chance, so to speak.

Comeback Athlete of the Year

Comeback Athlete of the Year! I appreciate the fact that the seventy members of the Laureus Academy, the likes of Ed Moses and Pelé, decided in my favor, that they knew how to gauge the level of severity of my injury. Martina Navratilova, a beaten competitor in my category, acknowledged that with respect. She said that my comeback was even greater than that of Lance Armstrong, and I felt honored by her statement. I had already received such an honor once, during the year 2000, when I was crowned Winter Sports Athlete of the Year in London's Royal Albert Hall. But the award here is yet a step above that. Comeback Athlete. That means you must have been at the very top once, and that you've managed to fight your way back after a grave setback.

It is an unbelievable feeling to stand up here on the podium and be allowed to gaze down on these famous sports figures. I am looking at Boris Becker, who has invited me to his TV show moments earlier; Emerson Fittipaldi is sitting down there, as are Michael Johnson and my former skiing buddy Alberto Tomba, stars of whom I was once in awe because they had

(continues)

(continued)

accomplished so much. The gala is being broadcast to sixty countries; almost three hundred million people are watching their televisions. I want to do a perfect job and disappoint no one. Everyone who helped me on my way back deserves a mention: my doctors, my coaches, my family. It is as though I am in a trance. My head and my body are no longer in harmony. An odd feeling, like just before a downhill premiere. But I love a challenge, especially one that I consider as preparation for life after sports. Who knows, maybe someday I will be nominated for an Oscar. That would really impress Arnie.

That serves as a motivator for me. I have only five complete World Cup seasons on my back, three world championships, and I've been to the Olympics only once. That's where I still have an open account. The last big goal is the 2006 Olympic Games in Turin. If I can swing the world championships during the year before and the year after, I'll gladly take them. With forty-seven World Cup victories (forty-eight, according to my private tally) I'm lacking only three (two) to reach Alberto Tomba's record, who occupies second place in the record books behind the great Ingemar Stenmark (eighty-six). Yes, and I'm missing only one big crystal ball to draw head to head with Marc Girardelli's overall World Cup record. However, working toward these goals is becoming more and more difficult. The consequences of my accident trigger a chain reaction during my training. Since the titanium rod has been removed from my right lower leg, the patella tendon, which had been split in the process, is hurting on a regular basis. This turns running into a problem activity. If the rounded step doesn't work right, my back starts hurting. In contrast to the "olden days," when I could work out as hard as I wanted without reservation, I now frequently have to switch over from training to rehabilitation. That really puts a damper on things. The "old" Maier, the one with the back-to-back victories and the huge leads, will never again exist. My nerve receptors, the "sensors" in the soles of my feet that we skiers call our "sixth sense," no longer function properly since the accident. The feeling down there is completely numb. I realized this once again only recently when I was sitting on my ergometer for two hours and failed to notice that I had forgotten the hotel key in my sneaker throughout the entire training session. I have no illusions in this regard. That sensation will never return to normal. How much I have lost is hard to put into numbers. As a rule of thumb, I would guess about 1.5 seconds per race, sometimes more, sometimes less.

The victories were something the old Maier had come to take for granted. I felt like I could do nothing wrong. Sure, it was a beautiful era, but I would not want to exchange it for the present. All the frightening experiences I had to undergo after the accident, the pain, the depression, the hopelessness, the setbacks—all that has turned me into what I am now.

The true victories are the quiet ones, says the voice-over in what is surely my most emotional commercial. I celebrate such victories even now in my normal life week by week. For instance, I have been able to balance on my right leg in the shower for a while now. Each day after getting up I test the range of motion of my right ankle; important impulses originate from there in the sport of ski racing. That, too, continues to get better.

Yes, I have learned again to win on the slope, though without taking it for granted. However, these victories were not the goal that drove me to my comeback. It was the will to learn how to walk again, to be able to live a normal life, maybe even to ski again. The victories are the icing on the cake—in the race of my life.

11

ENCORE: ONE MORE HAPPY ENDING

August 2004. I am the warlike dwarf Gimli from the Oscar-winning epic *Lord of the Rings* as I charge toward the photographers with my sword drawn. I am in the very region where star director Peter Jackson brought Middle Earth to life. Some Austrian reporters who have followed me around the globe have taken care of all the props and ushered me into this magical and mysterious realm.

This is the perfect opportunity for me to get away from the usual hubbub at snow camp during the first real snow-based training of the season, right in the middle of the New Zealand winter. I am sitting on a hill at the famous "Ribbon" vineyard on the South Island. As my gaze wanders over Lake Wanaka, I can see sheep grazing among the picturesque scenery. I am lost in my thoughts and absent-mindedly think back over the last few months. Indeed, the story of my comeback season could just as well have flowed from the pen of *Lord of the Rings* author J. R. R. Tolkien. It has taken me some time to realize just how much had to happen for my personal skiing fairy tale to come true and have a happy ending. Before undertaking my first full skiing season after the accident, I would never have dared to think about winning the overall World Cup. If you take a close look at my point total, the five races that I won and the 1,265 points on my account amounted to the worst score of my entire World Cup career. Even during the one season when I lost against Lasse Kjus and Kjetil-Andre Aamodt (1998/1999), I had 42 points more on my list. But for me personally after all that had happened, it was a very precious victory and for sure the one I've worked for the hardest.

I had certainly reached my major goal of winning the overall World Cup sooner than I expected. What now? Do I have anyone, including myself, to prove anything to at this point? I might as well just retire right now. Why does Lance Armstrong still compete after winning the Tour de France so many times? Why does multiple Formula 1 champion Michael Schumacher risk his life season after season? And hasn't Andre Agassi earned more money by now than Mike Tyson could ever squander?

Maybe this is what we have in common: the champion gene. A true champion can never get enough; we just set ourselves new goals, at least so long as the adrenaline and the joy of competing can let us forget the pain and the numerous injuries. The most important factor, though, is to find motivation at just the right moment. I have to admit that this gets harder and harder for me as the years go by. After my fourth overall World Cup victory, I took more time off than usual. I partied with friends, I enjoyed sunsets in Tuscany. It was mid-May, and I was relaxing after the Laureus Comeback Athlete of the Year ceremony in Portugal, when Heini called and congratulated me on winning the award. He cleverly guided the conversation toward his favorite subject: "When will we start training?" My brief answer: "Be patient, my friend, I need a few more days. I'll get a car and drive around this beautiful place." After scuba diving in the Atlantic Ocean, I felt that my batteries were charged enough to dive once again into my training routine. And believe me, the first rounds on the ergometer were at least as hard as they had been in years past. But after less than three months' prep time, I was ready for the snow training camp in New Zealand.

I set myself new goals. Since my comeback in the downhill and super-G disciplines had worked out so well, I tried as hard as I could to catch up in the giant slalom. It is, after all, the discipline that initially brought me to the World Cup in 1996, when no one else believed in me, the discipline that is technically and physically most demanding. Right after my comeback season ended, I met with my skiing coach, Andy, and with Ed, my equipment specialist. Andy opened his briefcase and took out the printouts of the giant slalom analyses for the entire season. There was a small stack of paper for every race, and he laid them out in a row. On every single front page, one number was circled in red: 16–7–out–26–50–12. Those are not the kind of results a three-time GS overall World Cup champion can be proud of. "We can't muddle on like that," said Andy, and promptly started the brainstorming meeting, one of many to come. Night after night we talked about technique and materials, analyzed videotapes, and searched for untapped opportunities.

For the very first time during my World Cup career I started considering an equipment change. I looked at this exclusively from an athletic point of view. A team could offer me millions of dollars and I would still stick with the best type of ski. So now I was thinking about changing my brand of boots (not skis, as had been falsely reported by the press). I had been racing with the Italian brand Lange for almost a decade, before and after my accident. The only alternative that sounded reasonable for me was to use Atomic for all of my equipment, which would mean skis, boots, and bindings. How can I explain the importance of ski boots to a layman? What is most important are the "turning points." With these points you have to hit the turn at just the right speed in order not to cut it short. To put it simply: The Atomic shoes let you take tighter turns. Thus the obvious calculation: Shorter distance plus smaller radius equals less time. At least that's what I expected from the impending equipment change.

So, on my flight to New Zealand, I had in my luggage five pairs of (foamed) Atomic boots, specially designed for my damaged lower leg, in addition to my usual Lange equipment.

After our arrival in wintry New Zealand, there was one overriding priority: test the new equipment. I kept exchanging my boots: two runs with the new Atomic boots and the next one with Lange. Each time I switched shoes, there was a huge difference. Every race was filmed and timed. I told Andy what I felt, and he took notes of what he saw. At night, we analyzed every detail.

I got very confused because of all these changes. I raced the same way with the Lange boot as with the Atomic, and the other way around. Nothing came out right, it seemed. The slopes were a complete bummer as well; they were much too soft, and I was running out of time. We practically never had the chance to train under real racing conditions. We especially couldn't practice the long turns that are so important for the giant slalom and downhill events. I was never able to establish the right gliding speed and the soft, rounded turns that used to be my hallmark. The bumpier it got, the jumpier my skis felt. This would later be the biggest source of my problems. And that's why I made progress only with my giant slalom skills and not with the fast disciplines, as I had been able to in years past.

But it got worse. When I was still on the plane, I caught a cold that I would be fighting for the next three weeks. Thus, my late summer cardiovascular training was all about regeneration. Some people around me didn't seem to care at all. Because I didn't want to make a big deal about my somewhat compromised condition, our advertising strategists didn't hesitate about involving me in a new and totally crazy TV commercial.

September 3, 2004.   I was obviously not entirely in my right mind, since despite my cold, I agreed to do exactly what the others did. The amusing script wanted us to rip off our clothes after a jog through the woods and then jump into an ice-cold mountain lake—stark naked! They had offered us the alternative of wearing women's skin-colored thongs, an option that I politely declined. You have to picture this: four well-known athletes standing around naked, waiting for their next round of filming. There were hikers and school kids passing us by and staring in amazement. The people from the film crew were sitting on a little hill behind us and staring at our exposed backsides. As time went by, so did our inhibitions.

The best was yet to come. After the shooting, we had lunch (we were graciously allowed to wear bathrobes). But then, the director came up to us a bit sheepishly and said, "The placement wasn't quite right. Would it by any chance be possible for you guys to jump once again?" I couldn't believe it. But at that point I didn't really care anymore. At least they hadn't sewn any sponsor logos onto our bare skin.

At any rate, jumping in a cold lake was not necessarily what I needed at that point in time. Mentally, I was already preparing for the opening of the World Cup season in Sölden. Why couldn't I have just said no and stayed in bed to recover from my cold? As it was, it took me a while to get over my cold, which in turn caused a delay to the start of my glacier training.

Up on the glacier, it was more of the same muddling. It was much too warm, and the soft conditions weren't very helpful for our training. By now, I had decided for sure to stick with the new Atomic ski boot, while at the same time leaving a loophole. Since I hadn't signed any contracts, I had the great advantage of using my old Lange boot whenever I felt like it. Finally, I saw some progress with the Atomic boot; I started getting faster with every race, and I was starting to feel that I could even win the first giant slalom of the season.

When it came time for the actual event, though, everything was completely different. Up on the Rettenbachferner glacier in Sölden, at 7,800-feet elevation, the slope was rock hard, and our setup turned out to be completely wrong. After the first run I was 2.34 seconds behind Bode Miller, my new Atomic teammate. After a somewhat solid second run, I was fast enough to get in at fifteenth place, 2.20 seconds behind Miller, who seemed in complete harmony with his new equipment. I was now completely unsure of myself. Had I made the wrong decision after all? Had I done all that testing for nothing? Suffering my first great disappointment of the season, I spoke to the journalists, full of conviction: "In the giant slalom, I'm never going to be able to get onto the winner's podium again, let alone win a race." On my way home, I was able to look at things with a little more detachment. It became clear to me that I simply couldn't face my first downhill race of the new season with the same ruthless attitude as I had in years past. I had raced in a more brutal way before the accident, and now I would have to find a new way into the season.

In contrast to my pitiful achievements was the hype around me as a person. The gorgeous weather had enticed more than twenty thousand fans to come up to the glacier, and I couldn't take a single step without being followed. I didn't even have time alone in the starting area. The little porta-potty, which was set there just for us racers, was always occupied, so I decided to take a leak behind some ice floes. A journalist from a local Salzburg paper shamelessly took a picture of me. Walter, my new press guy, got really mad, and the wannabe paparazzo has never again appeared at any of my races.

The headlines the next day were all about Bode Miller, of course. Journalists made up stories to reinforce the image of the ultracool American boy. One story asserted that Bode was sent to the ski lift only a few minutes before his turn during the second run. But the truth was that Bode had prepared as usual with all the other racers in the starting area. I can even remember him coming up to me before I started to wish me good luck. I (nineteenth place after the first run) was twelfth to race and he was the last. This means that there were eighteen racers between my start and his, in addition to two breaks for TV commercials. This meant that Bode had been on top of the mountain forever before it was his turn to race. The next morning, when they said he had arrived at the last minute for the course inspection, he had in fact been there half an hour before me. And you can't tell me that anybody got hysterical over the American racer. But the media just show things differently. Bode was now experiencing some of what I suffered at the start of my career. The media make you look like somebody according to their ideas, and you can't get rid of the image easily. I certainly didn't invent the name "Herminator." (On the other hand, I haven't exactly discouraged it.)

The opening day of the World Cup season is traditionally extremely hectic for me. Everybody needs you to do something for them: an interview here and a little sponsoring event there, equipment setup and clothing issue. The Austrian swimmer Markus Rogan was chosen as "Athlete of the Year" during the big annual Austrian sports gala. It's not that Austria's journalists think it more impressive to win two silver medals than to win an overall World Cup title that bugs me. It's their justification that annoys me: "Hermann Maier has already won so many times," was a common response in a radio poll among Austrian reporters. "Well, if they think so," I thought, and congratulated Rogan the way I was supposed to. Next was a date that I really was looking forward to for a change: the presentation of my autobiography, the English translation of you're reading right now. The presentation took place up on Salzburg's famous Mönchsberg, which in my opinion boasts one of the most scenic views in all of Austria. Looking out over the roofs of Salzburg, we celebrated late into the night. Which meant that I was pretty knocked out when I climbed up into the Lear jet the next day on my way to Barcelona. Before going to the overseas races, my headgear sponsor made me squeeze in an ad shoot in sunny Spain.

I somehow found myself eagerly waiting for the departure for races that are held every year in North America. During my flight to Denver I had enough time for a thorough discussion with Andy about my situation. Somehow, it seemed to me that all hope was lost for the overall World Cup right after the first race. If you lose many points right at the beginning because you're not done testing yet, you can't set your hopes too high. I had one big goal left for the 2004/2005 season: the World Championships in Bormio. I had a season full of testing and technical fine-tuning in front of me, which meant a lot of work. I hadn't yet found the right equipment setup for the fast disciplines. After the summer snow training that had gone wrong, I had lost the right feeling for the long gliding curves. On top of that, I had the switch to Atomic boots to contend with. As soon as I realized that my time window for testing had come and gone, I started to focus all of my energy exclusively on the giant slalom. I have to admit that for the first time in my career, I had to hope for a bit of luck. As could be expected, the time in North America was a real challenge. During the long gliding curves on my favorite slope in Beaver Creek, I had huge problems with my boots; at this point, I became really desperate. No matter what I tried, nothing seemed to speed up my bottom line. Luckily, I was able to come in at second place in the giant slalom. For the first time in a long while, I felt comfortable about my rank again. It was a real satisfaction for me, as gratifying as when I used to win on this slope, which journalists had begun calling "Hermann Maier's signature slope." I was standing on the winner's podium with tears in my eyes, realizing that I had already proven wrong my pessimistic theory from Sölden.

The World Cup, however, seemed to be over for me. Bode Miller had won four times after only five races, and he had 480 out of 500 points on his account. Everything seemed rather obvious to me. Bode had what the Americans call "momentum," a series of races in which everything comes together just right. You are on a mental high, where everything comes easily and goes your way. I still remember this feeling from the times before my accident, when I seemed undefeatable in certain periods. And it was supposed to go on like this. Including the slalom (held at night) in Sestriere, Miller had won a race in every possible discipline within a phenomenal sixteen days. My hat's off to Bode. Nobody else has ever been able to do this! Considering his stellar seasonal debut, though, there were some surprising challenges ahead for the prodigy from New Hampshire.

GOING CAMPING WITH BODE

December 6, 2004. On my flight back to Europe, I had mixed emotions. I was going home with 274 World Cup points in the bag, along with Heini's meticulously worked-out plan, sent by e-mail, for beating jet lag and seamlessly adjusting to the time change (e.g., "stay awake for two hours, eye patch, four hours of sleep under a warm blanket"). I would have loved to celebrate my thirty-second birthday, but there wasn't even time to think about it. After four weeks in North America, the FIS mercifully gave us one whole night to make a pit stop at home and get some clean clothes before getting back on the road for the exhausting trip to Val d'Isère. On arriving home, I found that Zeus had prepared a birthday present of sorts for me: There was rain in the French Alps, and our first downhill training run was canceled. I thus had an additional day to recharge my batteries before we flew to France in a privately rented jet in preparation for the start of the European World Cup tour, which would take place for the next three and a half months in Val d'Isère, Gröde, Alta Badia, Flachau, Bormio, Chamonix, and so on. Everything seems to happen all at once: Monday or Tuesday we arrive and check in. We move things around in our room and put away our things. Team meeting. Press appointments. Slope inspection. One, two, or three downhill training runs. Downhill race, dope test. Super-G, dope test. Giant slalom, dope test. For those who do all-around and on the weekends with combination (a combined downhill and slalom event), we had an additional slalom on Sundays. After every racing week, we hurriedly pack our bags and quickly check in back home for a day or two with our families. They don't call it "ski circus" for nothing.

One of the racers takes the idea of a circus almost literally: Bode Miller, who travels with a big RV. During the 2004/2005 ski season, he had a Cruiser 880 F with 226 PS (twenty-eight feet long and eight tons heavy) at his disposal. It includes everything he could possibly need: a refrigerator and freezer, satellite TV with two flat-screen TVs, a hot water heater, and a "level equalizing system," in case Miller ever feels the sudden urge to sleep next to the "mousetrap." I really do think it's cool how Bode pulls it off. He makes the best of the hectic and demanding ski season by turning it into a camping trip of sorts. Within the Austrian Ski Federation, where everyone walks in a straight row, nobody could ever live like that. With the U.S. ski team, Bode can get away with doing this, and his victories give him the right to do so. Even if I could, this lifestyle wouldn't be the thing for me, though. I feel really comfortable having meals together with my teammates. We joke and have fun together. The only time I am envious that my American colleague is able to slip away into his own realm is between two downhill runs. Bode has been used to living in seclusion since his childhood in rural New Hampshire. His "support staff" consists of his girlfriend and a pal who doubles as his driver and cook. But living with two other people for weeks on end in such a small place and being together all the time isn't exactly everybody's cup of tea. There are sweaty clothes, ski boots, gloves, helmets, goggles, and other equipment lying around everywhere. But it seems that leading this type of vagabond life is in fashion with the Americans. Daron Rahlves has acquired his own converted tour bus in the meantime, and it's way more spectacular than Bode's RV. It could even fit into the NASCAR trailer parks. Isn't it just all about who has the biggest one?

THE DOPE SHOCK

December 17, 2004. There was something in the air during the downhill training sessions in Val Gardena, Italy. Somehow everybody had kind of a bad feeling. Everybody except Michael Walchhofer, who won the super-G (I placed second). Walter gave us a lift back to the hotel after the victory ceremony, and all of a sudden he said something you don't want to even think about: "There's a doping case in our team." Regarding who? My press guy didn't know. "But you'll get all the news in a few minutes at our team meeting." After the Austrian team members gathered in the Wolkenstein hotel, Toni Giger showed up with furrowed brow. "While we're sitting here, a press conference is taking place at the media center," he began. "It's about a drug case concerning an Austrian team member." When you hear something like that, you have hundreds of thoughts going through your head. How could something like this happen? What consequences will the accused colleague face? What does this mean for the other team members? And, can we rule out any error? Our head coach told us about the many circumstances that could lead to a positive drug test. Finally, he revealed the name: "It's Hans Knauss." He had tested positive three weeks ago after the downhill in Lake Louise, Canada.

Our foreign "friends" had just been waiting for a situation like this. The German Press Agency gloatingly released the breaking news about the "biggest dope case in alpine ski racing ever" over the telex machine. I think back to the "Baxter case." The guy from Scotland had his bronze medal from the 2002 Olympic slalom literally ripped from his neck. It was because of a nose spray he had used. A few months later the medal was given to Benni Raich, who had originally placed fourth. Our competition didn't like our serial victories, and this news was certain to please them. How could this happen to an old hand like Hans Knauss? Hans assured us, believably, that the only plausible explanation for this unfortunate incident was a contaminated dietary supplement. Of course, that is an act of extreme carelessness, something that should never happen to a professional athlete. Nevertheless, I couldn't help thinking right away, "Did I have every single mineral supplement and electrolyte tested for any possible contamination before mixing them into my sports drinks over the past few months? What medicine did I take during the fall when I had a cold? Had I drunk only out of factory-sealed bottles when I was on the road? Did things really go according to protocol during my last few dope tests?"

At the risk of boring you, here is my opinion on the doping control system as it is in place at the moment. For sure, I think that all-encompassing tests that cover all athletes are the best. I think that we can achieve our best results if we train continuously and thoroughly. It's not for nothing that I spend six or seven days a week at the Olympic Training Center. The rules are set, and we have to follow them. If I'm driving on the interstate highway at 90 mph and I get caught, I have to pay, even if I can prove that there was hardly any traffic on that particular day and I wouldn't have put anyone at risk even at 102 mph. In the same way, as a professional athlete, I have to double-check with my professional sports medicine coaches every time I have a cold: "Am I allowed to take this generic cold medicine?" While this level of caution is understandable and necessary, I think it is wrong that athletes sometimes are made to feel like criminals. It's a pretty sorry scene when I'm sitting at a table in a café and I hear people at the next table talking about different athletes and presumptuously asserting, "This guy is taking something and that other guy is taking something." The whole system of doping checks and balances is rather questionable at any rate. Sometimes, as a top athlete and international role model I feel that I am treated like a prisoner on parole: I have to fill out a form in advance that reveals exactly where I am planning to be every single day. And if by chance I should decide to spend the night at a friend's house after a party and drive home a day late, I have to call in and notify the "powers that be" of the change in plans.

Since I have a clean conscience, I can play it safe by having everything that I consume tested in advance. But sometimes you simply don't have enough time to do that. I have to be careful when I shop and with everything that I consume when I travel or when I'm at the team hotel. Ever since the Knauss incident, all the drinks of the Austrian ski team are under close watch all the time.

DÉJÀ VU IN KITZBÜHEL

January 18, 2005. Kitzbühel. It's the usual chaos, the last racing weekend before the World Championships in Bormio, which is the most important of the season. I arrived without a single season victory. I knew this sort of feeling only from my legendary comeback in 2003, and the coming days would remind me of it a few times more. It started off very promising, with my best downhill training runs ever on the Streif, Kitzbühel's phenomenal downhill course. But the better I felt, the worse the weather became. Finally, it was so bad that they canceled the downhill race altogether. What a shame! It would have been a great chance. The super-G was rescheduled for Monday, just as it had been two years earlier. The last chance before the world championships to see how I stood up against the competition really felt strange to me, like I'd been there, done that.

I decided to do everything just as in 2003, and on Saturday night I escaped all the hubbub of the "Hahnenkamm." On Sunday, when the slalom was scheduled, we trained at an exclusive local ski resort in

Salzburg; then we went back to Kitzbühel. When I looked out the window Sunday morning, it was snowing, and I thought, "Everything is coming together in just the right way. The masses of people are gone, the craze is over, and I can now look forward to an enjoyable and laid-back race." Indeed, everything was going right this time. As in 2003 I was racing close to perfection in the middle section of the course, and I won! I had been waiting for this moment for ten months and through seventeen races, and now I was savoring it. Out of five super-G races in Kitzbühel, I achieved four victories and one second place. Try to copy that if you can!

January 27, 2005. We flew to Bormio for the world championships by helicopter. My expectations were high. After all, this is where I skied the best super-G of my life, thereby finalizing the overall World Cup win in 1999/2000 with a record score of 2,000 points. I was looking forward to racing again on the demanding Pista Stelvio, and to feeling the unique Italian flair.

Unfortunately, everything went differently. The overall mood of the event was rather bland. Compared to the World Cup finale in the spring of 2000, there were hardly any spectators in the stands. No wonder, since the ticket prices were absurdly high. Right after the super-G, the organizers made some quick price adjustments to boost attendance. Even in the lovely historical center of the town there was hardly anything going on. It seemed like they had scared away the real ski tourists with the world championships. Once again, the organizers seemed to be shooting themselves in the foot. The world championships had been extended for commercial reasons. Two weeks is just too long. I would shorten the event to ten days; that would make it thrilling from the first day to the last. The way it is now, the people there have too much time to ponder. Journalists don't have enough work, and they start thinking up needless stories. Even the most loyal fans are happy when it's finally over.

I let myself get sucked into the general sullen mood, which wasn't exactly enhancing my performance. Once you're running in the wrong direction, Murphy's Law kicks in, and things start going wrong. I raced the super-G picture perfect, but unfortunately it was a slow-motion picture and I came in fourth, barely missing the bronze medal. This was a big disappointment to my fans. Having been dubbed "Mr. Super-G" after winning a medal in every race in which I took part at the Olympics and world championships, I was now being measured by higher standards. "Oh no! Now the world championships are going to start totally messed-up too!" was the first thing that came to mind. I started secluding myself. The next day, while my teammates got together at the Hotel Miramonte for their daily press session with local journalists, I rode my ergometer bike in my hotel room to soothe my soul. I didn't feel like having journalists ask me questions, especially when they had already predetermined the answers anyway. Instead, I turned into somewhat of an observer. From this point of view the bland championships looked completely different. It was really interesting to see how certain people react when it looks like you've hit rock bottom. Food for thought. I knew exactly what would be coming up for me next: the traditional discussion about the downhill qualification, which usually tops the headlines for days in Austria's newspapers.

One of the radio reporters started the process with an especially clever question by asking me what decision I would make regarding the coveted downhill slots if I were a soccer coach. In marked contrast to the sport of skiing, you don't have any training test runs in soccer, and a good coach knows who will be the strongest man on "day X." This is sort of what I answered him with a smile. I didn't know that they would turn the whole long interview into a single sentence, which they kept repeating on Austrian radio stations: "I think my coaches decided a long time ago that they will give me a slot." When I walked to my breakfast table the next morning, there was a fax with the newspaper headline, printed boldly across two pages, lying next to my plate: "The Coaches Have Decided Already—It's Me!" Now they had their perfect story, and they made a big fuss about it. We had emergency meetings with the coaches of the Austrian ski team and radio reporters. We tried to make things right and had discussions about the brutal qualification system, about who would get to race and who wouldn't. The former German slalom racer Christian Neureuther added fuel to the flames when he voiced his opinion in a German newspaper, which the biggest Austrian daily compounded: "Maier's Time Is Over," screamed the headline, and that made me even more upset. Why does everyone who put himself forward as an expert get so much attention? Who is this dude Neureuther, anyway? "Neureuther better stick to soccer or whatever sport he comes from," is what I said when I was confronted by journalists with his statement; it was my first angry reaction. One journalist said matter-of-factly, "You know as well as I that he was a ski racer." That might be true, but it was at a time when I was maybe two or three years old. Later, I was told that he had been part of the jury of a popular German–Austrian TV quiz show, where the contestants were presented with such challenging tasks as to see how many plastic goldfish could be tossed into an aquarium in a minimal amount of time (I think it was seven or eight). Seems to me like he was better qualified to judge contestants on that show than to become a self-styled sports analyst.

It was no wonder that all this upheaval almost made me late for my training start. As soon as I had my boots buckled, they hurried me onto the track. Then something happened that is typical for a situation such as this: I had other things going on in my head. Since the ability to focus is such a crucial factor in ski racing, being distracted can have fatal consequences. I raced halfheartedly to the St. Peter jump and took off like a rocket. For a split second I thought of my crash at Nagano. Then I hit the ground. I was sliding across the slope when suddenly I could feel this twitching pain on my left shinbone. Apparently, the steel corner of my loose ski had hit me. When I finally stopped, I mentally located and examined each limb and breathed a sigh of relief. The bleeding bruise on my lower leg wasn't too bad; Artur would put six stitches there later.

What now? I didn't really feel like competing in the downhill under these circumstances; somebody else might as well use my starting position.

As always when there is a touchy situation, Peter Schröcksnadel found just the right words to calm me down and encourage me. Of course I raced, and came in seventeenth. I was so far away from winning a medal that I didn't even beat myself up over my poor performance: forget about it and look ahead.

"Ahead" was the giant slalom that took place two days before the closing ceremony of this lackluster world championships. During the practice I whined and got on Andy's nerves. "Nothing is working right," I complained. "Things have been working way better than this already this year." My coach looked at me the way a father looks at his sullen son and said, "It's not as bad as you think. To be honest, I don't see any mistakes. Just race as you have been and you'll be among the top finishers." Then Heini called me from Obertauern to encourage me. "Anything is still possible with the giant slalom! Go and ride your ergometer; that will help your regeneration." Now I was fed up. "I'm done biking," I shouted angrily. "I need to go outside, get some fresh air, go for a walk, and try to get my mind on other things." I borrowed a BMW scooter and drove around the vernal, snowless landscape. I stopped at a grove of larch trees, which I love, and started to walk around. That really helped to calm me down. I suddenly felt the buildup of competition pressure again, and indeed, I couldn't even wait to attack once more in my new favorite discipline. Because of an unforeseen strike by the Italian state-run television crews, the race was postponed one day, and I had even more time to enjoy the beautiful landscape.

The actual giant slalom had an almost mystical quality to it. I was completely calm, and at the same time had that incredible feeling of being invincible. I knew that I would accomplish something special. Before run two, I was placed second, right after Daron Rahlves, and I went for an all-out attack. I was already waiting in the starting box when the race was interrupted because the Canadian competitor Roy had crashed and been injured. Unexpected additional minutes like that can throw you off balance. But I waited patiently until the race resumed. I heard them say, "One more minute." I focused and then just went for it. Behind me I noticed Rahlves's coach, who was taking one snapshot of me after another. I still don't know whether he wanted to get me off balance or was just a huge fan of mine. But no matter. I managed to race close to perfection. I knew I had given my best, and I couldn't possibly have done more for my victory.

When Daron came in third right after Benni Raich, I grabbed my skis and sank into the snow with tears in my eyes. I had so many things going through my head. Memories of my previous victories were passing by in slow motion. It's unbelievable to think about all that had happened since my last gold medal at the World Championships in Vail. Then I thought of the man who had invented the ski with which I had been winning for ten years now: Alois Rohrmoser, the founder of Atomic Skis, had passed away a few days before. I dedicated this victory to him, the victory that in my first euphoria I called "the most important one of all." None of the five gold medals I had won before was earned as hard as this one.

During the right moment things had gone right again. It couldn't have been better. It may sound odd, but I preferred this one gold medal amid all the drama a lot more than if everything had gone perfectly from the start and I had won three gold medals just like that. The giant slalom meant a lot more to me than it might seem at first. It is the discipline I had started out with, and the one that I fought my way back to the World Cup with. I was very lucky to be able to accomplish great feats even after my accident, but it just didn't seem that I had enough for a victory in the giant slalom. Is there anything else that would seem better than this happy ending?

In contrast to the World Championships of 2001 in St. Anton, where I arrived as a top favorite and then broke down, in Bormio I was able to redeem myself. To be able to start over at the bottom and make my way back to the top is my trademark. And this doesn't apply only to my athletic life; it applies to my life in general. It's a basic attitude: Don't ever write off anybody, because nothing is impossible. After a very long party I dropped into bed and thanked the good Lord that I was allowed to reach my goal for the season at last. I had known from the beginning that the overall World Cup wasn't going to be a possibility this year. Now I have the one gold medal that probably no one had considered me capable of winning.

SUDDENLY EVERYTHING WORKS OUT

That one party was all the celebrating we could afford. Although the chase after World Cup points continued after the world championships, I decided to take things easier. I confirmed my world championships performance in Kranskja Gora and finished second. I decided from now on to focus on the fast disciplines. What was also important now was to look toward the Olympics in 2006. What was my goal? What could we improve? I had everything set up inside my head, had clear ideas and assumptions of how it all could work out. I decided to squeeze in an additional training session on the Reiteralm and tested one of my old boot models. I immediately felt how it had a positive effect on my posture. So many times I had had these boots with me, but I wasn't brave enough to race in them. Finally, in Kvitfjell, Norway, I did. It's especially hard to win on the Olympic downhill slope of 1994 because of its long gliding passages. Usually, the time differences are so small that if you make the smallest mistake, you've given away the victory. But this time I did everything right, and with my old boots I won my first downhill race of the season. Didn't that feel good! In addition to that, I even won the super-G the next day. My lead (83/100 second) reminded me of my best times as a racer. With this, my fiftieth World Cup victory, I finally caught up with Alberto Tomba in the overall ranking list. This was definitely all I had ever wanted to accomplish during this season! During the World Cup final in Switzerland I congratulated Bode Miller for racing his huge lead in points across the finish line, and my teammate Benni Raich for his phenomenal finish. The only disappointment was that I had to yield to Bode the super-G trophy, which I was so close to winning. I had expected to win that trophy. After all, my American colleague had been without a victory in twenty-three World Cup races, but in this case he tied for first place with Daron Rahlves.

THE QUESTION IS, WHY?

After every season I give one or two big interviews. And every time I have to answer the same inevitable question: "In your career you have reached everything you've wanted to. Why do you still do this to yourself? What else do you have to prove?" It's very simple, really. Because of all the excitement, the joy of winning, and the pleasure of being able to do what I like most. I still need this "kick," and who knows how long it'll stay this way? Every season is one big adventure. What reason would there be for me to quit something I really like prematurely? I know that I have only a limited amount of time to continue to race at this level. But I do want to use this time to its maximum. You constantly learn new things and gain new knowledge, especially if you are at a top level. I am certain that there are not many racers who have been allowed to take so many precious experiences with them. And you learn from your mistakes, that's for sure. I probably would have gained some of my knowledge a lot earlier if it hadn't been for my motorcycle accident. The question is, would I still be racing then? Fate has been kind to me. I'm glad that I dropped my bricklayer's stuff in the garage and started living my dream.

How much time do I have left to live my dreams? Of course, things get more challenging as you get older. Injuries take longer to heal. Training takes a lot more effort. On the other hand, I benefit from my knowledge every single year. My routine gives me a great deal more satisfaction. And when you're in your thirties you appreciate the fact that you're still able to achieve certain things. Of one thing I am certain: It's really good for your mind always to be pushing your limits. As you get older, you learn to husband your energy. You kick back more often and focus on the really important things in life. If I imagine my achievements of the season on a graph, it starts looking a lot like an electrocardiogram: up and down, up and down. I can concentrate on the races that I'm truly interested in, and those I really enjoy. I can savor life even more than before. I am my own boss.

I know that as long as I am a racer, I will set trends. Because when it comes to material, skiing works like a team sport, since the others benefit from my experiments and experiences. One example: After using my "old new" boots in Kvitfjell, Norway, and winning two races in a row, Daron Rahlves copied me right away. But I have to live with that. Of course, I would have an advantage in developing my own equipment quietly, without anyone knowing. Now my teammates think, "If this works for Maier, then we should try it too!" Funny, though, it's always I who have to take the first step. Something like that wouldn't be possible with Formula 1. Michael Schumacher is able to enjoy absolute exclusiveness.

WHERE DO I WANT TO GO?

For how long will I be the one who sets the trends? Honestly, I don't know. I don't want to commit myself. Since my most important contracts run through 2007, you can assume that I will add another season after the Olympics 2006 in Turin.

The question is how the sport of skiing will evolve in general. When I look at my skiing DVDs in slow motion, I believe I can see a slight downward trend. Don't ask me why it is this way, but I think that things are similar with other sports. People say that Michael Schumacher drove Formula 1 into a dead end. So what now? Who will entice a world champion named Alonso to leave home? And what will happen to cycling after Lance Armstrong? Where is the basketball star who can compete against Michael Jordan? And where are the Joe Montanas, Dan Marinos, and John Elways in football? I sometimes get the feeling that sports is running out of stars.

AND WHAT COMES AFTERWARD?

I like to train, and that's not just because of skiing. It's because I care about my physical condition, my well-being, and my attitude toward life.

You should be in good condition and not lose your breath after taking a few steps. Every morning when I wake up I feel an innate urge to further myself. It will probably always be like that. After all, that is what I am used to from childhood, when I was constantly challenged but had to work hard for everything. And I am also used to being successful. All that is appealing to me, but at some point I assume that the drive will be gone, and that's okay. Then I can start kicking back and relaxing. That might be very nice for a while, but I am always looking for new challenges. I will never stay in the same spot treading water; that just wouldn't be me.

It's not just all about condition and coordination. I am already looking forward to the time when I can train differently. To bike up a mountain like the wind, to run long distances—I can't do that now. Now I carry a great amount of muscle mass around with me, because that's the only way to be a competitive skier. Later on, I will look at possibilities to enhance my body; but then I will do it as a way of finding balance.

OLYMPIC WINTER GAMES 2006

People always say that my last big goal will be a downhill gold medal. Every time I read about this somewhere, it makes me smile. It's not true; it's just one of those things the press makes up. Of course, the Olympics are a huge goal. But I am one of the few athletes who will be able to participate in the Olympics twice. Once is not enough! I am glad that I took two gold medals the last time, while other big athletes have tried to achieve this forever. My big goal, of course, is a gold medal, and I don't care what discipline it is in, even the slalom.

The men's races at the 2006 Olympics in Italy are going to be in Sestriere, which is 6,500 feet above sea level, and I have great memories of this ski resort. It is where I had one of the best super-G races of my whole career, in 2004, and I won the big crystal trophy not even two years after my near-fatal motorcycle crash. Italy seems to have the perfect soil for thrilling competitions, and I am certain that the Olympics are indeed going to be thrilling. I am curious to find out what people will expect from the competitors this time. Things won't go without conflict of some kind; that seems to be a given. There will be big discussions about qualifying, about accommodation problems, and about—who knows? You shouldn't look too far into the future. The Olympic Games are important, but as the name already says, we're talking about a game here, and that's exactly how I will always think about sports in general.

MY PERSONAL
RACING DIARY

AC	Austrian Championships	
EC	Europe Cup	
WC	World Cup	
OG	Olympic Games	
WCH	World Championships	
D	Downhill	
SG	Super-G	

GS	Giant Slalom	
S	Slalom	
CDS	Combined (Downhill + Slalom)	
DNF	Did Not Finish	
DNS	Did Not Start	
DSQ	Disqualified	
DNQ2	Did Not Qualify for Second Run	

SEASON 1994/1995

AC	24.03.1995	Ellmau	AUT	SG	40.

1. Salzgeber (AUT) 1:39.00, 2. Rzehak (AUT) +0.05, 3. Wirth (AUT) +0.22 (40. Maier +4.96)
I enter the race with the very last starting number; then there's a warming trend in the weather. Help!
The slope is flowing away from me!

AC	25.03.1995	Spital am Semmering	AUT	GS	18.

1. Reiter (AUT) 2:25.99, 2. Wirth (AUT) +0.94, 3. Mader (AUT) +2.47 (18. Maier +6.92)
I squeeze into my old, stretched-out racing suit from Anita Wachter and fight through the deep holes
with number 130.

AC	26.03.1995	Semmering	AUT	S	DNF1

1. Reiter (AUT) 1:29.42, 2. Albrecht (AUT) +0.54, 3. Voglreiter (AUT) +0.76 (Maier DNF1)
I am disqualified; however, I am accepted into Salzburg's "second-string" pool of ski racers (Landes-
Kader B).

FIS Race	28.03.1995	Château-d'Oex	SUI	GS	7.

1. Locher (SUI) 2:38.64, 2. Buechel (LIE) +0.44, 3. Kernen (SUI) +2.26 (7. Maier +3.20)
My first successful appearance abroad. I slept in a double bed next to my skis; did not have breakfast,
took too long for the slope inspection; nonetheless, I impress the Swiss national team.

FIS Race	29.03.1995	Château-d'Oex	SUI	GS	6.

1. Eggenburger (SUI) 2:46.02, 2. Plaschy (SUI) +0.52, 3. Kernen (SUI) +0.89 (6. Maier +1.55)
I come back with 12 FIS points. I have accomplished the leap out of nowhere into the top 100!

FIS Race	09.04.1995	Altenmarkt	AUT	D	24.

1. Schifferer (AUT) 1:24.18, 2. Fritz Strobl (AUT) +0.10, 3. Dreschl (AUT) +0.31 (24. Maier +3.38)
Atomic digs out a pair of 2.14-m-long skis for me; I had seen those only on TV thus far!

AC   10.04.1995   Altenmarkt   AUT   D   9.
1. Aubonnet (FRA) 1:20.01, 2. Vogt (LIE) +0.04, 3. Huber (GER) +0.06 (19. Maier +1.39)
Because I was too slow the day before, I walk into a sporting goods store and buy some Wet-Jet wax.
It works!

FIS Race   11.04.1995   Altenmarkt   AUT   D   6.
1. Huber (GER) 1:20.41, 2. Aubonnet (FRA) +0.11, 3. Lichtenegger (AUT) +0.15 (6. Maier +0.57)
I am on the move; if they had another downhill the next day, I would already be up on the winner's
podium!

FIS Race   09.12.1995   Neustift   AUT   GS   3.
1. Millet (FRA) 1:48.90, 2. Königsrainer (ITA) +0.27, 3. Maier (AUT) +0.40
My first race as a former bricklayer; I am donning a Spyder racing suit that I borrowed from snow-
boarder Maria Pichler. I triumph over the entire Austrian Ski Federation Europe Cup team.

SEASON 1995/1996

FIS Race   10.12.1995   Neustift   AUT   SG   9.
1. Bjornsson (ISL) 1:24.55, 2. Piccard (FRA) +0.07, 3. Schönfelder (AUT) +0.19 (9. Maier +1.24)
High starting number, giant pits; I know this is how it's going to be for a while.

FIS Race   14.12.1995   Predazzo Alpe di Pampeago   ITA   GS   7.
1. Holzer (ITA) 2:21.14, 2. Bormolini (ITA) +0.59, 3. Königsrainer (ITA) +0.60 (7. Maier +0.91)
I am perplexed by the incredibly fast gate placement; my skiing style is too rounded.

FIS Race   15.12.1995   Predazzo Alpe di Pampeago   ITA   GS   4.
1. Schönfelder (AUT) 2:22.84, 2. Bormolini (ITA) +0.52, 3. Belfrond (ITA) +0.98 (4. Maier +1.22)
Unbelievable how brutal the giant slaloms are in Italy!

FIS Race   20.12.1995   Altenmarkt   AUT   D   3.
1. Galli (ITA) 1:19.26, 2. Holzknecht (AUT) +0.10, 3. Maier (AUT) +0.16
My fourth downhill, and I'm up on the winner's podium!

FIS Race   26.12.1995   Abtenau   AUT   GS   DNF2
1. Mlekuz (SLO) 2:18.70, 2. Schilchegger (AUT) +1.25, 3. Ertl (GER) +1.34 (Maier DNF2)
My secret breakthrough. Even though I'm disqualified during the second round, I know that soon it
will be my turn to win!

EC   08.01.1996   Les Arcs   FRA   GS   2.
1. Locher (SUI) 1:58.27, 2. Maier (AUT) +0.88, 3. Curra (AUT) +1.19
I secretly do my warm-up on the racing slope, which is actually against the rules. Because of my old
racing suit, no one takes any notice!

EC   09.01.1996   Les Arcs   FRA   GS   1.
1. Maier (AUT) 1:57.18, 2. Locher (SUI) +0.13, 3. Buraas (NOR) +1.19
My first victory in the Europe Cup, against Locher, who had come in fourth in the World Cup two days
earlier in Flachau!

EC   11.01.1996   Serre Chevalier   FRA   GS   1.
1. Maier (AUT) 2:29.39, 2. Albrecht (AUT) +0.11, 3. Königsrainer (ITA) +0.24
From eighth place in the first round to victory!

EC   15.01.1996   Les Orres   FRA   D   13.
1. Holzknecht (AUT) 1:11.67, 2. Filischkin (RUS) +0.47, 3. Eberharter (AUT) +0.57 (13. Maier +1.14)
My first downhill on a glider's racecourse. I lack experience and struggle with the right equipment choice.

EC 16.01.1996 Les Orres   FRA D 6.
1. Fritz Strobl (AUT) 1:12.11, 2. Filischkin (RUS) +0.14, 3. Eberharter (AUT) +0.16 (6. Maier +0.43)
There's an upward trend: I've reduced my time lag to an acceptable degree.

EC 17.01.1996 Les Orres   FRA SG 16.
1. Kröll (AUT) 1:12.50, 2. Wirth (AUT) +0.26, 3. Albrecht (AUT) +0.39 (16. Maier +1.53)
Wrong wax; nothing works anymore!

EC 18.01.1996 Les Orres   FRA SG 14.
1. Kröll (AUT) 1:12.12, 2. Fritz Strobl (AUT) +0.29, 3. Millet (FRA) +0.47 (14. Maier +1.58)
The competition admires me because of my makeshift ski boot, which is held together by screws.

EC 21.01.1996 Altenmarkt AUT D 14.
1. Rupp (SUI) 1:18.93, 2. Bloomfield (USA) +0.50, 3. Fritz Strobl (AUT) +0.57 (14. Maier +1.05)

EC 22.01.1996 Altenmarkt AUT D 17.
1. Rupp (SUI) 1:18.34, 2. Oldfield (CAN) +0.13, 3. Deissenböck (GER) +0.69 (17. Maier +1,46)

EC 23.01.1996 Altenmarkt AUT SG 1.
1. Maier (AUT) 1:22.24, 2. Fritz Strobl (AUT) +1.05, 3. Seletto (ITA) +1.67
My first super-G victory, and with my signature Maier lead!

EC 24.01.1996 Altenmarkt AUT SG 1.
1. Maier (AUT) 1:23.93, 2. Eberharter (AUT) +1.38, 3. Koblar (SLO) +1.52
My self-confidence rises with each victory.

EC 27.01.1996 Veysonnaz SUI D 19.
1. Herrmann (SUI) 1:20.05, 2. Holzknecht (AUT) +0.09, 3. Rauffer (GER) +0.16 (19. Maier +1.31)

EC 27.01.1996 Veysonnaz SUI D 5.
1. Holzknecht (AUT) 1:19.55, 2. Seletto (ITA) +0.31, 3. Rosener (USA) +0.40 (5. Maier +0.50)

EC 06.02.1996 Altaussee   AUT S DNF2
1. Sykora (AUT) 1:51.40, 2. Furuseth (NOR) +0.63, 3. Simond (FRA) +0.96 (Maier DNF2)

EC 09.02.1996 Sella Nevea ITA GS 1.
1. Maier (AUT) 1:38.90, 2. Zucchelli (ITA) +0.70, 3. Schönfelder (AUT) +0.82
There's a race almost every other day; I am exhausted. Back pains, but I have to travel by car to my World Cup debut.

WC001 10.02.1996 Hinterstoder AUT GS 26.
1. von Grünigen (SUI) 2:40.61, 2. Kälin (SUI) +0.35, 3. Reiter (AUT) +0.94 (26. Maier +4.48)
Huge mistakes in the upper portion; 31st during the first round, but after a disqualification I get to start in the second round!

EC 12.02.1996 Kranjska Gora SLO GS 24.
1. Königsrainer (ITA) 1:53.17, 2. Holzer (ITA) +0.11, 3. Nana (ITA) +0.18 (24. Maier +3.06)

EC 14.02.1996 St. Johann AUT GS 9.
1. Buechel (LIE) 1:37.22, 2. Staub (SUI) +0.21, 3. Nana (ITA) +0.29 (9. Maier +0.51)

EC 15.02.1996 St. Johann AUT GS 4.
1. Schilchegger (AUT) 1:46.97, 2. Kleinlercher (AUT) +0.16, 3. Torpe (NOR) +0.35 (4. Maier +0.54)
I am now overall Europe Cup winner and, as the giant slalom winner, have a guaranteed spot in the World Cup.

WC002   07.03.1996   Kvitfjell/Hafjell   NOR   SG   11.
1. Aamodt (NOR) 1:33.15, 2. Alphand (FRA) +0.06, 3. Kjus (NOR) +0.30 (11. Maier +1.64)
World Cup finals; debut in my favorite event.

WC003   09.03.1996   Kvitfjell/Hafjell   NOR   GS   DSQ2
1. Kälin (SUI) 2:12.44, 2. Stiansen (NOR) +0.40, 3. Saioni (FRA) +0.74 (Maier DSQ2)
During the celebration, Austrian Ski Federation men's head coach Margreiter informs me that I have been accepted onto the national ski team. I had already ensured a starting slot for myself by virtue of my giant slalom overall World Cup victory.

SEASON 1996/1997
WC004   27.10.1996   Sölden   AUT   GS   DNF1
1. Locher (SUI) 2:03.20, 2. Von Grünigen (SUI) +0.31, 3. Aamodt (NOR) +1.00 (Maier DNF1)
The World Cup ski course begins; my "class teacher" is Toni Giger (trainer of the giant slalom/super-G group).

WC005   25.11.1996   Park City UT   USA   GS   6.
1. Josef Strobl (AUT) 2:31.42, 2. Knauss (AUT) +0.42, 3. Von Grünigen (SUI) +0.48 (6. Maier +1.18)
My relationship with the coaches is a difficult one; it is hard for me to let them press me into a mold.

WC006   30.11.1996   Breckenridge CO   USA   GS   22.
1. Nyberg (SWE) 2:11.83, 2. Kälin (SUI) +0.16, 3. Knauss (AUT) +0.20 (22. Maier +2.76)
I'm tired and feel more and more unwell during the long time period at high altitude in Colorado.

WC007   22.12.1996   Alta Badia   ITA   GS   16.
1. Von Grünigen (SUI) 2:32.66, 2. Locher (SUI) +0.77, 3. Nana (ITA) +1.49 (16. Maier +3.50)
After two weeks of "sick leave" I clench my teeth on the steepest giant slalom slope.

WC008   05.01.1997   Kranjska Gora   SLO   GS   14.
1. Von Grünigen (SUI) 2:13.42, 2. Voglreiter (AUT) +1.64, 3. Aamodt (NOR) +2.36 (14. Maier +3.01)
There's so little snow that you can't even do your warm-up runs next to the slope; at least I'm fit again!

WC009   11.01.1997   Chamonix   FRA   D   DNF
1. Ghedina (ITA) 2:01.56, 2. Skaardal (NOR) +0.01, 3. Franz (AUT) +0.11 (Maier DNF1)
My first World Cup downhill; overly motivated after strong performances in my training runs. Crash, broken arm. Forced time-out from competition. Starting as of right now, there's a new wind blowing in my training practices; Heini Bergmüller has become my endurance coach.

EC   04.02.1997   La Thuile   ITA   D   5.
1. R. Assinger (AUT) 1:47.45, 2. Greber (AUT) +0.27, 3. Eberharter (AUT) +0.50 (5. Maier +1.11)
Only three and a half weeks after the crash I get going again with a splint on my left hand.

EC   05.02.1997   La Thuile   ITA   D   3.
1. Assinger (AUT) 1:22.71, 2. Greber (AUT) +1.00, 3. Maier (AUT) +1.01
An awesome race; the trainers are exuberant. I am not quite so taken by my own performance.

EC   06.02.1997   La Thuile   ITA   SG   DNF
1. Salzgeber (AUT) 1:14.74, 2. Seletto (ITA) +0.23, 3. Piccard (FRA) +0.42 (Maier DNF)
Shock! A complete somersault on my way to victory. Total luck: The splinted hand on which the surgery was performed is intact.

EC   07.02.1997   La Thuile   ITA   SG   2.
1. Seletto (ITA) 1:14.29, 2. Maier (AUT) +0.11, 3. Fournier (FRA) +0.81
"Don't fall on your hand," rolls constantly around in my head. I'm content with second place.

EC   11.02.1997   Sella Nevea   ITA   GS   DNS2
1. Schilchegger (AUT) 1:43.66, 2. Belfrond (ITA) +0.15, 3. Covili (FRA) +0.23 (Maier DNS2)
Fever; I leave after the first round!

WC010   21.02.1997   Garmisch-Partenkirchen   GER   SG   2.
1. Alphand (FRA) 1:15.32, 2. Maier (AUT) +0.55, 3. Perathoner (ITA) +0.58
I request a starting slot and am allowed to go to the start instead of Werner Franz, who has also broken his arm. The famous pink fan pig makes its appearance for the first time, and has reason to celebrate right away.

WC011   23.02.1997   Garmisch-Partenkirchen   GER   SG   1.
1. Maier (AUT) 1:21.64, 2. Ghedina (ITA) +0.52, 3. Skaardal (NOR) +0.61
My Austrian Ski Federation colleagues are disappointed by the spoiled world championships. I am motivated, celebrate my first victory, and am annoyed: Surely, I would have won a medal during the world championships!

WC012   02.03.1997   Kvitfjell   NOR   SG   4.
1. Josef Strobl (AUT) 1:24.95, 2. Schifferer (AUT) +0.68, 3. Kjus (NOR) +0.92 (4. Maier +1.07)
Highly motivated from my victory in Garmisch, I feel that I can't do much wrong in the super-G.

WC013   08.03.1997   Shigakogen   JPN   GS   12.
1. Von Grünigen (SUI) 2:41.68, 2. Schifferer (AUT) +0.36, 3. Accola (SUI) +0.61 (12. Maier +1.38)
Dress rehearsal for the Olympics; could be better.

WC014   13.03.1997   Vail CO   USA   SG   19.
1. Schifferer (AUT) 1:33.76, 2. Josef Strobl (AUT) +0.04, 3. Ghedina (ITA) +0.12 (19. Maier +1.54)
Stopped by the strong headwind; luckily, the last speed event on the old racecourse in Vail.

WC015   15.03.1997   Vail CO   USA   GS   5.
1. Von Grünigen (SUI) 2:18.58, 2. Salzgeber (AUT) +0.99, 3. Schifferer (AUT) +1.39 (5. Maier +2.20)
My best giant slalom so far; during the subsequent World Cup party I am in top form with my cowboy hat.

SEASON 1997/1998
WC016   24.10.1997   Tignes   FRA   Parallel   3.
1. Josef Strobl (AUT), 2. Aamodt (NOR), 3. Maier (AUT)
Parallel giant slalom; because of the special turns (radii), I am using women's skis; the ploy works! After winning ahead of Jagge, Ghedina, and Kjus I lose during the semifinals against Pepi Strobl and have a victory over Sigi Voglreiter during the small finale.

WC017   26.10.1997   Tignes   FRA   GS   3.
1. Von Grünigen (SUI) 2:24.29, 2. Locher (SUI) +0.57, 3. Maier (AUT) +0.97
Because I show up for the start-number drawing at the last moment, I am fined 10,000 Austrian schillings for "being late." What an outrage!

WC018   20.11.1997   Park City UT   USA   GS   1.
1. Maier (AUT) 2:43.99, 2. Aamodt (NOR) +1.80, 3. Grandi (CAN) +2.32
Carving revolution; I, too, am going to the start with tapered skis; bad visibility; first victory of the season (giant Maier time margins are starting to happen); and, for the first time, my overall lead in the World Cup.

WC019   04.12.1997   Beaver Creek CO   USA   D   9.
1. Ghedina (ITA) 1:41.16, 2. Cretier (FRA) +0.22, 3. Kjus (NOR) +0.24 (9. Maier +0.92)
Toni Giger insists on a guaranteed slot for me in the downhill. Debut on the Birds of Prey run; even though I'm only ninth, I know that this will be my new favorite downhill.

WC020   05.12.1997   Beaver Creek CO   USA   D   2.
1. Schifferer (AUT) 1:41.17, 2. Maier (AUT) +0.17, 3. Eberharter (AUT) +0.28
Finally, we're the fastest team in the World Cup; along with success, jocularity comes all by itself.

WC021   06.12.1997   Beaver Creek CO   USA   SG   1.
1. Maier (AUT) 1:16.20, 2. Eberharter (AUT) +0.36, 3. Knauss (AUT) +0.38
A killer race; of the top 30 contenders, 17 are disqualified, and I am more than 100 points ahead of Aamodt.

THE PERFECT WORLD CUP DRESS REHEARSAL
WC022   14.12.1997   Val d'Isère   FRA   GS   DSQ2
1. Von Grünigen (SUI) 2:29.48, 2. Eberharter (AUT) +0.93, 3. Knauss (AUT) +1.09 (Maier DSQ2)
I'm counting this as a victory in my own private statistics. Even though I have the best time, I'm disqualified because I unbuckle one ski before crossing the "red line." This is a "dinosaur regulation," which supposedly was issued because of the overly long commercial breaks on television.

WC023   21.12.1997   Alta Badia   ITA   GS   3.
1. Mayer (AUT) 2:20.97, 2. Von Grünigen (SUI) +0.43, 3. Maier (AUT) +0.66
I can't find my starting number prior to the second round. Atomic serviceman Tom Bürgler lends me his Hardrock Cafe T-shirt, which I turn inside out, scrawl a big "4" on it, and subsequently sail right up onto the victory podium.

WC024   29.12.1997   Bormio   ITA   D   1.
1. Maier (AUT) 2:01.59, 2. Schifferer (AUT) +0.03, 3. Franz (AUT) +0.20
This is a racecourse without a chance to catch your breath. Love at first sight! On my way to the starting booth, I see the display board with the winners thus far, and I think, "I want up there!" I win my first World Cup downhill.

WC025   30.12.1997   Bormio   ITA   D   4.
1. Schifferer (AUT) 2:01.44, 2. Franz (AUT) +0.18, 3. Kjus (NOR) +0.66 (4. Maier +0.75)
Unfortunately, I am using the skis from the day before. I switch the right and the left skis, which wears down the wax coat.

WC026   03.01.1998   Kranjska Gora   SLO   GS   2.
1. Mayer (AUT) 2:12.70, 2. Maier (AUT) +0.52, 3. Von Grünigen (SUI) +1.10
Fog; I am skiing with such an extreme angle to the slope that I brush up against one of the edges in the terrain with my hip; a crazy sensation!

WC027   06.01.1998   Saalbach-Hinterglemm   AUT   GS   1.
1. Maier (AUT) 2:37.96, 2. Tomba (ITA) +2.44, 3. Salzgeber (AUT) +2.69
There's a hurricane blowing at the start. I want to wait. "I'm not going down now!" Starting official: "Then you're disqualified!" My response: "All right, I'll go then! I am swept up by a powerful gust of wind, and slammed down on my butt. Nevertheless, I win with a record lead!

WC028   10.01.1998   Schladming   AUT   SG   1.
1. Maier (AUT) 1:14.95, 2. Eberharter (AUT) +1.15, 3. Cattaneo (ITA) +1.41
I am revving up to top form. In order to get away from all the hubbub, I stay at my house in Flachau.

WC029   11.01.1998   Schladming   AUT   SG   1.
1. Maier (AUT) 1:14.84, 2. Schifferer (AUT) +1.19, 3. Eberharter (AUT) +1.30
For Ghedina, I've now become the "cannibal"; whether monster or cannibal, who cares.

WC030   13.01.1998   Adelboden   SUI   GS   1.
1. Maier (AUT) 2:20.08, 2. Von Grünigen (SUI) +1.24, 3. Accola (SUI) +1.25
A war between nations. Even on the most difficult giant slalom slope, I don't have an opponent. Despite my ski pole breaking!

WC031   16.01.1998   Wengen   SUI   D   1.
1. Maier (AUT) 1:44.89, 2. Burtin (FRA) +0.68, 3. Schifferer (AUT) +0.72
In the Wengeralp narrow-gauge railroad, everyone thinks I'm crazy because I'm hauling the ergometer along. Fifth victory in a row; only one is missing to beat the Klammer record! I have more World Cup points already than last year's winner, Alphand, had at the end of the season!

WC032   17.01.1998   Wengen   SUI   D   3.
1. Schifferer (AUT) 2:28.32, 2. Cretier (FRA) +0.97, 3. Maier (AUT) +1.33
Schiffi shaved the day before; I didn't!

WC033   18.01.1998   Veysonnaz   SUI   S   10.
1. Stangassinger (AUT) 1:38.12, 2. Bjornsson (ISL) +0.79, 3. Kimura (JPN) +0.80 (10. Maier +2.00)
Sensational tenth place in my only World Cup slalom ever, and second-best Austrian!

WC034   18.01.1998   Veysonnaz   SUI   CDS   1.
1. Maier (AUT) 3:25.01, 2. Kernen (SUI) +2.66, 3. Accola (SUI) +3.73
With my combination victory, I gathered 286 World Cup points in only three days!

WC035   31.01.1998   Garmisch-Partenkirchen   GER   D   3.
1. Schifferer (AUT) 1:54.82, 2. Burtin (FRA) +0.56, 3. Maier (AUT) +0.75
Because I was worn-out, to save the Olympics I skipped Kitzbühel, and came back with my batteries fully charged.

WC036   01.02.1998   Garmisch-Partenkirchen   GER   SG   1.
1. Maier (AUT) 1:19.79, 2. Knauss (AUT) +0.91, 3. Kjus (NOR) +1.09
Tenth victory so far this season; the media coin a new nickname for me: As of now, I am the "Herminator"!

OG   10.02.1998   Nagano   JPN   Kombi-S   8.
1. Reiter (AUT) 1:31.85, 2. Kjus (NOR) +1.81, 3. Bachleda (POL) +2.64 (8. Maier +4.05)
Combination slalom; many mistakes in the dense snowfall; nevertheless I am hoping to win a medal.

OG   13.02.1998   Nagano   JPN   D   DNF
1. Cretier (FRA) 1:50.11, 2. Kjus (NOR) +0.40, 3. Trinkl (AUT) +0.52 (Maier DNF)
My takeoff of the century!

OG   13.02.1998   Nagano   JPN   Kombi-D   DNS
1. Mader (AUT) 1:34.83, 2. Kjus (NOR) +0.16, 3. Mayer (AUT) +0.23 (Maier DNS)
I was glad that I was still able to walk; there was no way I could start in the combination downhill.

OG   16.02.1998   Nagano   JPN   SG   1.
1. Maier (AUT) 1:34.82, 2. Knauss (AUT) and Cuche (SUI) +0. 61
The realization of all my dreams!

OG   19.02.1998   Nagano   JPN   GS   1.
1. Maier (AUT) 2:38.51, 2. Eberharter (AUT) +0.85, 3. Von Grünigen (SUI) +1.18
The icing on the cake.

WC037   28.02.1998   Yongpyong   KOR   GS   3.
1. Von Grünigen (SUI) 2:22.35, 2. Mayer (AUT) +0.40, 3. Maier (AUT) +0.66
I am battered from my post-Olympic vacation in Guam. With my back pain, I feel like a crash-test dummy.

WC038   14.03.1998   Crans-Montana   SUI   GS   3.
1. Eberharter (AUT) 2:22.97, 2. Knauss (AUT) +0.23, 3. Maier (AUT) +0.92
It's only the "small" giant slalom crystal ball trophy; with third place, I am getting my way against my eternal rival, Michael von Grünigen!

SEASON 1998/1999

WC039   25.10.1998   Sölden   AUT   GS   1.
1. Maier (AUT) 2:10.74, 2. Eberharter (AUT) +1.60, 3. Schilchegger (AUT) +2.34
For the first time, I am donning the "Raiffeisen" sponsor logo on my helmet; stress during the preparations, since we flew to Innsbruck directly from the "Night of Sports." Nevertheless, I leave everyone behind in the lower portion, a record lead on this short racecourse!

WC040   20.11.1998   Park City UT   USA   GS   DNF2
1. Eberharter (AUT) 2:14.75, 2. Mayer (AUT) +0.52, 3. Buechel (LIE) +0.93 (Maier DNF2)
I want to bolster my halftime lead; in the aggressive, artificial snow, I risk too much and am disqualified!

WC041   27.11.1998   Aspen CO   USA   SG   2.
1. Eberharter (AUT) 1:11.81, 2. Maier (AUT) +0.52, 3. Mayer (AUT) +0.64
I find myself on smooth ice, catch on a rock; the grip from my edge is gone, and I barely make it home safe.

WC042   12.12.1998   Val d'Isère   FRA   D   36.
1. Kjus (NOR) 1:43.20, 2. Cattaneo (ITA) +0.28, 3. Seletto (ITA) +0.44 (36. Maier +2.41)
Fog; I ski "snow-blind," barely avoiding a crash; I have to laugh because the domestic reporters are completely working themselves up over an "Austrian debacle."

WC043   13.12.1998   Val d'Isère   FRA   SG   1.
1. Maier (AUT) 1:18.73, 2. Eberharter (AUT) +1.18, 3. Kjus (NOR) +1.37
I make things right again and read later in the paper: "The Herminator struck back with a vengeance!"

WC044   18.12.1998   Gröden   ITA   D   3.
1. Kjus (NOR) 2:02.18, 2. Franz (AUT) +0.91, 3. Maier (AUT) +1.10
Across the camel's humps for the first time; a childhood dream come true.

WC045   19.12.1998   Gröden   ITA   D   4.
1. Ghedina (ITA) 2:04.17, 2. Kjus (NOR) +0.14, 3. Franz (AUT) +0.28 (4. Maier +0.48)
I make a mess of the camel's humps; a gliding slope, which does not at all suit me. Will I ever win here?

WC046   20.12.1998   Alta Badia   ITA   GS   4.
1. Von Grünigen (SUI) 2:41.01, 2. Holzer (ITA) +0.76, 3. Schifferer (AUT) +1.25 (4. Maier +1.83)
The right starting number this time around. Bravo!

WC047   21.12.1998   Innsbruck   AUT   SG   1.
1. Maier (AUT) 1:23.52, 2. Mayer (AUT) +0.76, 3. Fritz Strobl (AUT) +0.77
Historic ninefold Austrian Ski Federation victory! The narrow slope reminds me of my teenage races; on the smooth ice, I feel right at home!

WC048   29.12.1998   Bormio   ITA   D   1.
1. Maier (AUT) 1:54.51, 2. Fritz Strobl (AUT) +0.70, 3. Eberharter (AUT) +1.28
Fabulous victory on one of my favorite downhill courses; incredibly taxing, but at the time, everything comes easy to me.

WC049   05.01.1999   Kranjska Gora   SLO   GS   20.
1. Holzer (ITA) 2:14.91, 2. Mayer (AUT) +0.24, 3. Knauss (AUT) +0.31 (20. Maier +2.87)
Maybe I celebrated Bormio and New Year's too exuberantly; one big disaster!

WC050   09.01.1999   Schladming   AUT   SG   1.
1. Maier (AUT) 1:16.54, 2. Salzgeber (AUT) +0.58, 3. Knauss (AUT) +0.77
I am starting to think that everything is forced; I can tell that the victories no longer come so easily.

WC051   10.01.1999   Flachau   AUT   GS   3.
1. Raich (AUT) 2:27.02, 2. Von Grünigen (SUI) +0.05, 3. Maier (AUT) +0.41
I am fighting to get back into the rhythm that I lost back in Kranjska Gora. The fastest time in the lower portion gives me some peace of mind.

WC052   12.01.1999   Adelboden   SUI   GS   1.
1. Maier (AUT) 2:12.66, 2. Aamodt (NOR) +0.28, 3. Raich (AUT) +0.82
A victory that I worked for!

WC053   16.01.1999   Wengen   SUI   D   4.
1. Kjus (NOR) 2:25.10, 2. Trinkl (AUT) +0.56, 3. Knauss (AUT) +0.57 (4. Maier +0.65)
Severe back pains; struggle in the choice of material. But I force my way through.

WC054   17.01.1999   Wengen   SUI   S   DNQ2
1. Raich (AUT) 1:41.10, 2. Von Grünigen (SUI) +0.10, 3. Kjus (NOR) +0.54 (45. Maier DNQ2)
First run +3.66. Started in the second run only for the combination ranking.

WC055   17.01.1999   Wengen   SUI   CDS   3.
1. Kjus (NOR) 4:07.04, 2. Aamodt (NOR) +2.83, 3. Maier (AUT) +7.09
Sixty World Cup points; reached my target number!

WC056   22.01.1999   Kitzbühel   AUT   D   DNF2
1. Kjus (NOR) 2:14.03, 2. Aamodt (NOR) +0.18, 3. Franz (AUT) +0.46 (Maier DNF2)
Debut downhill on the infamous Streif. Sprint downhill in two rounds; coach Margreiter warns me, but I want to pull my powerful line through in the second round, which results in a similar takeoff as the year before in Nagano!

WC057   23.01.1999   Kitzbühel   AUT   D   8.
1. Knauss (AUT) 1:54.18, 2. Rzehak (AUT) +0.15, 3. Franz (AUT) +0.17 (8. Maier +0.98)
Finally a Hahnenkamm downhill from the very top; finally made it to the finish.

WC058   24.01.1999   Kitzbühel   AUT   S   DNF1
1. Kosir (SLO) 1:36.40, 2. Plaschy (SUI) +0.04, 3. Rocca (ITA) +0.07 (Maier DNF1)
Hooked a gate; tears in my eyes, lost World Cup lead to Lasse Kjus!

WCH   02.02.1999   Vail/Beaver Creek CO   USA   SG   1.
1. Maier (AUT) and Kjus (NOR) 1:14.53, 3. Knauss (AUT) +0.01
My first world championships; one big point collection! Gold in the head-to-head battle of nerves with Kjus; poor Hansi!

WCH   06.02.1999   Vail/Beaver Creek CO   USA   D   1.
1. Maier (AUT) 1:40.60, 2. Kjus (NOR) +0.31, 3. Aamodt (NOR) +0.57
Second gold in the world championships; not my best downhill, but by far my most daring!

WCH   12.02.1999   Vail/Beaver Creek CO   USA   GS   DNF2
1. Kjus (NOR) 2:19.31, 2. Buechel (LIE) +0.05, 3. Locher (SUI) +1.48 (Maier DNF2)
After the downhill celebration, I'm as immovable as a beer keg. On top of that, the cold front hitting Vail irritates me.

WC059   27.02.1999   Ofterschwang   GER   GS   4.
1. Eberharter (AUT) 2:17.79, 2. Knauss (AUT) +0.27, 3. Von Grünigen (SUI) +0.28 (4. Maier +0.34)
At any rate, I retake the lead in the World Cup point count after almost crashing in the second round.

WC060   05.03.1999   Kvitfjell   NOR   D   16.
1. Schifferer (AUT) 1:46.36, 2. Eberharter (AUT) +0.10, 3. Aamodt (NOR) +0.32 (16. Maier +2.07)
I had imagined my first downhill in Kvitfjell a bit differently.

WC061   06.03.1999   Kvitfjell   NOR   D   11.
1. Schifferer (AUT) 1:46.78, 2. Kjus (NOR) +0.18, 3. Eberharter (AUT) +0.77 (11. Maier +1.65)
My second one as well.

WC062   7.03.1999   Kvitfjell   NOR   SG   1.
1. Maier (AUT) 1:30.70, 2. Eberharter (AUT) +0.47, 3. Schifferer (AUT) +0.59
In the super-G, I'm back in my element and preserve my chances for the overall World Cup victory.

WC063   10.03.1999   Sierra Nevada   SPA   D   9.
1. Kjus (NOR) 1:49.73, 2. Fleischer (USA) +0.16, 3. Groenvold (NOR) +0.27 (9. Maier +0.78)
Before us, the ladies are allowed to start, then the slope gets all soft, and we heavy boys have to ski in the slush.

WC064   11.03.1999   Sierra Nevada   SPA   SG   7.
1. Mayer (AUT) 1:28.71, 2. Schifferer (AUT) +0.35, 3. Josef Strobl (AUT) +0.82 (7. Maier +1.24)
Blown away by the wind.

WC065   13.03.1999   Sierra Nevada   SPA   S   16.
1. Stangassinger (AUT) 1:50.44, 2. Aamodt (NOR) +0.23, 3. Casanova (SUI) +0.75 (16. Maier +5.98)
I am fighting for any and all World Cup points, but during the finals, there are points to be had only for the top 15 contenders.

WC066   14.03.1999   Sierra Nevada   SPA   GS   DNF1
1. Von Grünigen (SUI) 2:04.33, 2. Locher (SUI) +0.07, 3. Schilchegger (AUT) +0.11 (Maier DNF1)
Back pains, breakdown; lost the World Cup. At least reached my season's goal with two world championships titles.

SEASON 1999/2000

WC067   31.10.1999   Tignes   FRA   GS   1.
1. Maier (AUT) 2:22.33, 2. Von Grünigen (SUI) +0.75, 3. Eberharter (AUT) +1.90
A perfect season's beginning!

WC068   24.11.1999   Vail/Beaver Creek CO   USA   GS   1.
1. Maier (AUT) 2:32.48, 2. Von Grünigen (SUI) +0.28, 3. Schifferer (AUT) +1.15
In order to escape altitude sickness, I escape for a few days to Boulder, 3,000 feet below.

WC069   27.11.1999   Vail/Beaver Creek CO   USA   D   1.
1. Maier (AUT) 1:43.77, 2. Eberharter (AUT) +0.91, 3. Ghedina (ITA) +1.12
It's easy to raise a stink with full pants!

WC070   28.11.1999   Vail/Beaver Creek CO   USA   SG   1.
1. Maier (AUT) 1:16.51, 2. Eberharter (AUT) +0.94, 3. Kjus (NOR) +1.13
Same winner, same second place, (almost) the same time difference; fourth victory during the fourth race of the season!

WC071   04.12.1999   Lake Louise AB   CAN   D   2.
1. Trinkl (AUT) 1:46.98, 2. Maier (AUT) +0.03, 3. Eberharter (AUT) +0.76
Lots of mishaps: "detour" into the deep snow, helmet banged-up on a gate so that a piece of the Raiffeisen logo is knocked off.

WC072   05.12.1999   Lake Louise AB   CAN   SG   1.
1. Maier (AUT) 1:30.21, 2. Nyberg (SWE) +0.95, 3. Josef Strobl (AUT) +1.13
Perfect ending to the North American races!

WC073   17.12.1999   Gröden   ITA   D   6.
1. Ghedina (ITA) 2:02.99, 2. Josef Strobl (AUT) +1.35, 3. Podivinsky (CAN) + 1.38 (6. Maier +1.45)
Finally made it fine across the camel's humps, but during the final jump into the finish I rose up like a hot-air balloon.

WC074   18.12.1999   Gröden   ITA   D   3.
1. Schifferer (AUT) 2:04.78, 2. Ghedina (ITA) +0.11, 3. Maier (AUT) +0.22
Am completely concentrating on the final jump, but I open up while going across the camel's humps. This racecourse is very unforgiving.

WC075   19.12.1999   Alta Badia   ITA   GS   2.
1. Chenal (FRA) 2:39.68, 2. Maier (AUT) +0.08, 3. Salzgeber (AUT) +0.27
After the downhill hardships in the training runs and two races, I am tired and content with second place.

WC076   22.12.1999   Saalbach-Hinterglemm   AUT   GS   2.
1. Mayer (AUT) 2:25.83, 2. Maier (AUT) +0.30, 3. Raich (AUT) +0.32
After the exertions of the past week, I need the brief Christmas break more than ever.

WC077   08.01.2000   Chamonix Mont-Blanc   FRA   D   1.
1. Maier (AUT) 2:00.51, 2. Eberharter (AUT) +0.05, 3. Trinkl (AUT) +0.17
Three years after my crash, my second appearance in Chamonix; one of my biggest victories. I know that I can succeed even on a gliding racecourse!

WC078   09.01.2000   Chamonix Mont-Blanc   FRA   S   DNQ2
1. Weiss (ITA) 2:01.27, 2. Aamodt (NOR) +0.44, 3. Vrhovnik (SLO) +0.48 (40. Maier 1. Lauf +3.66)
I struggle across the icy slope, and have to be content.

WC079   09.01.2000   Chamonix Mont-Blanc   FRA   CDS   2.
1. Aamodt (NOR) 4:04.00, 2. Maier (AUT) +4.41, 3. Accola (SUI) +5.59
With second place during the combination event, I am above my target point count!

WC080   15.01.2000   Wengen   SUI   D   2.
1. Josef Strobl (AUT) 2:29.17, 2. Maier (AUT) +0.16, 3. Podivinsky (CAN) +1.39
Skied perfectly up above; down below, could have been better. I'm already rejoicing when Pepi Strobl, that scoundrel, overtakes me!

WC081   21.01.2000   Kitzbühel   AUT   SG   1.
1. Maier (AUT) 1:19.07, 2. Franz (AUT) +0.62, 3. Cuche (SUI) +0.63
My first victory in Kitzbühel! It has got to be the super-G!

WC082   22.01.2000   Kitzbühel   AUT   D   4.
1. Fritz Strobl (AUT) 1:46.54, 2. Josef Strobl (AUT) and Ghedina (ITA) +0.65 (4. Maier +0.95)
New snow lottery; I am endlessly disappointed and annoy the Atomic people because I throw my skis down in the finish area. Nevertheless, I celebrate the super-G victory later and show up in the downhill suit.

WC083   23.01.2000   Kitzbühel   AUT   S   DNQ2
1. Matt (AUT) 1:42.79, 2. Vrhovnik (SLO) +0.98, 3. Raich (AUT) +1.23 (37. Maier 1. Lauf +2.31)
. . . for the-warmup. Was completely relaxed during the race. For speed races, I prefer to get enough sleep. Anything else would be too dangerous and irresponsible!

WC084   23.01.2000   Kitzbühel   AUT   CDS   3.
1. Aamodt (NOR) 3:31.98, 2. Nyberg (SWE) +3.71, 3. Maier (AUT) +4.32
Sixty World Cup points; met my target number!

WC085   29.01.2000   Garmisch-Partenkirchen   GER   D   1.1.   Maier   (AUT)
1:55.77, 2. Ghedina (ITA) +0.32, 3. Trinkl (AUT) +1.28
Three years after my first World Cup victory, I make a point in Garmisch even during the downhill and keep off my rival Ghedina in the fight for the downhill World Cup.

WC086   05.02.2000   Todtnau   GER   GS   1.
1. Maier (AUT) 2:13.75, 2. Nyberg (SWE) +0.86, 3. Von Grünigen (SUI) +1.02
After a spoiled first run I pull myself out of the swamp. A splendid victory!

WC087   12.02.2000   St. Anton   AUT   SG   DNF
1. Josef Strobl (AUT) 1:23.41, 2. Cuche (SUI) +0.13, 3. Eberharter (AUT) +0.14 (Maier DNF1)
After only 12 seconds I get into the snow with my boot at gate 6. World championships dress rehearsal is spoiled.

WC088   13.02.2000   St. Anton   AUT   SG   3.
1. Franz (AUT) and Fritz Strobl (AUT) 1:20.72, 3. Maier (AUT) +0.26
I am thrilled for Werner to have scored his first victory. I ski like a coward, and just want to get into the finish in order to redeem some certain World Cup points.

WC089   03.03.2000   Kvitfjell   NOR   D   3.
1. Rahlves (USA) 1:28.69, 2. Cuche (SUI) +0.09, 3. Maier (AUT) +0.26
After a totally messed-up training I experimented and still ended up third in the Norwegian icebox.

WC090   04.03.2000   Kvitfjell   NOR   D   4.
1. Rahlves (USA) 1:28.88, 2. Ghedina (ITA) +0.18, 3. Rauffer (GER) +0.37 (4. Maier +0.45)
I contain the damage against Ghedina in the fight for the downhill trophy and am friends again with this downhill.

WC091   05.03.2000   Kvitfjell   NOR   SG   2.
1. Ghedina (ITA) 1:28.56, 2. Maier (AUT) +0.38, 3. Schifferer (AUT) +0.96
Not even I can prevent the first Austrian defeat since my first victory on February 21, 1997.

WC092   08.03.2000   Kranjska Gora   SLO   GS   DNF1
1. Mayer (AUT) 2:11.17, 2. Chenal (FRA) +0.64, 3. Buechel (LIE) +0.99 (Maier DNF1)
After a perfect race, I get off track shortly before the finish on my way to the victory.

WC093   11.03.2000   Hinterstoder   AUT   GS   3.
1. Mayer (AUT) 2:46.17, 2. Buechel (LIE) +0.91, 3. Maier (AUT) +1.29
The World Cup is a sure thing now! Among the fans, I notice the blonde Gudrun.

WC094   15.03.2000   Bormio   ITA   D   2.
1. Trinkl (AUT) 1:58.31, 2. Maier (AUT) +0.40, 3. Greber (AUT) +0.79
My first overall downhill World Cup victory!

WC095   16.03.2000   Bormio   ITA   SG   1.
1. Maier (AUT) 1:40.08, 2. Fritz Strobl (AUT) +1.91, 3. Franz (AUT) and Schifferer (AUT) +1.98
The best super-G of my career; record lead! With 2,000 points, I have established a new record in the World Cup standings to date.

WC096   18.03.2000   Bormio   ITA   GS   DNF2
1. Raich (AUT) 2:25.64, 2. Mayer (AUT) +0.17, 3. Schilchegger (AUT) +0.24 (Maier DNF2)
I am ahead after the first round, and I take a total risk; then, I'm out in the second race; yet, I win the giant slalom trophy on top of the downhill and super-G crystal balls; unfortunately, one of the trophies breaks during the victory brawl!

AC   23.03.2000   St. Lambrecht   AUT   SG   19.
1. Schifferer (AUT) 1:12.45, 2. Gruber (AUT) +0.78, 3. Sparovec (SLO) +1.15 (19. Maier +2.65)
An entire class of school kids is standing right in my way, I have to make a detour to get to the finish.

SEASON 2000/2001

WC097   29.10.2000   Sölden   AUT   GS   1.
1. Maier (AUT) 2:16.89, 2. Eberharter (AUT) +1.01, 3. Nyberg (SWE) +1.04
Slept little during the night before because there was so much going on in the parking lot in front of the hotel. Luckily, the night lasts an hour longer due to the daylight-savings time change.

WC098   17.11.2000   Park City, UT   USA   GS   3.
1. Von Grünigen (SUI) 2:32.92, 2. Kjus (NOR) +0.55, 3. Maier (AUT) +0.58
Shocked over the glacier train tragedy in Kaprun; relieved after a phone call: Thank God my brother, who is training there on that day, is not on the disaster train. I ski an emotionless race.

WC099   25.11.2000   Lake Louise AB   CAN   D   15.
1. Eberharter (AUT) 1:40.79, 2. Beltrametti (SUI) +0.24, 3. Kjus (NOR) +0.42 (15. Maier +1.22)
After the best time during training, I decide on the wrong ski.

WC100   26.11.2000   Lake Louise AB   CAN   SG   1.
1. Maier (AUT) 1:29.53, 2. Kjus (NOR) +0.32, 3. Schifferer (AUT) +0.42
The super-G victory is balsam to my soul!

WC101   02.12.2000   Vail/Beaver Creek CO USA   D   1.
1. Maier (AUT) 1:40.66, 2. Kjus (NOR) +0.49, 3. Eberharter (AUT) +0.81
I always like to win on my favorite course!

WC102   03.12.2000   Vail/Beaver Creek CO USA   SG   6.
1. Nyberg (SWE) 1:21.18, 2. Gruber (AUT) +0.03, 3. Sivertsen (NOR) +0.47 (6. Maier +0.94)
Mentally, I'm already sitting on the plane on my way to Europe; I have to get to my birthday party on time!

WC103   09.12.2000   Val d'Isère   FRA   D   1.
1. Maier (AUT) 1:45.04, 2. Eberharter (AUT) +0.31, 3. Fritz Strobl (AUT) +0.55
Sensational! My best race on this downhill classic!

WC104   10.12.2000   Val d'Isère   FRA   GS   1.
1. Maier (AUT) 2:30.63, 2. Schilchegger (AUT) +1.36, 3. Schifferer (AUT) +1.37
Again, a perfect race; I cross the red line with both skis and kiss the stupid line.

WC105   16.12.2000   Val d'Isère   FRA   D   16.
1. Fattori (ITA) 1:52.25, 2. Ghedina (ITA) +0.32, 3. Fischnaller (ITA) +0.41 (16. Maier +1.64)
Cold; the ski slows you down so much that you get stuck during the gliding passage and can just about read the paper at less than 20mph; it was so slow that Schiffi talked to his coach on the sidelines during his descent.

WC106   17.12.2000   Val d'Isère   FRA   GS   DSQ1
1. Von Grünigen (SUI) 2:31.33, 2. Schilchegger (AUT) +0.59, 3. Miller (USA) +0.65 (Maier DSQ1)
Even though there is no official time-taking, I supposedly take too long to inspect the slope and am disqualified. Obviously, I am winning too much, and this is the only way to stop me. Schumi can count himself lucky!

WC107   21.12.2000   Bormio   ITA   GS   10.
1. Gruber (AUT) 2:12.33, 2. Schlopy (USA) +0.19, 3. Nyberg (SWE) +0.43 (10. Maier +1.03)
Am not completely concentrating on what I'm doing; because I still skied the course in Val d'Isère after the disqualification, FIS threatened to lock me out until shortly before the race.

WC108   06.01.2001   Les Arcs   FRA   GS   7.
1. Von Grünigen (SUI) 2:43.67, 2. Raich (AUT) +1.62, 3. Buechel (LIE) +2.13 (7. Maier +2.58)
Return to the site of my triumphant Europe Cup debut.

WC109   09.01.2001   Adelboden   SUI   GS   1.
1. Maier (AUT) 2:15.53, 2. Von Grünigen (SUI) +0.53, 3. Nyberg (SWE), +0.72
The third success in a row on the classic giant slalom on the most difficult GS slope.

WC110   19.01.2001   Kitzbühel   AUT   SG   1.
1. Maier (AUT) 1:21.72, 2. Josef Strobl (AUT) +0.95, 3. Franz (AUT) +1.17
Not even a detour to London (World Sports Award as Winter Sports Athlete of the Year) can take away from my fantastic form. Could I wish for a better start to the Hahnenkamm weekend?

WC111   20.01.2001   Kitzbühel   AUT   D   1.
1. Maier (AUT) 1:56.84, 2. Trinkl (AUT) +0.27, 3. Eberharter (AUT) and Rahlves (USA) +0.62
Now I've reconciled with the Streif for good!

WC112   27.01.2001   Garmisch-Partenkirchen   GER   D   DNF
1. Fritz Strobl (AUT) 2:00.93, 2. Rzehak (AUT) +0.29, 3. Cavegn (SUI) +0.38 (Maier DNF)
Crash! At one of the most dangerous passages in the entire World Cup the anchor bolt holding my bindings in place is ripped off my ski.

WC113   28.01.2001   Garmisch-Partenkirchen   GER   SG   2.
1. Gruber (AUT) 1:18.27, 2. Maier (AUT) +0.01, 3. Cuche (SUI) +0.56
Despite a safe run, I miss victory by only one hundredth of a second! Still, I am making my way to the world championships with mixed emotions.

WCH   30.01.2001   St. Anton/Arlberg   AUT   SG   3.
1. Rahlves (USA) 1:21.46, 2. Eberharter (AUT) +0.08, 3. Maier (AUT) +0.23
Stress; from one appointment to the next; headache. The championship on my home turf's the trick!

WCH   07.02.2001   St. Anton/Arlberg   AUT   D   2.
1. Trinkl (AUT) 1:38.74, 2. Maier (AUT) +0.20, 3. Eckert (GER) +0.52
Radio chaos; new snow; a lower starting point turns the strength-draining Karl Schranz course into a mediocre run.

WCH   08.02.2001   St. Anton/Arlberg   AUT   GS   4.
1. Von Grünigen (SUI) 2:23.80, 2. Aamodt (NOR) +0.35, 3. Covili (FRA) +0.38 (4. Maier +0.39)
Missed the bronze by a hundredth of a second; I missed three gold medals by a total of 0.82 second. Forget about it and move on!

WC114   15.02.2001   Shigakogen   JPN   GS   1.
1. Maier (AUT) 2:43.49, 2. Buechel (LIE) +1.74, 3. Raich (AUT) +1.83
I ignore the time difference, and win during my lightning-fast visit at the site of my Olympic triumph, with a Herminator lead to boot. Now, the world is in order once again!

WC115   02.03.2001   Kvitfjell   NOR   D   1.
1. Maier (AUT) 1:45.90, 2. Eckert (GER) +0.15, 3. Kjus (NOR) +0.19
After an unnecessary detour to the USA (Olympic test drowns in the snow), victory after experimentation during the training runs; Andy Evers is testing out my victory skis during his early-bird shift.

WC116   03.03.2001   Kvitfjell   NOR   D   5.
1. Eberharter (AUT) 1:45.17, 2. Eckert (GER) +0.09, 3. Fritz Strobl (AUT) +0.25 (5. Maier +0.44)
During the last jump, there is an upward lift that would make a ski jumper turn green with envy; the downhill World Cup will be suspenseful once again.

WC117   04.03.2001   Kvitfjell   NOR   SG   1.
1. Maier (AUT) 1:28.58, 2. Trinkl (AUT) +0.06, 3. Eberharter (AUT) +0.84
Minus 22 degrees Fahrenheit. I protect myself with a face mask.

WC118   08.03.2001   Aare   SWE   D   1.
1. Maier (AUT) 1:24.20, 2. Eberharter (AUT) +0.35, 3. Sivertsen (NOR) +0.42
After second-to-last place during training, I ski one of the best downhill races of my life.

WC119   10.03.2001   Aare   SWE   GS   1.
1. Maier (AUT) 2:31.23, 2. Schlopy (USA) +1.14, 3. Raich (AUT) +1.28
Fifth victory during the sixth race after the world championships. Any more questions? Michael von Grünigen is thrown off balance by our pretend remodeling of my ski boot shortly before the start. I now have the "small" giant slalom trophy in addition to the downhill and super-G crystal balls, utter an exuberant scream, and rip off my racing overalls.

24. 08. 2001
The accident!!

SEASON 2002/2003
WC120   14.01.2003   Adelboden   SUI   GS   DNQ2
1. Knauss (AUT) 2:29.68, 2. Von Grünigen (SUI) +0.09, 3. Aamodt (NOR) +0.25 (Maier DNQ2)
My comeback. My resolve ("If everything goes right, I'll win") unfortunately doesn't quite work out.

WC121   17.01.2003   Wengen   SUI   D   22.
1. Eberharter (AUT) 2:27.78, 2. Rahlves (USA) +1.11, 3. Kernen (SUI) +1.38 (22. Maier +3.15)
The first downhill! Will my leg hold up during the jumps?

WC122   18.01.2003   Wengen   SUI   D   7.
1. Kernen (SUI) 2:28.69, 2. Walchhofer (AUT) +0.23, 3. Eberharter (AUT) +0.45 (7. Maier +1.91)
The crucial moment. I can tell that things are starting to work again!

WC123   25.01.2003   Kitzbühel   AUT   D   6.
1. Rahvles (USA) 1:09.63, 2. Cuche (SUI) +0.05, 3. Aamodt (NOR) +0.08 (6. Maier +0.46)
I have to be content on the short sprint downhill.

WC124   27.01.2003   Kitzbühel   AUT   SG   1.
1. Maier (AUT) 1:20.48, 2. Gruber (AUT) +0.11, 3. Eberharter (AUT) +0.15
The most beautiful victory of them all!

WCH   02.02.2003   St. Moritz   SUI   SG   2.
1. Eberharter (AUT) 1:38.80, 2. Maier (AUT) and Miller (USA) +0.77
After the best split time, I get lost along the lower portion.

WCH   08.02.2003   St. Moritz   SUI   D   8.
1. Walchhofer (AUT) 1:43.54, 2. Aamodt (NOR) +0.51, 3. Kernen (SUI) +0.97 (8. Maier +1.22)
I am only missing 25/100 second for bronze; am ending the season with a small private celebration in the finish area.

SEASON 2003/2004

WC125   26.10.2003   Sölden   AUT   GS   16.
1. Miller (USA) 2:09.58, 2. Covili (FRA) +1.12, 3. Chenal (FRA) +1.18 (16. Maier +3.09)
Rib cracked during training. No wonder. For the first time in Sölden, no "1" comes up on the board next to my name.

WC126   22.11.2003   Park City UT   USA   GS   7.
1. Miller (USA) 2:20.84, 2. Schifferer (AUT) +0.86, 3. Knauss (AUT) +1.00 (7. Maier +1.38)
Still having trouble with that rib. Yet, finally, things are looking up in the giant slalom!

WC127   29.11.2003   Lake Louise AB   CAN   D   9.
1. Walchhofer (AUT) 1:51.16, 2. Guay (CAN) +0.69, 3. Deneriaz (FRA) +0.74 (9. Maier +1.21)
A strange race; equipment adaptation problems (skis) on the gliding racecourse.

WC128   30.11.2003   Lake Louise AB   CAN   SG   1.
1. Maier (AUT) 1:36.69, 2. Walchhofer (AUT) +0.26, 3. Eberharter (AUT) +0.55
With my victory, I even eclipse the bear alarm.

WC129   05.12.2003   Vail/Beaver Creek CO   USA   D   5.
1. Rahlves (USA) 1:39.59, 2. Eberharter (AUT) and Solbakken (NOR) +0.69 (5. Maier +0.79)
After a strong training, messed up choice of ski and still miss second place by only a tenth of a second.

WC130   06.12.2003   Vail/Beaver Creek CO   USA   D   1.
1. Maier (AUT) 1:39.76, 2. Knauss (AUT) +0.95, 3. Schifferer (AUT) +1.19
With the right type of equipment, I am showing who's boss in my own living room!

WC131   07.12.2003   Vail/Beaver Creek CO   USA   SG   2.
1. Solbakken (NOR) 1:13.05, 2. Maier (AUT) +0.39, 3. Knauss (AUT) +0.45
With starting number 28, nothing goes on this slope. Yet, I have to be content and am celebrating my thirty-first birthday up on the winner's podium.

WC132   14.12.2003   Alta Badia   ITA   GS   DNF2
1. Palander (FIN) 2:30.57, 2. Simoncelli (ITA) +0.92, 3. Covili (FRA) +1.08 (Maier DNF2)
During the second run I am out despite the leading split time up above; unfortunately, my strongest giant slalom of the season remains unrewarded.

WC133   19.12.2003   Gröden   ITA   SG   3.
1. Kjus (NOR) 1:36.94, 2. Eberharter (AUT) +0.10, 3. Maier (AUT) +0.48
First super-G in Gröden, though my worst since my comeback. The top three are 100 years old altogether!

WC134   20.12.2003   Gröden   ITA   D   5.
1. Deneriaz (FRA) 1:52.99, 2. Walchhofer (AUT) +0.89, 3. Knauss (AUT) +0.92 (5. Maier +1.19)
As long as superior glider Deneriaz is starting, I will never win on this racecourse!

WC135   21.12.2003   Alta Badia   ITA   GS   26.
1. Simoncelli (ITA) 2:33.90, 2. Palander (FIN) +1.03, 3. Miller (USA) +1.21 (26. Maier +4.64)
Out of power! I'm just taking a Sunday stroll on the slope. Yet World Cup leader for Christmas!

WC136   03.01.2004   Flachau   AUT   GS   DNQ1
1. Raich (AUT) 2:22.54, 2. Blardone (ITA) +0.70, 3. Solbakken (NOR) +0.82 (Maier DNQ1)
My favorite home race; here of all places everything goes wrong!

WC137   10.01.2004   Chamonix   FRA   D   13.
1. Eberharter (AUT) 1:59.08, 2. Kjus (NOR) +0.31, 3. Walchhofer (AUT) +0.75 (13. Maier +1.33)
Am struggling with a weather downturn and have to start worrying about the overall World Cup rankings.

WC138   11.01.2004   Chamonix   FRA   S   DNQ2
1. Rocca (ITA) 1:29.09, 2. Bourgeat (FRA) +0.08, 3. Miller (USA) +0.43 (55. Maier 1. Lauf +6.23)
The slalom stints are becoming more and more difficult.

WC139   11.01.2004   Chamonix   FRA   CDS   13.
1. Miller (USA) 3:30.91, 2. Raich (AUT) +0.03, 3. Kjus (NOR) +0.06 (13. Maier +9.41)
Can't exactly brag about this combination.

WC140   22.01.2004   Kitzbühel   AUT   D   4.
1. Kjus (NOR) 1:58.78, 2. Eberharter (AUT) +0.01, 3. Rahlves (USA) +0.20 (4. Maier +0.48)
Back pain, Kitzbühel hubbub; not so bad, all things considered.

WC141   23.01.2004   Kitzbühel   AUT   SG   2.
1. Rahlves (USA) 1:23.08, 2. Maier (AUT) +0.03, 3. Walchhofer (AUT) +0.39
One year after my comeback victory I contain my joy over second place.

WC142   24.01.2004   Kitzbühel   AUT   D   9.
1. Eberharter (AUT) 1:55.48, 2. Rahlves (USA) +1.21, 3. Hoffmann (SUI) +1.30 (9. Maier +2.19)
Acknowledgment without envy of a perfect race by the winner!

WC143   25.01.2004   Kitzbühel   AUT   S   DNQ2
1. Palander (FIN) 1:30.63, 2. Grandi (CAN) +0.08, 3. Schönfelder (AUT) +1.06 (67. Maier 1. Lauf +5.37)
A pitiful slalom; unfortunately, I am making a fool of myself with my silly rooster hat on the Hahnenkamm.

WC144   25.01.2004   Kitzbühel   AUT   CDS   14.
1. Miller (USA) 3:31.43, 2. Raich (AUT) +1.01, 3. Kjus (NOR) +3.24 (14. Maier +8.08)
My worst combination.

WC145   30.01.2004   Garmisch-Partenkirchen   GER   D   5.
1. Cuche (SUI) 1:59.49, 2. Rahlves (USA) +0.08, 3. Eberharter (AUT) +0.21 (5. Maier +0.83)
Idyllic quarters right on Bader Lake. After the stress of Kitzbühel I feel like I'm on a relaxing vacation.

WC146   31.01.2004   Garmisch-Partenkirchen   GER   D   5.
1. Eberharter (AUT) 1:58.70, 2. Fritz Strobl (AUT) +0.09, 3. Fattori (ITA) +0.45 (5. Maier +0.79)
Head to head with Trinkl and Gruber in fifth place; except for place number 13 in Chamonix, I am within the top 10 during all the speed events!

WC147   01.02.2004   Garmisch-Partenkirchen   GER   SG   1.
1. Maier (AUT) 1:18.09, 2. Dalcin (FRA) +0.07, 3. Grünenfelder (SUI) +0.37
Important victory; on my way to the pesky doping control I slow everyone else down and am allowed to go home first.

WC148   07.02.2004   Adelboden   SUI   GS   8.
1. Palander (FIN) 2:32.15, 2. Blardone (ITA) +0.74, 3. Gruber (AUT) and Schilchegger (AUT) +1.12 (8. Maier +1.55)
During my drive to Adelboden, I'm constantly on the phone due to a misleading report in connection with my motorcycle accident; good race on my favorite slope. My footprints are being put in cement.

WC149   14.02.2004   St. Anton   AUT   D   1.
1. Maier (AUT) 1:56.09, 2. Eberharter (AUT) +0.32, 3. Grugger (AUT) +0.37
Finally, I'm allowed to get going from the very top and show what is possible on this, the most draining of all downhills.

WC150   28.02.2004   Kranjska Gora   SLO   GS   12.
1. Miller (USA) 2:13.01, 2. Schieppati (ITA) +0.25, 3. Ploner (ITA) +0.60 (12. Maier +1.60)
Big to-do during the trip to Slovenia; at least they let me cross the finish line without a passport.

WC151   06.03.2004   Kvitfjell   NOR   D   9.
1. Eberharter (AUT) 1:43.41, 2. Fritz Strobl (AUT) +0.04, 3. Deneriaz (FRA) +0.36 (9. Maier +0.86)
Twenty-five degrees warmer than during my last start in the "deep freezer."

WC152   07.03.2004   Kvitfjell   NOR   SG   3.
1. Rahlves (USA) 1:34.00, 2. Solbakken (NOR) +0.15, 3. Maier (AUT) +0.17
Barely missed the victory; hopefully, the lost 40 points won't cost me the overall World Cup.

WC153   10.03.2004   Sestriere   ITA   D   18.
1. Rahlves (USA) 1:51.88, 2. Fritz Strobl (AUT) +0.10, 3. Eberharter (AUT) +0.13 (18. Maier +2.08)
Such a catastrophic combination of equipment; no one else would have made it to the finish with this choice of ski.

WC154   11.03.2004   Sestriere   ITA   SG   1.
1. Maier (AUT) 1:18.73, 2. Eberharter (AUT) +0.63, 3. Gruber (AUT) +0.75
Thank you, Edi; the revenge was sweet! With absolutely perfect equipment choice! After my fourth overall World Cup victory, I am celebrating for a week straight. Maybe longer.

WC155   24.10.2004   Sölden   AUT   GS   (Maier 15. + 2.20)
It's Walter's first time with me; he's my new press guy. I have to hurry him up the winding road leading up to the glacier, or else I'll be late! My first race is a great disappointment!

WC156   27.11.2004   Lake Louise AB   CAN   D   5. (+1:34)
My first downhill with Atomic boots. I didn't do so bad on the "superhighway." I must be content with the first downhill of the season.

WC157   28.11.2004   Lake Louise AB   AN   SG   2. (+0.14)
After the course inspection I drive back to my hotel, where I'm waiting for a TV broadcast of the super-G. I wait too long and almost miss my start. The commercial break finally saves me and I barely make it to the start. My first super-G defeat on this course.

WC158   2.12.2004   Beaver Creek CO   USA   SG   8. (+0.74)
Everything goes wrong in my "living room." Lane grooves make it impossible to succeed with number 30. I was about to stop during the race! Mario, the sorcerer's apprentice in our group, uses his good number 3 to make it to the podium.

WC159   3.12.2004   Beaver Creek CO   USA   D   9. (+1.09)
I have huge problems with my materials, especially during the long turns. I lose the race exactly on those sections where I usually win!

WC160   4.12.2004   Beaver Creek CO   USA   GS   2. (+0.45)
I reconcile with my favorite World Cup resort. For the first time this season I feel optimistic, and I'm happy with my Norwegian "elk friend" Lasse.

WC161   11.12.2004   Val d'Isère   FRA   D   26. (+2.03)
I'm a big fool and switch boots again after being fastest in the training run. I then had to pay for it. I should have learned my lesson by now!

WC162   12.12.2004   Val d'Isère   FRA   GS   3. (+0.33)
My first lead during halftime since the motorcycle accident; for the first time with a lead like this I can't rescue a win. Very unnecessary (I cruised around too much).

WC163   17.12.2004   Gröden   ITA   SG   2. (0.12)
Even though I make a lot of little mistakes, my equipment choice starts working out better and better. I am shocked when I get the news of the positive doping test of Hans Knauss (from three weeks ago in Lake Louise).

WC164   18.12.2004   Gröden   ITA   D   37. (+2.23)
Wind roulette; at least the Germans are having a reason to celebrate. The wind is blowing so hard that I hardly make it over the third camel jump.

WC165   19.12.2004   Alta Badia   ITA   GS   3. (+0.01)
A most satisfactory finish after an exhausting week. A great second run! I get to wear the red jersey of the overall leader of the giant slalom.

WC166   21.12.2004   Flachau   AUT   GS   28. (+9.59)
My press guy "parks" his car in a snowbank, so I have to take the ski lift through a whole lot of fans in order to get to the course inspection. During the second run I cross my skis.

WC167   29.12.2004   Bormio   ITA   D   11. (+1.65)
Nothing goes right, and on top of that I have strong headwind; my worst race on this course!

WC168   8.1.2005   Chamonix   FRA   D   8. (+0.51)
Until the last intermediate time I'm ahead. Now I know that everything is possible, even in the downhill!

WC169   11.1.2005   Adelboden   SUI   GS   18. (+1.99)
The last giant slalom before the world championships. My hand gets tangled up a few gates before the finish, and I give away what should have have been a better result.

WC170   14.1.2005   Wengen   SUI   CDS   9. (+3:28; Slalom 15./Downhill 4.)
A combined with only one slalom run and a downhill on one day; that was fun! It was great to wear my short skis again.

WC171   15.1.2005   Wengen   SUI   D   4. (+0.62)
It turns out better and better with my long skis!

WC172   24.1.2005   Kitzbühel   AUT   Super-G   1.
It seems like déjà vu from two years ago, where I celebrated my comeback victory.

WCH   29.1.2005   Bormio   ITA   Super-G   4. (+0.85)
No mistakes, but still, there's no beauty prize, and I miss the bronze by 17/100.

WCH   5.2.2005   Bormio   ITA   D   17. (+1.73)
What a miracle that I'm even starting the race; after having big discussions over my qualification, crash, and hospital, Peter Schröcksnadel, president of the Austrian Ski Federation, talks me into competing. With a huge lag like this, I didn't even have to think about it.

WCH   9.2.2005   Bormio   ITA   GS   1.
I start the race as the loser of the world championships; stay cool and just do everything right!

WC173   18.2.2005   Garmisch   GER   D   2. (+0.99)
My best downhill result of the season is like a victory for me.

WC174   19.2.2005   Garmisch   GER   D   7. (+1.04)
I should be content with this result, but after World Cup gold I can relax and have fun.

WC175   20.2.2005   Garmisch   GER   SG   8. (+0.36)
On this course you're lost with number 30!

WC176   26.2.2005   Kranjska Gora   SLO   GS   2. (+0.45)
World Cup gold approved from Bormio. I make mistakes but I still make it onto the victory podium; it feels almost like the old days!

WC177   5.3.2005   Kvitfjell   NOR   D   1.
My unofficial fiftieth. It feels good to finally win a downhill competition again. I finally know what racing boot I need for the fast races!

WC178   6.3.2005   Kvitfjell   NOR   SG   1.
I have found my set-up and the statistics have their official fiftieth. We celebrate together with former slalom great Ole-Christian Furuseth in his cabin.

WC179   10.3.2005   Lenzerheide   SUI   D   4. (+0.68)

I end up as third in the downhill overall ranking, even after the devestating start of the season.

WC180   11.3.2005   Lenzerheide   SUI   SG   9. (+0.39)

It's a game for hundredths of a second, and I have to yield Bode Miller the super-G trophy. Was that really necessary?

WC181   12.3.2005   Lenzerheide   SUI   GS   4. (+0.84)

Once again I give all that I can give and I make it from seventh place to fourth. My personal highlight at the season finale is the great World Cup party, including a bonfire at the Wanner Bar in Lenzerheide.

WC182   23.10.2005   Sölden   AUT   GS   1.

1. Hermann Maier (AUT) 2:17.60, 2. Bode Miller (USA) +0.07, 3. Ranier Schönfelder (AUT) +0.18.

When I saw Bode passing the finish line and realized I had won, I felt like a bull in the ring seeing the red flag, and freaked out. I thought I would never win a World Cup opener again!

GLOSSARY
FROM A TO Z

Austrian Ski Federation: Its president is Professor Peter Schröcksnadel, with Hans Pum heading up the alpine racing division. Homepage: www.oesv.at.

Bib drawing: The top fifteen contenders in the giant slalom and slalom draw their respective starting numbers for the race that is to take place the next day; they do this in two groups (world ranking numbers 1–7 and 8–15).
   Downhill: The top thirty from the last training run in reverse order.
   Super-G: The top thirty from the super-G World Cup starting list start in reverse order; that is, the best contender has number 30.

Bricklayer's trout: A knackwurst; an indispensable culinary delight for any decent bricklayer's lunch break.

Europe Cup: The European version of the Continental Cup and, in a manner of speaking, the B league of skiing; contestants can use the respective events (downhill, super-G, giant slalom, slalom) in order to gain a firm slot in the World Cup for the following season.

FIS: Federation Internationale de Ski, the international skiing federation. Homepage: www.fis-ski.com.

FIS points: These are granted during each FIS, Continental Cup, and World Cup race (and even in the Olympic combination slaloms); however, the point allotment is so complicated to figure out that it can be done only by computer or with a calculator. Whoever has one of these devices at his disposal and wants to dig deeper can go to the following link online: http://www.fis-ski.com/reglementeundpublikationen/alpinerskilauf/alpinefispunkte.html.

Olympic Training Center: My training home base in Obertauern. Heinrich "Heini" Bergmüller is the sports supervisor. Homepage: www.olympiastuetzpunkt.at.

Time Limit Overrun: Before each race, the competitors inspect the race-course; anyone who takes more than the allotted amount of time is disqualified according to the rules; at least that's how it's done in Val d'Isère.

Tuning: Perfect harmony among ski, binding anchor, and ski boot. This is much more important than the (by the media) often-touted waxing process.

World Championships: This, the second-most-important large-scale event, takes place every other year (every odd year, 2005 in Bormio, 2007 in Aare, 2009 in Val d'Isère).

World Cup: The highest league of competitive skiing. French journalist Serge Lang is considered the inventor of the World Cup, which he himself headed up for more than two decades. During the summer of 1966, the idea was taken up by FIS during the world championships in Portillo, Chile. The first World Cup race took place in January 1967 in Berchtesgaden.

World Cup Point Distribution:

1. place	100 points	16. place	15 points
2. place	80 points	17. place	14 points
3. place	60 points	18. place	13 points
4. place	50 points	19. place	12 points
5. place	45 points	20. place	11 points
6. place	40 points	21. place	10 points
7. place	36 points	22. place	9 points
8. place	32 points	23. place	8 points
9. place	29 points	24. place	7 points
10. place	26 points	25. place	6 points

11. place	24 points	26. place	5 points
12. place	22 points	27. place	4 points
13. place	20 points	28. place	3 points
14. place	18 points	29. place	2 points
15. place	16 points	30. place	1 point

WORLD CUP
OVERALL RANKINGS

MEN'S RACES FROM
1967–2005, WITH POINTS WON

1967
1. Jean-Claude Killy (FRA) 225
2. Heini Messner (AUT) 114
3. Guy Perillat (FRA) 108

1968
1. Jean-Claude Killy (FRA) 200
2. Dumeng Giovanoli (SUI) 119
3. Heini Huber (AUT) 112

1969
1. Karl Schranz (AUT) 182
2. Jean-Noël Augert (FRA) 123
3. Reinhard Tritscher (AUT) 108

1970
1. Karl Schranz (AUT) 148
2. Patrick Russel (FRA) 145
3. Gustavo Thöni (ITA) 140

1971
1. Gustavo Thöni (ITA) 155
2. Henri Duvillard (FRA) 135
3. Patrick Russel (FRA) 125

. . .
7. David Zwilling (AUT) 86

1972
1. Gustavo Thöni (ITA) 154
2. Henri Duvillard (FRA) 142
3. Edmund Bruggmann (SUI) 140
. . .
8. Karl Schranz (AUT) 83

1973
1. Gustavo Thöni (ITA) 166
2. David Zwilling (AUT) 151
3. Roland Collombin (SUI) 131

1974
1. Piero Gros (ITA) 181
2. Gustavo Thöni (ITA) 165
3. Hans Hinterseer (AUT) 162

1975
1. Gustavo Thöni (ITA) 250
2. Ingemar Stenmark (SWE) 245
3. Franz Klammer (AUT) 240

1976
1. Ingemar Stenmark (SWE) 249
2. Piero Gros (ITA) 205
3. Gustavo Thöni (ITA) 190
4. Franz Klammer (AUT) 181

1977
1. Ingemar Stenmark (SWE) 339
2. Klaus Heidegger (AUT) 250
3. Franz Klammer (AUT) 203

1978
1. Ingemar Stenmark (SWE) 150
2. Phil Mahre (USA) 116
3. Andreas Wenzel (LIE) 100
4. Klaus Heidegger (AUT) 95

1979
1. Peter Lüscher (SUI) 186
2. Leonhard Stock (AUT) 163
3. Phil Mahre (USA) 155

1980
1. Andreas Wenzel (LIE) 204
2. Ingemar Stenmark (SWE) 200
3. Phil Mahre (USA) 132
...
5. Anton Steiner (AUT) 130

1981
1. Phil Mahre (USA) 266
2. Ingemar Stenmark (SWE) 260
3. Alexander Zhirov (SOV) 185
...
8. Harti Weirather (AUT) 115

1982
1. Phil Mahre (USA) 309
2. Ingemar Stenmark (SWE) 211
3. Steve Mahre (USA) 183
...
10. Harti Weirather (AUT) 97

1983
1. Phil Mare (USA) 285
2. Ingemar Stenmark (SWE) 218
3. Andreas Wenzel (LIE) 177
...
9. Franz Gruber (AUT) 112

1984
1. Pirmin Zurbriggen (SUI) 256
2. Ingemar Stenmark (SWE) 230
3. Marc Girardelli (LUX) 222
...
5. Anton Steiner (AUT) 148

1985
1. Marc Girardelli (LUX) 262
2. Pirmin Zurbriggen (SUI) 244
3. Andreas Wenzel (LIE) 172
...
8. Helmut Höflehner (AUT) 116

1986
1. Marc Girardelli (LUX) 294
2. Pirmin Zurbriggen (SUI) 284
3. Markus Wasmeier (GER) 214
...
6. Leonhard Stock (AUT) 174

1987
1. Pirmin Zurbriggen (SUI) 339
2. Marc Girardelli (LUX) 190
3. Markus Wasmeier (GER) 174
...
7. Leonhard Stock (AUT) 97

1988
1. Pirmin Zurbriggen (SUI) 310
2. Alberto Tomba (ITA) 281
3. Hubert Strolz (AUT) 190

1989
1. Marc Girardelli (LUX) 407
2. Pirmin Zurbriggen (SUI) 309

3. Alberto Tomba (ITA) 189

…

6. Rudi Nierlich (AUT) 144

1990
1. Pirmin Zurbriggen (SUI) 357
2. Ole-Kristian Furuseth (NOR) 234
3. Günther Mader (AUT) 213

1991
1. Marc Girardelli (LUX) 242
2. Alberto Tomba (ITA) 222
3. Rudi Nierlich (AUT) 201

1992
1. Paul Accola (SUI) 1,699
2. Alberto Tomba (ITA) 1,362
3. Marc Girardelli (LUX) 996

…

6. Günther Mader (AUT) 797

1993
1. Marc Girardelli (LUX) 1,379
2. Kjetil-Andre Aamodt (NOR) 1,347
3. Franz Heinzer (SUI) 828
4. Günther Mader (AUT) 826

1994
1. Kjetil-Andre Aamodt (NOR) 1,392
2. Marc Girardelli (LUX) 1,007
3. Alberto Tomba (ITA) 822
4. Günther Mader (AUT) 820

1995
1. Alberto Tomba (ITA) 1,150
2. Günther Mader (AUT) 775
3. Jure Kosir (SLO) 760

1996
1. Lasse Kjus (NOR) 1,216
2. Günther Mader (AUT) 991

3. Michael von Grünigen (SUI) 880

…

106. Hermann Maier (AUT) 29

1997
1. Luc Alphand (FRA) 1,130
2. Kjetil-Andre Aamodt (NOR) 1,096
3. Josef Strobl (AUT) 1,021

…

21. Hermann Maier (AUT) 379

1998
1. Hermann Maier (AUT) 1,685
2. Andreas Schifferer (AUT) 1,114
3. Stephan Eberharter (AUT) 1,030

1999
1. Lasse Kjus (NOR) 1,465
2. Kjetil-Andre Aamodt (NOR) 1,442
3. Hermann Maier (AUT) 1,307

2000
1. Hermann Maier (AUT) 2,000
2. Kjetil-Andre Aamodt (NOR) 1,440
3. Josef Strobl (AUT) 994

2001
1. Hermann Maier (AUT) 1,618
2. Stephan Eberharter (AUT) 875
3. Lasse Kjus (NOR) 866

2002
1. Stephan Eberharter (AUT) 1,702
2. Kjetil-Andre Aamodt (NOR) 1,096
3. Didier Cuche (SUI) 1,064

2003
1. Stephan Eberharter (AUT) 1,333
2. Bode Miller (USA) 1,100
3. Kjetil-Andre Aamodt (NOR) 940

2004

1. Hermann Maier (AUT) 1,265
2. Stephan Eberharter (AUT) 1,223
3. Benjamin Raich (AUT) 1,139

2005

1. Bode Miller (USA) 1,648
2. Benjamin Raich (AUT) 1,454
3. Hermann Maier (AUT) 1,295

Because the method of determining points was changed during the 1991/1992 season, the number of points that could be acquired quadrupled: earlier, there were only 25, 20, and 15 points for places one, two, and three.

THE GREATEST WINNERS IN THE WORLD CUP

1. Ingemar Stenmark (SWE): 86 wins (46 GS, 40 slalom)
2. Hermann Maier (AUT): 51 wins (14 downhill, 22 super-G, 14 GS, 1 combination)
3. Alberto Tomba (ITA): 50 wins (15 GS, 35 slalom)
4. Marc Girardelli (LUX): 46 wins (3 downhill, 9 super-G, 7 GS, 16 slalom, 11 combination)
5. Pirmin Zurbriggen (SUI): 40 wins (10 downhill, 10 super-G, 7 GS, 2 slalom, 11 combination)

VITAL STATISTICS
FOR "HERMINATOR"
HERMANN MAIER

Born: December 7, 1972, in Altenmarkt, Austria

Astrological sign: Sagittarius

Fan mail: Hermann-Maier-Strasse 1
           A-5542 Flachau

Height: 5 feet, 11 inches

Weight: 207 pounds

Hobbies: Shark diving, helicopter piloting, motorcycling, jet skiing

Favorite food: Kaiserschmarren (sweet pancakes) with stewed plums

Favorite drink: Sparkling apple juice

Racing Suit: Spyder

Skis: Atomic

Binding: Atomic

Shoes: Atomic

Poles: Leki

Helmet, goggles: Carrera

Gloves: Reusch

Functional underwear: Löffler

Socks: Falke

Recreation: Adidas

Heart rate chronograph: Suunto

Nourishment: Herminator Power Bar

Private sponsor: Raiffeisen, My Bank

WINS

Olympic Games 1998 in Nagano: gold super-G, gold GS
World Championships 1999 in Vail: gold downhill, gold super-G
World Championships 2001 in St. Anton: silver downhill, bronze super-G
World Championships 2003 in St. Moritz: silver super-G
World Championships 2005 in Bormio: gold GS

WORLD CHAMPIONSHIPS 2004

Fourteen Crystal Balls
Season 1997/98: overall, super-G, GS
Season 1998/99: super-G
Season 1999/2000: overall, downhill, super-G, GS
Season 2000/2001: overall, downhill, super-G, GS
Season 2003/2004: overall, super-G

51 (52*) Wins

WORLD CUP RACES (AS OF DECEMBER 2005)

22 super-G
14 downhill
14 (15*) GS
1 combination (Wengen/Veysonnaz)

---

* Including a GS win on December 14, 1997, at which I was disqualified for un-
  buckling a ski before the "red line."

ACKNOWLEDGMENTS

My sincere appreciation goes to Hermann Maier, a remarkable athlete whom I admired even during my days as a journalist, for his natural talent, determination, and training discipline. I especially enjoy his wit, which has made for a number of perfect headlines and stories. During my time as his press spokesman, I got to see altogether new dimensions in Hermann: his faith, his patience, his focus. A few weeks after the accident, he mentioned in an interview (and would reiterate the same thing many times later on) that he was grateful for his fate. During his unbelievably difficult road to recovery, which I was privileged to share with him, I could see in person that this statement was not a hollow phrase, but a life philosophy put into practice. My thanks and appreciation further go to Ivie and to Stevie and Bianca, who never let me feel that there simply wasn't enough time for parental obligations while I was caught up in Hermann's vortex. On the contrary, by virtue of their independence and inspiration, they, too, made a contribution to a biography, which took long into the summer to complete after an exhausting World Cup winter.

Knut Okresek

The authors would like to thank also Toni Giger, Hans Pum, and the whole staff of the Austrian Ski Federation, Werner Margreiter, Thomas Rilk, Toné Mathis, Kurt Niederegger, Franz Pammer, Ursula Statzinger, Susie Ehrentraud, Ernst Lacker, Rupert Silbergasser, and to Laura Walden.

Last but not least, we would like to express our sincere gratitude to David Kramer and Barbara Swartzwelter for their tireless efforts at providing an authentic English translation, and to Patrick Lang, who made it possible for this book to be available across the Atlantic.

ABOUT THE AUTHORS

Hermann Maier was born in 1972. He was apprenticed as a bricklayer and worked as a skiing instructor before starting his incredible career as a ski racer: two-time Olympic champion in 1998, two-time world champion, three-time overall World Cup winner, all before almost losing his right leg as the result of a serious motorcycle accident. Only 521 days after the accident he was able to celebrate his sensational comeback victory in the super-G at Kitzbühel. In March 2004, he captured his fourth overall World Cup victory, and in 2005, his third World Championships gold medal.

Knut Okresek, born in 1965, sportswriter and author, was Hermann's spokesman for three years. He accompanied Hermann from his accident to his comeback as overall World Cup champion and recorded his every thought, every minute.